A.B. MITFORD AND THE BIRTH OF JAPAN
AS A MODERN STATE

Portrait of Mitford c1865 shortly before he left for China

A.B. Mitford
and the Birth of Japan
as a Modern State:

Letters Home

ॐ

by

Robert Morton

RENAISSANCE BOOKS

A. B. MITORD AND THE BIRTH OF JAPAN AS A MODERN STATE
LETTERS HOME

First published 2017 by
RENAISSANCE BOOKS
P O Box 219
Folkestone
Kent CT20 2WP

Renaissance Books is an imprint of Global Books Ltd

ISBN 978-1-898823-48-3 Hardback
      978-1-898823-53-7 e-Book

The Publishers, wish to express their thanks to the Great-
Britain Sasakawa Foundation for their support in the making
of this book.

British Library Cataloguing in Publication Data
A catalogue record for this book is available
from the British Library

Set in Garamond 11.5 on 12.5 pt by Dataworks
Printed and bound in England by CPI Antony Rowe Ltd., Chippenham, Wilts

CONTENTS

ℰↃ

FOREWORD

by

Sir Hugh Cortazzi

℅

THE JAPANESE REVOLUTION of 1868, euphemistically called by the Japanese The Meiji Restoration, marked a significant turning point in Japanese history. The revolution was achieved without the intervention of any of the Western powers and Japan did not fall under the dominance of any foreign state.

The Americans had taken the lead in 1853 in forcing the re-opening of Japan but in the 1860s America was torn apart by civil war and the British and French, whose primary interests were in furthering trade, had displaced the Americans as the leading foreign powers interested in the outcome of the revolution.

The British minister and consul general was the thrusting Sir Harry Parkes. His French opposite number was the swashbuckling Leon Roches. Their competitive antics were little more than a minor sideshow in the dramatic events of 1867–8, but they had significant if minor parts to play in Japan's drama.

The tiny British legation in Japan had 'front seats' for some of the most important acts in this drama and, when shipping was available, reported on developments in some detail to London. The official despatches were supplemented by private letters, in particular from A.B. Mitford, second secretary in the legation, to his father.

This book draws on these letters to paint a fascinating picture of the events, which brought feudal Japan into the modern world.

In so doing it complements and clarifies the detailed narrative of events given by Ernest Satow in his memoir *A Diplomat in Japan.*

A.B.Mitford (Algernon Bertram Mitford to give him his full aristocratic and rather pompous names) became in due course the first Baron Redesdale, whose granddaughters were the famous Mitford sisters. In 1867, he was an ambitious young diplomat, cultured, well educated and highly intelligent. He embraced the chance of adventure in a country, which at that time was almost completely unknown to his compatriots.

Life in Japan in those days was dangerous and unhealthy and living conditions were primitive. He accepted this as inevitable in the circumstances of the time. As a schoolboy at Eton he had become inured to violence in the rough and tumble of life.

He was a good linguist and almost unique among British diplomats at the time he studied hard to master the local language (Japanese) and became a fluent speaker and interpreter and a competent translator. The Foreign Office in its usual meanness refused to compensate him for the rigours of his life and for the efforts, which he had put into learning Japanese.

Despite occasional complaints to Parkes and his father he revelled in his life in Japan. He was sociable and became a close friend of Ernest Satow who went on to become a distinguished scholar-diplomat, and of William Willis, the doctor to the mission. His interest in people ensured that he soon got on good terms with the young samurai who would become the leaders of Japan in the following decades.

As there was no first secretary or deputy to Parkes in the mission Mitford was thrust, despite his youth and junior rank, into assuming responsibilities, which would normally have fallen to an older and more experienced diplomat. In particular, he was largely on his own for a few months in Osaka in 1868 where he acted not only for Britain but also for other Western powers in some important diplomatic actions including attempts to mitigate Japanese government measures against the 'hidden Christians' of Japan.

Mitford was proud of his aristocratic origins and was conscious of his class. It helped him to understand the emphasis, which Japanese traditionally placed on honour. As a gentleman, 'born and bred', he knew how to put at ease those who were from less distinguished origins and his instinctive snobbery was generally well disguised while he was in Japan. The caricature of him published in *Vanity Fair* in 1904 suggesting a dandified aristocratic snob is amusing but not a fair portrait of him as young man.

Robert Morton through his study of Mitford's original letters throws valuable light on a fascinating and important moment in Japanese history. These letters also show that while Mitford's lengthy two volume *Memories,* published in 1915, is generally accurate in its depiction of his time in Japan and contains many well written descriptions of Japan and its people, there were a few occasions when his memory was at fault and he remembered things as he would liked them to have been, but this is a common fault of old age.

Mitford, like so many foreigners who came to live in Japan in subsequent decades, went through the usual phases of a love-hate relationship with Japan and its people. But whatever his personal feelings at any one time he was anxious above all that we should strive to know and understand Japan and its people.

PREFACE

༄

WHAT WAS JAPAN and who were the Japanese? In 1870, when the thirty-three-year-old Algernon Bertram Mitford (1837–1916) returned to England after three and a half years as a diplomat there, this question was being asked across the Western world. Japan had taken it by storm. There has never been another time in history when a distant culture so invaded the drawing rooms of Western Europe and North America in such a sustained way. A British journal commented:

> Our women are Japanese in costume; the Japanese top-spinners and posture-masters are an institution; Japanese umbrellas, fans, trays, silks, and jewelleries have occupied the old bric-à-brac market ... In a word taste ... just now adopts all Japanese things.[1]

Everybody was familiar with the country's arts and crafts, but were in 'profound ignorance' of the nation itself, as a newspaper of the time put it.[2] A trickle of Westerners had visited since the 1850s and had created the impression of a strange, unknowable place. They would stress how different it was to the West and how contradictory it seemed. Japan was portrayed as a land of toy people and toy houses but at the same time its people were perceived to be brutal and bloodthirsty, with a casual indifference to life and death. The Japanese were seen to have plenty of beliefs and customs, but no proper religion and therefore no basis for their morality. There was no 'right' or 'wrong' in Japan – only what was acceptable in their labyrinthine code of behaviour and what was not. Above all, its people were different: singular – unknowable – inscrutable.

Mitford would come to reject this view out of hand. While at first he was bewildered by the country and indeed felt contempt for it, with remarkable speed he learned the language and started to embrace Japanese traditions. He came to feel that the Japanese were, in many respects, superior to Westerners, particularly in their views of honour and duty. The beliefs underpinning their culture were entirely different to those in the West, but once they were understood, Mitford believed, their behaviour was completely reasonable. Nobody before him had described the Japanese in these terms, nobody before him had shown them yet as human beings that Westerners could relate to. When he did this it caused a sensation.

Mitford had charm, looks and – very important in Japan – excellent social graces. Together with these assets, his status as a diplomat gave him access to the highest levels of Japanese government and society, just when they started tolerating the presence of outsiders. He met with the Emperor face-to-face when almost everybody else, including the Shogun, could only talk to him behind a screen. He became friendly with the Shogun and witnessed a *hara-kiri*, his atmospheric account of which is now a classic, and is included in this volume. Above all, he played a part in one of the great turning points in world history – the 1868 revolution that saw the demise of the 250-year-old feudal dynasty ruled over by a Shogun and its replacement by a modern state, the so-called Meiji Restoration. Mitford also had an important role in its aftermath when the lives of persecuted Japanese Christians depended on his personal negotiations with the new Government.

He had remarkable courage – he almost drowned, could have burned to death, was shot at, and was nearly cut down by samurai swords, but he did not flinch. He did not relax either – he 'never wrote a note without having a revolver on the table and never went to bed without a Spencer rifle and bayonet' at his hand'.[3] He survived more mundane risks – a colleague of his own age was suddenly struck down by a stomach ailment and was dead winin a week. Another could not stand the strain of life there and shot himself. In Japan, one minute you were alive and the next you were dead.

Four qualities make Mitford feel like the perfect guide to the stirring but confusing events of the late 1860s: his sense of adventure, which meant he gained experiences a more cautious person would have missed; his sense of people, which allowed him to form close relationships with Japanese of every class, helping him to penetrate to the heart of the country; his sense of history, which enabled him to perceive the significance of the events he was witnessing and put them into context; and, perhaps most important for posterity, his sense of narrative. He knew how to craft descriptions in a memorable way, knew how to make Japan seem real to his readers, and thereby left the most immediate record of the events surrounding the Restoration.

Mitford was not, of course, a perfect judge of what he was witnessing and his views shifted greatly in the three and a half years he was in the country, running the gamut from contempt to adoration. The Japan of the late 1860s was exceptionally complex and chaotic with a cacophony of clashing opinions. Mitford did not worry too much about this diversity – his voice on Japan is nearly always certain, even when he has just changed his opinion about it. He made mistakes, and he certainly simplified, but he ended up getting the essentials right. He saw further than many of his contemporaries by rejecting the attitudes of those who had gone before him and presenting a picture of the country as he viewed it with his own eyes. He did better than most at parking his cultural baggage at the door and accepting Japan on its own terms. I have tried to do the same in my attempt to chart the confusing course of Japan's Meiji Restoration, while relating the opinions and adventures of the person who has certainly become my, and I hope by the end of this book my reader's, favourite foreign gentleman in Japan.

Robert Morton
Tokyo, January 2017

LIST OF PLATES

ଏ

1

YOKOHAMA

October – December 1866

~

For someone as prone to sea-sickness as Mitford, any sea voyage was an ordeal. 'I thank my stars,' he once told his father, 'that you did not send me to sea when I was a youngster.'[1] He was an unlucky sailor, always seeming to encounter storms, and his voyage from Shanghai to Yokohama was one of his worst, his ship, the P&O steamer *Cadiz*, hitting a typhoon head on: the force of the wind was so great that it blew the foam like a carpet spread over the waves.'[2]

Even in calm weather, Mitford found the motion of boats uncomfortable, but in the extreme conditions of a typhoon, it became terrifying. The ships would take on water at a terrific rate, not just from waves, but from the sea seeping in through cracks created by the violent rocking and the shifting of the cargo. Crews would fight a desperate battle to prevent the fires going out in the engine room. If this happened, they lost power and therefore lost control of the ship, and then anything could happen.

Mitford was accompanied by his Chinese servant, Lin Fu, who he was bringing over from Beijing, and was travelling in a First-Class cabin. This made the journey expensive, but was necessary, not so much for comfort, as for keeping up his position. While the storm was raging, he was no doubt fervently wishing the Foreign Office had let him stay in China. Before his departure, he had written that he was 'sorry and glad mixed' to be leaving it; 'sorry to leave China and Chinese – glad to leave Peking and its dust.'[3] Most Westerners found the annoyances of China far outweighed its pleasures, and Mitford wrote: 'I believe I am the only person that ever liked it.'[4] Among its negatives was the 'Beggar's Bridge,' which Mitford had to pass every time he went out. Gathered there was a collection of the 'most degraded specimens of humanity,' which formed 'the most loathsome and stinking exhibition that it ever was my fate to come across'. It was a sight Mitford thought would stay with him as 'a nightmare' for the rest of his life.[5]

You had to be able to overlook a lot of this kind of thing to like China, but if you were prepared to engage with the country, it offered some remarkable experiences: 'Among the great monuments of the world there can be few more striking than those of the North of China,' thought Mitford. Beijing itself, 'that grim and grey city with all its mysteries and tragic secrets, is difficult to beat.'[6] Japan might turn out to be more comfortable than China, but it would have to work hard to compete with that country for top place in Mitford's imagination. He did not think it would: 'I don't expect to like it or the people as much as I did the country folks in China.'[7]

But Mitford was not thinking so much about enjoyment as plotting his future. Just before he left China, he outlined to his father what his plan was:

> I want to gain as much as possible by my Eastern trip. Having sacrificed a valuable portion of my life I don't want to have done the thing by halves. If I stay a reasonable time in Japan, I believe I can make myself an efficient interpreter in both the Chinese and Japanese languages – I can continue the study of the former in Japan, and, the written language of Japan being based on that of China, having mastered the rudiments of the one is so much gained towards the other. If there are to be Chinese and Japanese embassies in Europe, the F[oreign]. O[ffice]. will need their own interpreter. There is no one now qualified to interpret in both languages.[8]

In fact, Chinese and Japanese have little in common, aside from the writing system, so Mitford was setting himself a fantastically difficult challenge in attempting to become competent enough in both languages to interpret in them. Furthermore, written Japanese was very much more difficult than it is today, having little in common with the spoken language, and there were no proper dictionaries to refer to. Why would he do all this? Perhaps the roots of Mitford's determination lie in the insecurity of his upbringing. Before China, his life had been chequered: his mother had abandoned the family when he was just four and he was sent away to board at Eton at the age of nine, where he struggled. He recovered, however, going on to Christ Church College, Oxford, and then entering the most prestigious government department, the Foreign Office. As a young adult, he had everything going for him: he was tall and handsome, always immaculately dressed, with large blue eyes and an elegant pointed, slightly hooked nose, set off by a carefully-groomed moustache. He had no trouble getting invitations to the best parties and the Prime Minister's wife, Lady Palmerston, treated him as one of her special favourites. He had seemed set to follow the same course as his father by taking a congenial overseas posting (in his father's case, Florence), before settling to a calm aristocratic existence in Britain. But then Mitford did something strange. The top civil servant in the Foreign Office casually mentioned that he was having trouble finding someone for a junior attaché position in Beijing and Mitford amazed him by actually volunteering for it. Beijing was considered the ultimate hardship posting: remote, lonely, dangerous and uncomfortable. In addition, the job was a lower position than a temporary third secretary post Mitford had already held, in Russia.[9] Why did he take it? He did not have debtors or scandals to escape from. But he did not have anything in particular keeping him in Britain either – there was no sweetheart who it was a wrench to leave. He certainly had a sense of adventure and wanted to escape dreary Foreign Office desk work in London. But I think the main reason is that he wanted to make his life extraordinary.

*

It was a relief when the *Cadiz* entered the safety of Edo Bay. This is a fine sight on a sunny day, with Mt Fuji looming in the background and the coast full of picturesque coves. However, when Mitford arrived, on 3 October 1866, it looked miserable under grey skies and lashing rain. 'Could this be the fairy land of whose beauties we had heard from … earlier travellers?,' he asked himself.[10]

Mitford borrows a typical image of Japan presented by Westerners who had briefly visited the country and had found it full of charming customs and sights. But his new colleagues at the British Legation (it became the Embassy in 1905) would have quickly told him that Japan was no fairy land. They were in a country where many, perhaps most, felt that their presence was a desecration – the British representatives had been driven out of the Shogun's capital, Edo (now Tokyo), their buildings having been attacked in 1861 and 1862. Two British guards had died in each attack and the fatalities could have been much worse. The head of the Legation wrote after the first one that it was only 'by the merest chance' that they had escaped a massacre.[11] A new, more secure Legation had been built, but was burnt to the ground before they had the chance to occupy it. Consequently they had to stay in Yokohama, a small port thirty kilometres from Edo, which the Japanese Government had decided was a good place to confine the Westerners.

It had only been seven years earlier that the Government had chosen a strip of marshy land along some shoreline for the new town. It was cobbled together; an American businessman, Francis Hall, noted that the name – Yokohama – which means simply 'beside a beach,' fitted it at the start, because the place was nothing more than this.[12] Even when Mitford left Japan, in 1870, Yokohama was still only a relatively small place: it was home to about 25,000 Japanese and 3,000 Chinese residents, with around 1,000 more or less permanent Westerners, and about three times that number of transitory sailors and soldiers. The military, however, were a major presence there; Hall recorded on 30 November 1863 that 'resonant fife and drum fill the quiet air … for today, as I write, twelve hundred British soldiers and marines are parading our streets, to give the Japanese an impress of their strength'.[13]

As Mitford docked, on his left he would have seen the Western area with its spacious compounds belonging to the different Powers, along with substantial houses for rent to Westerners. On his right were densely-packed Japanese streets, jammed with higgledy-piggledy wooden buildings, 'laid out,' as one of Mitford's colleagues put it, with 'little thought of the general convenience'.[14] Mitford would end up living in the cheaper Japanese section, the skinflint Foreign Office not wanting to spend more than it had to on accommodating its diplomatic staff. Luckily, Yokohama turned out to be a good site for a port and is now Japan's second-largest city, with a population of more than three and a half million. Although Western diplomats resented being forced to live there, they had to admit it had its advantages, with its sheltered, deep-water harbour, which was much better than that at Edo.

The most striking sight in Yokohama was the ships in the harbour; on the day Mitford arrived, his was one of twenty-four merchant ships in port and there would have been around a dozen naval vessels there as well. Of the merchant ships there on that day, nineteen were British, two French, two Dutch and one American. Woodblock artists included the ships again and again in their prints – they were a novel sight to the Japanese who would have found them both intimidating and awe-inspiring, the means by which Europeans dominated the world. They were nearly all hybrids, using a mixture of steam and sail – they still had the beauty of traditional tall ships, but they also represented the latest technology. To us, they would have seemed small; the *Cadiz* had a tonnage of 816, making it the third biggest merchant ship in the harbour. (For comparison, the *Titanic's* tonnage was 46,000, and the world's biggest ships now are five times that.)

The most interesting thing to Mitford was the people he saw on the dock, untouched as they were, by any Western influence: the government employees carrying their two swords, 'clad in sad-coloured robes with quaint lacquer hats'; the coolies, with rain-coats made of straw, looking like 'animated haycocks', and women with babies that were 'sorely afflicted with skin diseases slung behind their backs'.[15] Reeling from sea-sickness, Mitford was in no mood to be charmed by them, rather thinking them a 'melancholy' sight that was 'sufficiently depressing'.[16] He was disappointed in Japan; he knew that it would be a far from easy place to live, but he had thought it would at least be beautiful. As it appeared not to be, it seemed to have nothing going for it. Two months after his arrival, he was writing, 'I can take no interest or pleasure in the country,' and doubted if he even had the capacity to like it, because 'the edge of' his 'wondering-at-new-scenes power had been taken off in China'.[17]

If Mitford had later been challenged to explain why he was so negative about Japan at the start, he would probably have blamed being in Yokohama which, with its jumble of nationalities, was 'about as much like Japan as Regent Street'.[18] In his memoir, written fifty years later, he gives a very different impression, portraying Japan as a country he had fallen in love with virtually at first sight. This is how he described his feelings on his second day there:

> Suddenly coming in full view of Mount Fuji, snow-capped, rearing its matchless cone heavenward in one gracefully curving slope from the sea level, I … was caught by the fever of intoxication … – a fever which burns to this day, and will continue to burn in my veins to the end of my life.[19]

Mitford is not exactly lying here – this is how Japan no doubt seemed to him in hindsight. But in reality, it took a long time for him to even accept the country, much less fall in love with it. Mitford, like most people probably, fairly quickly decided what his feelings about a place were and then viewed all his experiences there through those lenses. Where Mitford is different from others is that he did not like mild emotions, preferring to bounce between extremes. He was not comfortable unless what he felt was either love or hate.

*

Mitford joined a team of six or seven officers (the number was slightly fluid) at the British Legation; three diplomats – Mitford was the most junior of these –, a doctor, and two or three translators/interpreters. They were assisted by 'student interpreters', whose main task was to study Japanese. At the start, Mitford's work was menial, mostly copying out despatches and taking messages up to the Government in Edo, although opportunities would soon open up for him.

The overwhelming concern at the time was commerce. Britain's trade with east Asia was worth a relatively modest £40 million or so a year; China, where most of this money was made, accounted for less than 5% of total British trade.[20] As it was in China, Britain was in a dominant position in Japan: in the mid-1860s, its merchants were responsible for 60% of Japanese exports and 75% of its imports, although the volume was small because of onerous restrictions imposed by the Japanese Government.[21] The priority of the British Government was consequently to get rid of the barriers and free up trade with Japan. Mitford, on the other hand, was more interested in Japan's political future, with the feudal system falling apart and revolutionary change in the air. In any case, he hated the obsession with profit: 'We have set up an idol of mammon and sacrifice to it every weak people whose resources excite our cupidity,' he wrote, adding:

> Here I have been writing rank blasphemy against the god in whose temple I am a small Levite, for diplomacy is now only the exponent of the commercial creed. Unfortunately I put the national honour before the gains of a few individuals.[22]

Mitford's boss, Sir Harry Parkes, was one of the 'Levites', mainly focused on trade and less concerned with Japan's politics except in so far as they affected British interests. He was the Envoy Extraordinary and Minister Plenipotentiary (this position was upgraded to Ambassador in 1905), usually simply known as the 'Minister'. Still only in his thirties, he was, in almost every respect, exceptional.

Mitford described him like this: 'small, wiry, fair-haired … with a great head and broad brow, almost out of proportion to his body; his energy was stupendous, he was absolutely fearless and tireless'.[23] His story is like something out of Dickens: he had lost his mother and father by the age of five and the uncle who became his guardian after that died when he was ten. His older sisters had gone to Macao, to join a cousin who ran a school for blind Chinese girls there, and at thirteen, having nobody who cared about him in England, Parkes set sail for China to join them. He quickly made good there, starting working for the British consular service at fourteen, and becoming so proficient in Chinese that at sixteen, he was appointed Interpreter at the port of Amoy (now more commonly known by its Mandarin name, Xiamen). As Mitford put it, he 'was doing important work ... at an age when other boys are yet wondering whether they will get into the school eleven'.[24] In 1860, during the Second Opium War, he was captured, imprisoned, chained from the throat, wrist and leg to a low beam and repeatedly threatened with execution. He showed great courage during this ordeal, refusing to leave until all the other prisoners had been released. This turned him into a hero in Britain and put his career on to the fast track. By the time Mitford met him, his reputation was such that he was almost above criticism; as one of Mitford's colleagues later wrote, he 'came to us invested with the prestige of a man who had looked death in the face with no ordinary heroism, and in the eyes of all European residents in the far east held a higher position than any [other] officer of the crown'.[25]

In spite of all this, he was loathed by most of his staff because he was hard-driving and temperamental. The doctor at the Legation, William Willis, believed that the premature death of a first assistant, John Macdonald, had been brought on by the strain of working under Parkes.[26] He was, however, generally well regarded by the Japanese and when he left Japan on leave in 1871, Sanjō Sanetomi (the *Udaijin* or 'Minister of the Right') broke with diplomatic etiquette by telling the British Foreign Secretary that

our Government have trusted profoundly to him as a support, and have frequently received his aid in different matters with various nations, and it is truly impossible to express our sense of gratitude ... I have been commanded by His Majesty the Tennō [Emperor] to take the opportunity of telling Your Excellency of his merits during his period of office, and I have the honour to request that you will lay these facts before Her Majesty the Queen of England.[27]

At the same time, he left bitter feelings for the lack of respect he showed when he disagreed with his counterparts. When he left, a Japanese newspaper wrote that he 'advanced the interest of his nation by humiliating and oppressing other states ... Smashing of glasses at our prime minister's table; physically assaulting ... an individual now of elevated rank; insulting the ex-minister for foreign affairs, Terashima.'[28] In 1864, while he was still in China, he mused: 'I am afraid that I do not take things sufficiently easily ... I *can't* take things quietly, and the worry they occasion me destroys all my peace very often'. 'I sometimes wish I were a cleverer man; but contentment would be a far more valuable gift.'[29]

Mitford did not complain as much about Parkes as other people – the worst he wrote about him was that he was 'a very bustling man and always actively engaged upon something or another'.[30] Parkes seems to have respected Mitford, who was hard-working and highly competent. He was the only member of the Legation who had contacts at the highest level in London – maybe Parkes was circumspect with him because he knew that Mitford could have gone over his head. Or perhaps Parkes identified something of himself in Mitford who had also lost his mother when he was very young. Could there have been an unspoken bond between them created by the recognition that they had both experienced the same loss? Whether this was true or not, they never became close and certainly at the start, Mitford found being with Parkes uncomfortable, having to not only work with him, but also live with him until his own place was ready. A month after his arrival, he was telling his father, that he had no table to sit at and was 'altogether in a worse state than a visitor'.[31]

A more positive presence for Mitford than Parkes was the man who would become his closest friend in Japan, Ernest Satow. At the time Mitford met him, he was working as an interpreter – while Parkes was fluent in Chinese, he spoke little Japanese – meaning he had to follow Parkes around, explaining to him what was going on while withstanding his blasts of temper. Mitford thought they were a good team: 'with all his energy and force of character, [Parkes] would never have succeeded as he did without Satow'.[32] In spite of this, Satow never felt at ease with Parkes and wrote this about him years later:

> He was strict and severe in service matters, but in his private relations gracious to all those who had occasion to seek his help, and a faithful friend to all who won his goodwill. Unfortunately I was not one of these, and the result was that from the beginning we were never friends.[33]

Satow was six years Mitford's junior, but had far more experience of East Asia, having arrived at the age of eighteen in China (living in Shanghai and Beijing), from where he went on to Japan. He was gangly and socially awkward, but he was Mitford's intellectual superior, being an even better linguist, and he went on to become a significant scholar. He wrote the definitive account of the Meiji Restoration from the British viewpoint, *A Diplomat in Japan*, which complemented Mitford's books, providing all the detail and analysis that Mitford found boring. Their status was very different. Mitford was in the diplomatic service, which was entered by nomination and effectively restricted to the upper classes. They were the men who eventually became Ministers or Ambassadors and it was very rare for them to learn local languages because they were likely to be moved after a few years. The immense effort Mitford made to learn both Chinese and Japanese was exceptional. Ex-pat society in Japan was much more focused on using free time to do sport or horse-riding than studying the language and in any case the British, as a contemporary newspaper put it, 'seldom make any attempt to arrive at a knowledge of what is … around them, and, when they do, they rest satisfied with the scanty information they are able to pick up through the medium of the broken English of their native servants'.[34]

Satow was in the consular service, which was entered by competitive examination and was open to men of more humble origins. Consular officials were normally specialists who spoke local languages and, in the case of China and Japan, would usually stay in whichever country they knew the language of. In spite of their inferior position, consular staff were not necessarily paid less than diplomatic; when he was promoted to Japanese Secretary on 1 January 1868, Satow's pay went up to £700 a year, while Mitford, in spite of being promoted from third to second secretary two months later, stayed on £400 a year. It was thought that the 'gentlemen' of the diplomatic service did not need the money.

It was unusual to transfer from the consular service to the diplomatic because it was thought that middle class men would fail to command enough respect in a senior position. Mitford agreed with this with regard to Japan and China, advising a House of Commons committee soon after his return to England that,

> no people in the world have such a keen eye for a … man of high breeding as the Asiatics; and certainly in dealing with them I would employ men of as high breeding and birth as I could get to represent this country.'[35]

In other words, people like him. Nevertheless, Satow, like Parkes, broke through the class barrier, rising to become Minister to Japan and then China. Despite their differences, Mitford and Satow formed a close bond and Mitford later wrote that it was largely due to Satow that 'the sun shone so brightly' on his days in Japan.[36]

*

When Mitford finally moved into his own house, it was a cause for celebration. His housewarming was a 'feast *à la japonaise*' which his neighbours, Satow and Willis, along with a couple of officers from the ninth regiment, shared sitting on the floor. The food was all fish and rice, served on lacquer trays from the best local restaurant by an old woman with shaved eyebrows and blackened teeth; after dinner some younger women treated them to a musical entertainment.[37] Mitford was happy to have a try at living like a local, but at first wanted to eat Western food as well, until he found out how expensive and difficult to obtain it was. Milk, beef and bread were all an exorbitant price, and 'a leg of mutton, when it arrives from Shanghai, is a thing which people dance for days at, for Japan has no sheep'.[38] He and Satow soon gave up on eating Western food; it was far cheaper to eat local food – freshly-caught fish, along with vegetables and rice – albeit with European wine.[39] For most foreigners, this would have been considered impossible, or at any rate a terrible hardship. Isabella Bird, who travelled around Japan in 1878, wrote that Japanese food could 'only be swallowed and digested by a few' Westerners, and that 'after long practice'.[40]

In fact, aside from a lack of calcium, the diet for most urban dwellers was reasonably healthy, if simple; it included grains, often a mixture of barley, rice and millet; a variety of vegetables and seaweed; pickles; tofu and other soybean products as well as occasional fish from the sea and rivers, supplemented by seasonal fruits. It was the Westerners, particularly the British, with their insistence on having meat every day, over-boiling vegetables, and eating sweet desserts, that probably had the less healthy diet, but they would have refused to believe it.[41] The Japanese seemed tiny to them – the average man was only a little over 1.5 metres (around five feet) tall, about 15 centimetres shorter than the average Briton, so it was reasonable for them to think there was something wrong with what the Japanese were eating.[42]

Parkes did not like being in Yokohama, thinking it 'most undignified and anomalous' for the representatives of the world's most powerful country not to be able to live in the seat of government.[43] But even he had to accept that, unlike in most of the world, Westerners did not have the upper hand in Japan, a country that was not the kind of weak, backward, placid place ripe for colonisation. Japan was chaotic and divided, but it had a powerful sense of its own destiny – it was the sacred land of the gods, into which, unfortunately, some very unwelcome guests had forced their way. Western imperialism met its match there, Japan's self-belief ensuring that it would remain master of its own fate.

Occasionally the Japanese Government would deign to send a senior official to Yokohama to meet with the foreign representatives. Mitford was present at the second ever visit of a member of the governing council, the *rōju* (one rank lower than the Shogun), with the British Legation on 12 November 1866. In order to impress him, Parkes took him on board the *Princess Royal* and invited him to inspect the ninth regiment. It was probably the first time he had been on a ship; senior Japanese did not travel by sea between cities, moving around in uncomfortable palanquins, which were large, enclosed boxes carried on bearers' shoulders – the roads were not smooth enough for wheeled transport. Horses would have been quicker, but the Japanese pony was 'the worst horse in the world', thought Mitford, the Japanese were the 'worst riders' and the roads were 'utterly unsuited to riding'.[44] Moreover, time was not important; it was considered unthinkable to travel in a hurry and, worse, in a way that left any risk of being seen by the lower classes. As Satow put it, 'Etiquette prescribed that a great man should neither see nor be seen.'[45] Parkes subscribed to none of this; he travelled on horseback in full view and always wanted to move as quickly as possible, whether on the sea or on land. A sign of this was his being rapped over the knuckles for the spending of £84,141 on coal to power ships during the years 1867–8 rather than relying on the wind, which was slower – the Admiralty told him to use sail except in cases of 'urgent necessity and great political importance'.[46]

Mitford was not impressed by the *rōju*, telling his father that the 'great man' was 'small in stature, mean in appearance and seemingly of very ordinary intellect'.[47] Although powerful, he seemed like small beer – Mitford would not have to wait long before he met with Japanese who impressed him far more.

*

Yokohama was a rough and contradictory place, the diplomats and military men being joined by missionaries, and traders out to make their fortune. Mitford was appalled at the behaviour of this last group, calling them 'such a scum of the earth'.[48]

Adventurers would scrape together the funds to come to Japan, lured by stories of easy profits, and would cut any corner to make money. Everyone seemed out to cheat everyone else: silk, which accounted for around 70% of Japanese exports, was adulterated with sand to add weight; tea, the second-biggest export item, would never be like the sample was. Corruption was rampant, the Custom House officials demanding huge bribes in return for allowing merchants to escape paying duties. Businesses were unstable and in the second half of the 1860s, more than 60% of foreign trading firms went bust.[49]

The Western part of Yokohama was overwhelmingly male, Japan being considered too difficult and dangerous for Western women to live in. It was also too shocking, with explicit sexual images everywhere. There was not the distinction observed in the West between art and pornography and households of any class would have both around. The man who is now Japan's most celebrated artist, Hokusai, famous worldwide for his iconic image of the 'Great Wave' with Mt Fuji in the background, also produced what even now looks like hard-core erotica. Francis Hall noted how strange it was that such 'vile pictures' should be of such excellent artistry and concluded that this showed the 'blunted sense and degraded position of the Japanese as to the ordinary decencies of life'.[50] It did not occur to him that the 'ordinary decencies' were simply different to the Japanese. Mitford felt that the Japanese were entitled to follow their own moral code, and anyway realised that they were not as free and easy about sex as they appeared. In his book, *Tales of Old Japan*, published in 1871, soon after he returned to England, he told of how 'not a man is allowed to approach the daughter of a gentleman; and she is taught that if by accident any insult should be offered to her, the knife which she carries at her girdle is meant for use'.[51] However, he noticed that his servant Lin Fu, coming from China, was 'very much shocked at Japanese morality or rather immorality'.[52] Some Westerners would whip themselves into a fury of indignation over it; the traveller Edward de Fonblanque warned visitors that when shopping in Japan, the greatest care must be exercised to guard against the acquisition of indecencies which are found not only in books and pictures, but are painted on their porcelain, embossed on their lacquer, carved in their ivory, and surreptitiously conveyed into their fans ... I was deeply grieved to learn that even ... the Bishop of Victoria [Hong Kong] ... had neglected the precaution of minute examination [of some porcelain cups] ... Had not an acquaintance providentially examined his ... cups, they would, in all probability, have been stopped at the English Custom-House.[53]

The Bishop himself lambasted Yokohama, writing that it was a 'deplorable scene of demoralisation and profligate life', where a considerable portion of the foreign community lived in a 'state of dissoluteness exceeded in no part of the East' and the 'native officials' contributed 'every facility for the perpetration of domestic vice and impurity'.[54]

At the time, the Japanese Government could not have cared less what Westerners thought of the country's morals and anyway assumed that foreigners would want pleasure quarters as much as the Japanese. But after the fall of the Shogun in 1868, the new Government became concerned about how Japan was viewed by outsiders, wanting it to be seen as a virtuous, principled nation. They moved the Yokohama pleasure quarter away from where the Westerners lived and in 1871, banned nakedness outdoors. It was explained, 'Westerners consider it shameful to reveal their bodies, and they do not do it ... If this ugly practice is left as it is, it will bring shame upon our nation.'[55] Mitford thought there was nothing wrong with it: 'having been used to the scene from their childhood, they see no indelicacy in it; it is a matter of course, and *honi soit qui mal y pense* [shame on him who thinks ill of it]'.[56]

In the contemporary woodblock prints of Yokohama, the pleasure quarter stands out like an immense theme park would today – an artificial fantasy world which contrasted with the everydayness of the town it was near. It was beautiful, the most famous of the brothels in it, the Gankirō, was, in de Fonblanque's description, 'all lacquer and carving and delicate painting', built around an artificial lake, crossed by an ornamental bridge, and it was a favourite subject for artists.[57] It even had its own little theatre.

To those who were not involved in the trade, the quarter conjured up an image of poetic, wistful beauty – a 'floating world', defined like this by Asai Ryōi in 1661:

> Living only for the moment, turning our full attention to the pleasures of the moon, sun, the cherry blossoms and the maple leaves, singing songs, drinking wine, and diverting ourselves just in floating, floating … like a gourd floating along with the river current.[58]

The offer of an abundance of guilt-free pleasure was very seductive and a missionary wrote that the 'temptations in this country are fearful … [and] very few indeed … have not fallen.'[59] Was Mitford one of the few that did not fall? He never wrote of visiting the pleasure quarter in Yokohama, but it was such a major part of the life of the town, it is inconceivable he did not go. However, it is unlikely that he had sex with the prostitutes because sexually transmitted diseases were rampant among them, and he seems never to have caught one, going on to live healthily into old age and father at least nine apparently healthy children. It was probably not so much morals, or even health concerns that stopped him; he despised the Yokohama prostitutes who, with their few crude words of English and aping of Western ways, he felt had been corrupted: 'strange as it seems, our contact all over the East has an evil effect upon the natives'. Moreover, Mitford did not think that Japanese women were beautiful – 'if judged by our standards' – they only had any charm for him if they preserved their Japanese manner and 'dainty little ways'.[60]

At the same time, we can be fairly sure he was not living a monk's life, judging by a diary of his time in Beijing. It was discovered by his granddaughter, Diana Mosley, who told her sister Deborah that it had 'dread SEX mentioned & [was] not mealy mouthed like the published books'.[61] Frustratingly, the diary has been lost, but it looks as if Mitford described his sexual experiences in China in it. Probably in both China and Japan he avoided anyone who consorted with Westerners, instead pursuing more refined women who normally would not have looked at one. Doing this, however, was illegal in Japan – until 1873, sex between foreigners and women who were not prostitutes was strictly forbidden, although only the women (and sometimes their fathers), were punished for it.

Mitford was not a hypocrite and unlike many other writers on Japan, did not get on a high horse about its sexual mores. Rather, he did what he could to counter the impression in the West that the country was a moral cesspool. He did not deny how widespread prostitution was there, but in *Tales of Old Japan*, he defended the women who were engaged in it. In that work, he urged his readers to understand that if a woman went into prostitution to save her family, that she had performed a virtuous act. There was, he wrote, 'no greater act of filial piety, and, so far from incurring reproach among her people, her self-sacrifice would be worthy of praise in their eyes'.[62] This was a very rosy way of looking at it and was rubbished by the journalist and traveller Henry Norman. He wrote that there was 'not one case in hundreds' where prostitutes were not 'unwilling and unhappy victims' and that therefore the 'pleasing belief' that a prostitute serves her term at a brothel and then 'returns to the bosom of her family as if nothing had happened, indeed with the added halo of filial piety', was 'unmitigated rubbish'.[63]

The women were bonded labourers, bought by a brothel for a fixed term like three years, for which the owner would pay the family a cash advance. If the woman had earned enough to cover that amount, plus expenses, during the term, she could leave, but this was rare – the brothels had little incentive to let their higher earners go. The prostitutes themselves would receive virtually no money and often had to enter into debt to survive. Around a third of them died before they gained release from their contract.

Mitford approved of confining prostitution to a certain quarter of a town, arguing that it was better than having 'vice jostling virtue', as happened in the West.[64] The virtuous man 'may live through his life without having this kind of vice forced upon his sight', which was not true in London.[65] Mitford ignored the downside of a delineated area – that the women were effectively imprisoned there, unable to leave without a police pass. In addition, he was leaving aside the fact that there were plenty of prostitutes working illegally from teahouses outside the pleasure quarters.

The biggest and most celebrated pleasure quarter was the Yoshiwara, on the outskirts of Edo, about an hour from the centre by rickshaw. When Japan became safe to walk around in, it was probably Edo's main tourist attraction and was certainly worth a visit – Norman described its buildings as being the finest in the city.[66] Mitford liked it, writing that it was seen at its best just after nightfall, when the lamps were lighted and the women emerged, having spent the previous two hours 'gilding their lips and painting their eyebrows black, and their throats and bosoms a snowy white, carefully leaving three brown Vandyke-collar points where the back of the head joins the neck'.[67] He thought that where Japanese prostitution went wrong was in 'the harlot of Yokohama', where foreigners were involved. But (with his rose-tinted glasses firmly in place) he went on, in the Flower District of Edo 'and wherever Japanese customs are untainted, the utmost decorum prevails'.[68]

*

Yokohama was pretty safe because it was entirely surrounded by water and guards controlled who entered. Nevertheless, there were drunken brawls that got out of hand and on one occasion, the American Minister was manhandled by a mob protesting about rice shortages. Parkes urged the Japanese to publicise the fact that Western ships could supply grain, thus helping to make the locals more positive about the presence of foreigners. Mitford did not worry about these protests, telling his father, 'the mob are not the class whom we have to keep a sharp look out for'.[69]

It was the samurai class, who carried two swords, that were far more frightening, having on their person the ready means to attack foreigners. Westerners would mainly encounter them when they left Yokohama, which Mitford often did, having to go to Edo to transact Legation business with the Shogun's officials there. The Government so dreaded the consequences of a foreign diplomat being murdered that it would surround them with a phalanx of Japanese guards. Mitford told his father, 'marching in the middle of these wretches, I felt very criminal, as if I had done something wrong and was being taken up for it'.[70] These men were, however, essential. From time to time Mitford would meet long *daimyō* trains – processions of feudal lords travelling between Edo and their home domains. They had to make obeisance to the Shogun in Edo, but back in their power bases they were absolute rulers, used to being treated with the highest respect. Proceeded by men shouting 'Get Down!', locals would have to prostrate themselves, foreheads pressed to the ground, when they went past. In 1862, a British group had tangled with such a procession from Satsuma, in southern Kyushu, leaving one of them dead and two wounded. The British demanded reparations, but Satsuma refused and the Shogun's Government could not make them pay. Eventually the British took matters into their own hands and punished this domain by bombarding its capital, Kagoshima. The nation learned two lessons from this: the first was that if there was a showdown with a foreign power, the Japanese side would probably come off worse. The second was that the once impregnable Shogunate was now so weak that it could no longer enforce its power over the bigger domains. The country was ripe for revolution.

Mitford believed that the British action had made the roads safer for Westerners, although when he encountered these processions, he would still put his hand on his revolver. Often he would have to stop and send one of his Japanese guards to ask leave to go on, which would be grudgingly granted. 'The outrageous pride and vanity of the Japanese character' he told his father,

passes all belief, and we have to give in to it, or risk a row, in which we should be sure to get the worst of it in the first instance; and I don't think it would be much consolation to me after I had been killed, that Great Britain should exact an indemnity and blow up a town or two of wood and paper to avenge me.[71]

At the same time, Mitford had some understanding of why they behaved as they did. He knew that like the Chinese, most Japanese felt that the presence of Westerners in their country was an affront. He found a handbill urging people to preserve the land sacred to the descendants of the gods from being defiled by the barbarians, who were the offspring of dogs, cats and apes.[72] Mitford accepted that 'The Japanese did not want us; they were rich, at peace, and happy in their own way' before the Westerners came.[73] Furthermore, the behaviour of many of his countrymen justified the Japanese attitude. The Legation doctor, William Willis, commented:

> We [British] have all the air, if not the insolence, of a dominant race; the facility with which we use our hands and feet in support of argument may elicit respect but not esteem … To the proud Japanese it must be painful to see the air of superiority the commonest foreigner assumes in his presence.[74]

*

A month and a half after his arrival in Yokohama, Mitford was woken by a violent gale which blew in a pane of glass. He got up normally and while he was shaving, Lin Fu came in to tell him there was a fire about two-thirds of a mile away. Mitford said he would go and have a look once he had dressed, not realising that typhoon-strength winds were spreading the fire at tremendous speed; it was 'leaping from roof to roof, driven before the wind in sheets of flame' and

> little Japanese crazy cottages built of wood and paper, shrivelled up like gun cotton passed through a candle. There was no falling of timbers, no creaking or noise like in an ordinary fire; the flames passed and when they had been driven by, there was nothing but a few tiles to mark where the houses stood.'[75]

Mitford thought that the fire had started in the pleasure quarter, probably because it suffered the greatest loss of life, but in fact it seems to have originated in a butcher's shop. As the pleasure quarter was surrounded by water, it would have been spared had the road to it not been lined with teahouses – once the first caught fire, the next went up in flames and then the next, like a row of dominoes. The fact that there was only one bridge to get out of the quarter meant there was a terrible crush to escape and over a hundred of the women who lived there were killed. The fire ended up destroying more than two-thirds of the Japanese part of the town, but the wind died down before it could engulf the foreign section as well, although the new American consulate was lost (it was the first US consulate in the world). Unfortunately, Mitford's house was in the Japanese sectionand was completely burnt out. He explained to his father the scale of his losses:

> I ... was unable to save anything and in fact had just time to escape with my life. I have lost nearly seven hundred pounds [around £50,000 today] worth of effects, all my papers (including my translations from Chinese which were ready for the press and I intended to publish on arriving in England), all my little odds and ends, gifts of friends, some of which date back from before the time when I went to Eton. Nothing could be saved. The fire was too rapid.[76]

Luckily he had stored most of his collection from China in the Legation buildings, which were undamaged (he thought it was worth more than £1,000), and he soon sent it back to England for safety. But the losses were still overwhelming. Perhaps the most painful of all was his beloved black retriever which he had brought with him from China. The dog had followed Mitford when he rushed out of the house, but 'lost his head and ran back home. Poor beast!'[77] From a professional point of view, it would have been the loss of the translations that was most devastating. He had compiled them by employing a 'learned Chinese' to write a series of papers on 'different manners and customs, rites and ceremonies of the Chinese', then asking a 'jealous Chinese critic' to review them, so he could be sure they were trustworthy.[78] After this, he translated them into English. Mitford had hoped that this book would get him noticed in Britain, although it sounds from his description that it would have been much less interesting than *Tales of Old Japan*. But he could have hoped to have acquired a reputation as an expert on China. He explained to his father (when feeling negative about both China and Japan), 'To pretend to like living in the East would be absurd', But, he went on: 'It suits me for the present … looking to what I have done here as a means to an end, and … ensure advancement.'[79] Having lost his Chinese translations, it had to be through Japan that he would make his name. Considering how successfully he did this, the loss might have been a blessing in disguise, if it spurred him on to trying all the harder with Japan.

Everybody in Japan seemed to be burned out at some point. Parkes had come through this fire unscathed, but lost everything a year later when his roof caught fire, and in half an hour, his house was burnt to the ground. 'These houses,' thought Mitford, 'seem made for burning. Being almost entirely built of wood which gets very dry and rotten, a spark getting under the tiles of the roof is sufficient to set a whole quarter on fire.'[80] Luckily there was little wind and a light rain was falling when Parkes lost his house, so the fire did not spread.

Mitford was amazed at how casual the Japanese seemed to be about fires – in Edo, they were almost daily events during the winter, the main season for them, being the driest time of year. 'It is the most original thing', he told his father,

> the way in which a native comes up to one and announces with a grin that his house is burnt. One of my servants came to me today to ask leave to go to Yedo [Edo] and see if his father and mother were burnt as if it were the best of jokes.[81]

Mitford was still new to Japan and did not know how to read the Japanese yet – the smiles would have been a brave face. Mitford concluded that they were 'utterly careless' to the danger of fires, but this was untrue.[82] In Edo, there was a system of watchtowers and when a distant fire was spotted from one, a bell would be rung and all the local firefighters would rush to try to stop it spreading.

Where the Japanese really differed from Westerners in their attitude to fires was in the speed with which they picked up the pieces afterwards. While the Westerners in Yokohama were still wringing their hands over their losses, Mitford noted that 'almost before the embers have ceased to smoulder' the Japanese had calmly set about rebuilding their houses.[83] The opportunity was taken to make Yokohama safer, a wide street between the Japanese and Western towns being made, which would act as a firebreak. The pleasure quarter was moved and the old one turned into a public park, the first in Japan, still called simply 'Yokohama Park'. Today, the park's origins are modestly remembered – in a quiet corner there is a lantern, inscribed 'Gankirō', with a sign explaining that the area had been noted for its 'sociable establishments'.

Mitford, who always seemed to be so resilient, found the experience traumatising. Four months after the disaster, he told his father, 'at every step, whether of pleasure, private or public business, sleeping, eating, drinking, sitting or lying, I feel the loss of that fire'.[84] The fire and its aftermath hardened Mitford's view of Japan, but he did not say why. One reason may have been the widespread feeling among the Westerners in Yokohama that the Japanese residents had done little to save anyone but themselves and nothing to stop the flames spreading. Whatever the cause, Mitford was writing two weeks after the fire: 'It has disgusted me with Japan', adding, 'I hate the Japanese. Treachery and hatred are the only qualities which they show to us.' He was, however, impressed by the 'lowest class,' who seemed '*bons enfants* enough'.[85] In fact, they had shown exceptional honesty after the fire, having hidden valuable items to keep them safe, then returned them to their masters, when they could easily have kept them.

A good thing to come out of the fire was the generosity of the other Britons there: Mitford immediately had offers of a place to stay and a Vice-Admiral, who barely knew him, was prepared to write him a cheque for $1,000 (equivalent to more than half Mitford's annual income) and give him six shirts.[86] Mitford accepted the shirts but refused the money. From this point onwards, clothes would be a constant problem, partly because he was very particular, but also because he thought it necessary to have large quantities of them. He would wear Japanese-made clothes for travelling and as casual wear, but he wanted to dress like a gentleman in England whenever he was doing anything official, meaning he had to ask his father to send him things. A shopping list he wrote eight months after the fire gives an idea of what he thought he needed and could not be obtained in Japan:

> One pair of brushes (long bristles)
> One comb
> One dressing roll with good shaving tackle. Stout and not too expensive, say £5.
> Twelve flannel shirts as thin as possible. Striped gray and white or lilac and white ... (to wear with false collars).
> Twelve India gauze under waistcoats: short sleeves ...
> [Ditto] drawers
> Two suits of light-gray flannel clothes
> Two gray winter suits from Ball's ...
> Also any quantity of pocket handkerchiefs.[87]

He got back on his feet fairly quickly, staying for three weeks with the British Consul in Yokohama, Francis Myburgh, and they 'had a very jolly time of it'.[88] Myburgh had been in Japan since 1859, and spoke Dutch, which in the early days was the only European language known to the Japanese (the Netherlands had been the only Western nation allowed to trade with Japan after the country was closed). He died tragically in 1867, struck down, as were so many in the East, by a sudden illness. Mitford mourned him, reflecting:

> There are so few, so very few, men whom one meets in these far countries with whom one becomes really intimate that such a loss is deeply felt. Myburgh was a man of my own age, one of the handsomest men I ever saw, and a thorough English gentleman.[89]

Mitford was angry that he had been unable to insure his possessions; to save public money he and his colleagues had been put in, what he called, 'tinder cottages', which no company would insure.[90] It should be said that before the fire, he had been much more positive about his 'little Japanese cottage', which had been 'really very pretty in a tiny way with its clean mats and paper'.[91] It was only when he realised how unsafe it had been that he felt differently about it. His new dwelling was no improvement on the previous one, being the 'queerest little bit of a shanty you ever saw. That it should hold together at all is the mystery to me, so dilapidated is it.'[92] In the end, he was compensated for his losses, but this was seven months later, and not when he really needed the money – he had to borrow $1,000 commercially, at an interest rate of 10%, to tide him over.

Overall, very little impressed Mitford during his first months in Japan. An exception was the huge bronze statue of Buddha in Kamakura, 'certainly one of the most, if not the most wonderful monument I have ever seen … it has the merit of being perfect'.[93] However, he had a low opinion of the rest of the town, which had been the capital of Japan from 1192 to 1333; for Mitford, only a 'few old temples' indicated that there was anything special about the place.[94] Kamakura stands out now because unlike the surrounding cities, it was not bombed in the Second World War, and its historic sites have been preserved. This is in contrast to Yokohama, where frequent disasters, combined with a culture of casually knocking things down and rebuilding them, has meant there is not a single building that Mitford would have recognised existing today – the oldest intact building remaining in the city dates to 1904.[95]

One other thing that Mitford thought was good about Japan was the cleanliness of the lodgings. He had been used to filthy inns in China, and in comparison, the Japanese ones were spotless: 'instead of the dirty fireman who waits upon you in the former, here there is sure to be some neathanded little maiden, hideous but scrupulously clean and very flirtatious'.[96]

The trouble was that Japan was boring compared to China and Mongolia with none of their 'wildness and variety'. Mitford thought the countryside around Kamakura was 'all so very small, and so same. One valley is just like another … On the whole I believe no country has ever been more lied about than Japan. For my part I never got so little for so much expectation anywhere.'[97] After Mitford had decided he liked the country, the way he responded to its scenery was very different. On a return trip to Kamakura in 1872, he wrote: 'Can anything be more lovely in its way than the ride from the Great Buddha over the richly wooded hills to the sea?'[98] The views were the same but Mitford had changed.

2

EDO

October 1866 – May 1867

ဆ

AN ENTIRELY WHITE, perfectly-formed Mt Fuji in the background; a sketchy castle in the middleground, and in the foreground, the common people going about their daily business beside Nihonbashi – the 'Bridge of Japan'. This picture of the Shogun's capital was how the woodblock artist Ando Hiroshige (1797–1858) started his series *One Hundred Famous Views of Edo*. These images – now considered among the greatest achievements of Japanese art – have shaped the way we view Edo. They show its inhabitants living a peaceful existence in often idyllic settings, with nothing ugly or unpleasant intruding.

In fact, the Edo that Mitford saw had been through the wringer. There had been a big earthquake in 1855 that had seen the destruction of 50,000 houses, although this was just a large-scale version of a routine Edo experience.[1] More devastating were the most severe outbreaks of cholera in Japan's history, which hit in 1858 (both Hiroshige and the Shogun died in this epidemic) and again in 1862.[2] It was not lost on the citizens of Edo that just before the first outbreak, the treaties between Japan and the Western powers, which opened certain Japanese ports to foreign ships, had been signed. The timing was a coincidence, but it brought home the fact that in the two hundred years that Japan had been closed to foreigners, it had been almost completely spared devastating diseases that other parts of the world were repeatedly exposed to. Westerners tend to look upon those Japanese who resisted the opening of the country as backward, ignorant bigots, and Mitford certainly did, but it cannot be denied that isolation had some big advantages.

Mitford, who in these early days was still not engaged by Japan, could not work up any enthusiasm for Edo: for him it was 'another disappointment' with 'nothing grand or magnificent'.[3] His attitude would change when he became caught up in the tumultuous events that were about to occur, and he began to see Japan as an opportunity rather than a series of annoyances. But at this time, Beijing was firmly lodged in his mind as the model of how a great Asian city should look. It was on a monumental scale, its walls, 'high, ruinous, battlemented, and picturesque …' capped at intervals by towers of fantastic Chinese architecture … with their lofty gates'.[4] Edo could not compete with this. A visitor in 1879 wrote: 'It is hard to realize that Tokio is a city … It looks like a series of villages … There is no special character to Tokio, no one trait to seize upon and remember.'[5] It was certainly big, with a population of more than a million people, but, Mitford thought, 'So far as architecture is concerned it is the most featureless place in the world.'[6] He thought that a bird's-eye view of Edo would be 'exactly like the view one gets when some Lowland farmer takes one to a small eminence and shows one his cattle sheds in interminable parallel lines. This is Yedo [Edo] – low narrow buildings in straight lines round dirty squares.' He adds: 'I say dirty advisedly – for although there is great cleanliness inside the houses the filthy stenches and abominations outside are as bad as China.'[7] The smells came from the large-scale use of human excrement to fertilise fields – it was collected every night in Edo and transported to the countryside. Mitford hated the system:

> … the whole of what should form the sewerage of the city is carried out on the backs of men and horses … and, if you would avoid the overpowering nuisance, you must walk handkerchief in hand, ready to shut out the stench which assails you at every moment.[8]

The low narrow buildings would have been the 'long houses' that accommodated the retainers of the feudal lords, or *daimyō*.[9] The most powerful *daimyō* had very big entourages; the domain of Chōshū in western Honshu alone had more than two thousand men stationed in Edo. Mitford described the great *daimyō* as 'men with pedigrees lost in the clouds, with incomes that could buy our richest nobles and possessing the power of life and death over thousands and thousands of human beings'.[10] Their long processions were a common sight in the city and Mitford was entranced by them – the retainers dressed 'in armour with crested helms', and 'fiercely moustachioed visors' – even though he hated their arrogance when it was directed at him.[11] He described the terror these processions instilled, with the attendants 'ready to punish with instant death any insolent fellow who might presume to cross their line of march,' adding that they scowled 'fiercely at us western barbarians, intruders, sorcerers and devils'.[12]

The *daimyō* retainers were all of the samurai class, which obliged them to wear two swords, one long and one short, held through a sash at the waist. It was not easy walking with them, and they developed a distinctive hips-forward stride to enable them to do so with a swagger. Their hair was tied in a special topknot and the smartly-dressed ones wore stiff-shouldered jackets (*kataginu*) and baggy but elegant trousers (*hakama*). Such men created an air of menace and Satow wrote that Europeans looked on any of them 'as a possible assassin, and if they met one in the street, thanked God as soon as they had passed him and found themselves in safety'.[13] It was not only foreigners who feared them – they could attack anyone from a lower class with impunity, and it was not unknown for them to slice through beggars, just to test the sharpness of their blades and keep their hand in (every male samurai was expected to be able to cut off a head). The upper classes were not much safer, Parkes writing that 'the liability of assassination seems to be accepted by everyone in Japan from a Prime Minister downwards.'[14]

More unpredictable were samurai whose feudal lord had been defeated or disgraced, known as *rōnin*. They had lost their income and had great difficulty finding lawful employment.

Mitford wrote a romanticised description of these men: 'persons of gentle blood, entitled to bear arms, who, having become separated from their feudal lords ... wander about the country in the capacity of somewhat disreputable knights-errant, without ostensible means of living'.[15] In reality, they could be little more than well-bred thugs, armed with razor-sharp swords, inevitably bearing some kind of grudge, and if homeless as well, with little to lose.

Mitford leaves readers of *Tales of Old Japan* with the impression that Japan was a violent country, peopled with such characters, but it was mostly peaceful. Only male samurai were allowed to carry swords and they constituted only three per cent or so of the population and were concentrated in Edo – eighty per cent of the population was involved with farming. Therefore, the sword fights were not as widespread as he implied. But Mitford did tend to focus on those with 'gentle blood'.

Within Edo, the lower classes – divided into craftsmen and merchants – lived in a completely separate part of the city from the samurai class, the result of, as Mitford later put it, the 'Asiatic prejudice of keeping persons of one calling in one place'.[16] Tokyo is still a bit like this, with shops selling things like electronic goods, books or sports equipment, each concentrated in their respective areas. Although the lower classes constituted around two-thirds of Edo's population, they were squeezed into a fifth of the city, around the edges.

In *Tales of Old Japan*, Mitford launched into an effusive account of what has been called the 'Low City' where the ordinary people lived. About Sensōji temple in Asakusa, which was the spiritual heart of Edo, he writes that the main hall was adorned with such 'curious workmanship of gilding and of silvering ... that no place can be more excellently beautiful'.[17] He also describes a rich street life which included 'wild beasts, performing monkeys, automata, conjurers, wooden and paper figures ... acrobats, and jesters'.[18] In fact he did not visit Asakusa himself – rather he relied on a Japanese book entitled 'Guide to the Prosperous City of Edo' (*Edo Hanjōki*), along with other Japanese sources. It must have irked him that he missed seeing probably Edo's most interesting neighbourhood, but it would have been very difficult for him to get there – he would quite likely have had stones thrown at him, even surrounded by guards, and it would have been a ten kilometre ride from the British Legation through some crowded streets to reach it.

He did, however, make it to Ueno, which is nearly as far, but this was in the safety of a large group, led by Parkes, to see the burial ground of the Shoguns. In spite of Parkes' rank, they had great difficulty gaining entrance, but eventually succeeded because, as Mitford put it, 'we are more masters here than we were, and they dare not refuse us admittance as they used to'.[19]

After his initial feelings of disappointment, we see Mitford gradually start to warm to Edo. Six months after his first visit, he was conceding to his father that the castle was a 'splendid remnant of feudality which, with its deep broad moat and solid walls of masonry forms a great contrast to the bourgeois appearance of the town'.[20] It was indeed a formidable construction, the biggest castle complex in the world, but its inhabitants had crumbled at the sight of Commodore Perry's eight 'black ships' when they sailed into Edo Bay in 1853, determined to reopen Japan. To Mitford it seemed 'outside the bounds of possibility' that the country should 'have been thrown into an agony of panic by so puny a force … with no show of hostile intentions'.[21]

But the Shogun's Government believed that if it forced a showdown with the Western powers it would almost certainly be humiliated, as China had been in the two Opium Wars – in the first of these wars, Britain defeated a country with ten times Japan's population, while losing only sixty-nine men dead. At the same time, the Government had to placate those who were determined to expel the foreigners, whatever the cost, convinced that they were polluting the sacred land of the gods. There were no good options for the Shogun's regime. Its response was described by Fukuzawa Yukichi, now seen as one of the key founders of modern Japan, like this:

> Our government was simply worrying over the threats and bullying of the European diplomats, and could not decide what to do … As

matters became more acute, the senior officers pretended they were
ill … Finally, only the minor officers were talking the matters over
in a series of confused arguments.[22]

*

Britain's first Minister to Japan, Rutherford Alcock, established
his mission at a temple called Tōzenji, in the south of Edo, in
1859. A temple may seem an odd choice for a Legation, especially as they had to share the premises with monks, but it was
one of the few available complexes of buildings in Edo that was
big enough to house all the staff. It took about an hour to trot
to Edo Castle from Tōzenji, so it was not very convenient for
meetings with the Government, but it had exquisite gardens, was
close to where ships could dock, and was on the way to Yokohama. It also turned out to be a rare survivor: many of the buildings the Legation used there are still standing today.

The trouble with it was that it was not secure. It had no wall
around it and its construction was flimsy. Westerners used to
brick houses and solid doors with locks were horrified by how
insubstantial Japanese buildings were – many of them could have
been pushed down with a decent shove. Mitford wrote of how
during a gale, he had to have a servant sit on the roof of his
house to stop it blowing away.[23] Thin sliding doors meant that
you knew exactly what all the people around you were doing –
there was no such thing as a private moment. Mitford explained
to his father how the Japanese dealt with this: 'Paper slides open
at the tops divide the rooms and there is no privacy nor means
of ensuring a confidential talk without point-blank ordering the
profane out of hearing. Luckily this is not considered impolite.'[24]

In addition, Tōzenji was close to Shinagawa where, according to Mitford, every house was 'a den of infamy'; it was a
'horrible suburb which we had to ride through every time to or
from Yedo, never venturing there after dark without the greatest
precaution'. He added that it was 'not an uncommon thing in
the early morning to see a dead body hacked to pieces thrown

out before a teahouse door'.[25] When the area burned down, on 30 January 1867, Mitford thought it was a cause for celebration, although he knew how quickly the Japanese recovered from fires: 'in a fortnight they will be flourishing again as merrily as ever'.[26] It was in Shinagawa that the plot had been hatched to attack Tōzenji on a hot July night back in 1861. A group had crept unnoticed through sliding doors left open to keep the building cool. Laurence Oliphant, who had just arrived as a secretary, was woken by a dog barking. The only weapon he had to hand was a hunting crop, and he went out into a dark corridor to be faced by a sword-wielding samurai. The intruder slashed at him twice, missing both times, and Oliphant managed to strike him with his whip. However, with a third blow, the samurai cut Oliphant's shoulder. Oliphant would have been killed had a colleague not come out into the corridor and shot the attacker.

In a despatch to the Foreign Seretary in 1860, Alcock explained the feeling of living in Edo like this:

> With a perpetual menace of assassination on the one hand, and incendiarism on the other, while earthquakes almost every week shake the houses to their foundations, I cannot say the post of Diplomatic Agent in Yedo is to be recommended to nervous people.[27]

None of this put off Alcock's successor, Sir Harry Parkes, who was determined to move the Legation back to Edo, regardless of the risks and difficulties. So the Japanese Government erected a temporary building for them in the grounds of another temple, Sengakuji, which was very close to Tōzenji and they moved there in November 1866.

Sengakuji was more secure than Tōzenji, being surrounded by a high wall, and indeed the buildings had the look of a low-security prison. Mitford described them as being 'long, straggling crazily built huts of glass ... letting in every blast of the bitter cold winds, and utterly unfit for a Japan winter'.[28] They were, however, in a beautiful setting and when Mitford came to write about it in *Tales of Old Japan*, he described it as a 'fair, smiling landscape: gentle slopes, crested by a dark fringe of pines and firs, lead down to the sea ... the bay studded with picturesque fisher-craft ... and beyond ... Fuji-Yama, the Peerless Mountain, solitary and grand'.[29] As we have seen, Mitford veered from one extreme to the other in his descriptions – he was incapable of thinking a place so-so.

Whether he was loving it or hating it, Sengakuji, more than any other temple in Japan, had the power to capture Mitford's imagination. In order to understand why, we need to go back to the beginning of the eighteenth century and to the story that has been described as Japan's 'national legend'.[30] It is known in Japanese as *Chūshingura* (literally, the Treasury of Loyal Retainers), and in English as *The Forty-Seven Rōnin*. It is performed every year in *kabuki* and *bunraku* puppet versions and endless television and film productions of it have been made. Mitford, who was the first to translate it accurately into English, used it to open his retellings of classic Japanese stories, *Tales of Old Japan*. This is a summary of how he told it:

A *daimyō*, Asano Takumi no Kami and a noble, Kamei-sama, needed to be trained in the etiquette of receiving an Imperial envoy, and a high official, Kōtsuke no Suke, was appointed to teach them it.[31] The two men brought gifts, as custom dictated, but Kōtsuke no Suke was greedy and decided that they were inadequate. He provoked Asano with sneers and insults and eventually Asano could stand it no longer and tried to stab him with his short sword, but only managed to lightly wound him. Nevertheless, he had committed a grave crime by attacking a man inside Edo Castle. His lands and property were confiscated and he was sentenced to perform *hara-kiri*, which he did honourably, and he was buried at Sengakuji.

This turned all his retainers into *rōnin* – masterless samurai – and forty-seven of them decided to dedicate their lives to avenging their master. Kōtsuke no Suke expected this, and was so well guarded that it was impossible to get to him. The forty-seven were led by Asano's chief councillor, Ōishi Kuranosuke; he became a drunkard and frequented brothels so that it would look like he had given up on any idea of revenge. He even divorced his wife and took a mistress. One day, he was found lying in the street and passers-by, recognising him, mocked him. A man trod on his face as he slept and spat on him. Kōtsuke no Suke's spies reported this to their master, who decided that he was now safe, and dismissed half his guard.

But Ōishi and the other forty-six *rōnin* were only biding their time. Eventually, on a cold winter's night, they attacked Kōtsuke no Suke's residence and after fighting their way past all the guards, they found their quarry, hiding like the coward he was. Ōishi respectfully explained why they were there and begged him to perform *hara-kiri*, so that he might die the death of a nobleman. But he refused, so Ōishi cut off Kōtsuke no Suke's head with the same dagger that had been used for Asano's *hara-kiri*. The *rōnin* took the head to Sengakuji and the abbott led them to their master's grave. They washed the head in a well (which can still be seen there), placed it on Asano's tomb and awaited their fate. They were all sentenced to perform *hara-kiri*, which they did courageously, in the correct manner. Their bodies were taken to Sengakuji and buried in front of the tomb of their master. Almost like saints in Catholic Europe, they were immediately venerated, and flocks of people came to pray at their graves. These included the man who had trodden on and spat at Ōishi, who came to seek pardon and atonement for this at the temple; he stabbed himself there and was buried with the forty-seven.

Mitford felt that this story presented a 'terrible picture of fierce heroism which it is impossible not to admire'.[32] When he describes Ōishi 'in his zeal to slay his lord's enemy' thinking 'nothing of divorcing his wife and sending away his children', he adds 'Admirable and faithful man!'[33] Mitford sees loyalty to the honour of a dead master as being above loyalty to a living family. Probably most of his Western readers would not have agreed with such a high price being paid for an act of revenge. However, the *rōnin* are still admired in Japan and the historian Tsurumi Shunsuke has said, 'if you study Chūshingura long enough, you will understand everything about the Japanese'.[34] But while the story does show impressive devotion and the complete dissolving of personal concerns into that of a group, it also reveals what was missing from the samurai code: reverence for human life (including one's own), forgiveness, compassion, and above all, the ability to move on.

When Mitford expressed an interest in the story at the temple, he was allowed a private inspection of the relics of the *rōnin* kept there. The chief priest took out carefully-labelled boxes and showed him the contents: rags of clothing, and scraps of metal and wood. These were armour, which the *rōnin* had had to improvise, because if they had bought it, Kōtsuke no Suke would have found out that they were planning to attack him. There were also plans of Kōtsuke no Suke's house which one of them had obtained by marrying the daughter of the builder. Another was a receipt made out to the priests who had given Kōtsuke no Suke's head to his son; it read: 'Memorandum: Item. One Head.' Mitford made a translation of a note explaining their conduct, which was found on each of the forty-seven: 'It is impossible to remain under the same heaven with the enemy of lord or father … If any honourable person should find our bodies after death, he is respectfully requested to open and read the document.'[35]

Mitford experienced the power of the story when, in September 1868, a man came to pray at the grave of Ōishi, and then performed *hara-kiri*, stabbing himself in the throat after cutting his belly, as he had no second to cut off his head. He had been a *rōnin* who had decided that the position was hateful to him and he would rather die with honour. Mitford visited the spot soon afterwards and saw the man's blood on the ground. 'What more fitting place', he asked, 'could he find in which to put an end to his life than the graveyard of these Braves?'[36] Mitford seems to have had no idea what the man's story was, but because it was connected with the *rōnin* tale, he was determined to see this death as heroic, rather than the grave crime it would have been seen as in Britain at the time (suicide was a capital crime there, being considered equivalent to murder).

The story was used in Japan for propaganda during the Second World War, held up as an example of the loyalty and self-sacrifice that was expected. US intelligence analysed it and decided that it was evidence that Japan would never surrender – the conclusion that justified the dropping of the atom bombs. However, an American Admiral, Ellis Zacharias, who had lived in Japan before the war and spoke Japanese, pointed out that of almost four hundred retainers, only forty-seven had sought revenge. He argued that what the story really showed was that while there would be a few hold-outs, most Japanese would give up the fight.

Mitford's interest in the story of the *rōnin* did not reconcile him to living at Sengakuji in winter, where the wind 'whistled unhindered through long passages and chilly rooms, so it almost seemed as if we should be better off in the open'.[37] On their first night, which was only in November, there was 'no temptation to sit up late; shivering and shaking, we went to bed very early, but it was long before even a pile of blankets could bring enough warmth to enable me to sleep'.[38] While it was still dark, Mitford was wakened by a loud noise; he jumped up with his revolver to see what it was, and it turned out to be a reveille – a daily routine that compounded the misery. It was a bleak, comfortless place. He told his father, 'Books, music, society, carpets, arm-chairs, curtains, good eating and drinking, cosy fires, are pleasures of memory only and of hope. I never was in such a place in all my life.'[39]

Another annoying thing about being in Edo was that because it was so dangerous, they had to be surrounded by Japanese guards. Even Parkes, who presented an irritating image of someone who did not care about discomfort (and therefore expected his subordinates not to complain about it), grumbled about them to the Foreign Office, writing that they made living at Sengakuji 'very like penitentiary life'.[40] These men were not very effective at protecting them – one hundred and fifty of them had been guarding Tōzenji, but not one had seen the attackers who had entered the buildings and wounded Oliphant. This was probably because, as Mitford explained, 'they were far more concerned with spying' on them than fighting for them.[41] The Shogun's Government wanted to know what everybody was doing and these men were part of an immense network of inspectors who were constantly searching for signs of plots or corruption in everyone from the *daimyō* down. Officials who checked on the *daimyō* were called *ōmetsuke* – literally 'big attached eye' – and those who watched everybody else were *metsuke*, or 'attached eye'. 'Nowhere', Mitford wrote,

> was espionage carried out in such perfection as it was in Japan, where ... it attained the dignity of a fine art. No native official, whatever his rank might be, went forth on his business alone ... [I]t is not to be wondered at that we also should have been unable to move a step without our 'eyes in attendance'.[42]

Mitford saw nothing wrong with the Legation being in Yokohama and for staff to go up to Edo when business needed to be transacted, the city being 'a curious place enough to pay a flying visit to', but 'a dreary residence'.[43] He thought Parkes' insistence on being there was meaningless – the country was in such a state of flux that Edo would probably not remain the centre of government for long, Kobe or Osaka being more probable sites for it. Parkes, Mitford wrote, 'being full of whims, and seeming to seek out discomfort as he does danger for its own sake, must needs compel all of us to sacrifice every little comfort, and Heaven knows there are not too many anywhere in the East'.[44] In his memoir Mitford changed his tune, writing that Parkes 'argued, and I quite agreed with him', that it was wrong to 'practically ... waive the right of residence in what, if not the true capital of that country, was, at any rate, at the moment the seat of Government'.[45] For the older Mitford, it would have been very difficult to admit that he had not wanted to live in Edo because he was not comfortable there.

Matters improved when Mitford and Satow persuaded Parkes to allow them to rent a place outside the Legation, 'a delicious ... little shrine ... commanding a lovely view over the bay', at a sub-temple of Sengakuji called Monryōin, now long gone.[46] Mitford emphasised how small it was: 'a lovely little wee temple on a tiny hill', but it sounds much more extensive in Satow's description, probably because Mitford was used to bigger houses than Satow.[47] But people like Mitford – and the even taller Satow for that matter – would have been constantly banging his head and having difficulty getting through entrances, so buildings felt confined, even if they were not particularly small. According to Satow, the house sat on about two-thirds of an acre and, as well as numerous rooms, had three staircases to facilitate escape from the upper floor in case of attack.[48] It was, Satow thought, 'one of the oddest houses imaginable' and was less safe than Sengakuji because their only protection there was three or four guards in a hut.[49] He wrote that they thought themselves 'very plucky in thus braving the risks of midnight assassination'.[50] For a little added security, Mitford had the garden laid with cockle-shells so that they would be able to hear any intruders coming.

Mitford and Satow still had to be accompanied by their guards when they went out, but at least they were further away from the wretched reveille. Another benefit of being outside the Legation was that they could receive visits from *daimyō* retainers, whose presence in the main buildings would have attracted unwelcome attention. This meant that Mitford and Satow could find out what was happening in the crucial domains far from Edo, where plots to overthrow the Shogun's regime were fomenting. It looks like Satow and Mitford walked a fine line in these meetings. They thought the feudal system should be overthrown and replaced by a parliamentary government along British lines. But Parkes' instructions were to assist in maintaining the stability of the Shogun's Government and to keep out of any internal conflict. For all his temper tantrums and colourful ways, Parkes was very obedient to his superiors. Typical of his written style is the following: 'I shall be most careful to observe Earl Clarendon's [the Foreign Secretary] instructions as to neutrality of action and of opinion.'[51] He was anyway principally concerned with trade, not politics. Mitford's official reports leave the impression that he and Satow maintained this line but Saigō Takamori (who would become one of the great heroes of the Meiji Restoration), wrote after a meeting on 12 January 1867 that Satow had actively encouraged him to challenge the Shogun's regime.[52]

Mitford was senior to Satow which is why it was he who had to write the reports of these meetings for Parkes. Many in Mitford's position would have simply used Satow as an interpreter and taken the credit for what was found out. But Mitford let the more experienced Satow do the talking, and was happy to later admit that 'his was the brain which was responsible for the work which I recorded'.[53] However, Mitford was determined to take part in these conversations and therefore studied Japanese with, according to Satow, 'unflagging diligence', making rapid progress.[54] Mitford later said that it took a year and a half for him to become able to conduct business in Japanese – often studying eight to ten hours a day. He found that unlike a European language, you could not just pick up Japanese – 'there is no such thing …; it is a matter of close application … every day'.[55] Between them, Mitford and Satow would make Parkes much the best informed of the foreign Ministers; something which would prove very useful as the Shogun's regime started to fall apart.

As the weather got warmer, in his 'really a little gem' of a cottage, Mitford started to feel comfortable. Edo had been 'a perfect horror … in winter', but he was 'quite in love' with it in the summer.[56] It seemed even better when he heard of a typhus epidemic in Yokohama, 'which of all stinking ill-drained holes that ever invited a pestilence is about the worst. Here we have delicious sea breezes and cool pure air to breathe.'[57] Mitford was beginning to think that Edo, and even Japan, might not be so bad after all.

3

THE SHOGUN

January – April 1867

∽

We are subjected to the insults of five arrogant Powers; conquest by them seems certain to be our fate. Thinking of this, I can neither sleep ... nor ... swallow food ... The subjugation of the hated foreigner is the greatest of the national tasks that faces us ... if, through idleness, we fail to achieve success, how much the greater will be our crime! The deities of the universe themselves would punish us. Be most diligent, therefore![1]

THE SEVENTEEN-YEAR-OLD SHOGUN Iemochi must have felt in despair when he received this harangue from Emperor Kōmei in 1864. His predecessors had enjoyed unquestioned authority since the Tokugawa dynasty had been founded in 1603 and the Emperors were consigned to impotent irrelevance in Kyoto. But the diminishing power of the Shogunate meant that Iemochi was too weak to argue with Kōmei but also too weak to do anything to expel the foreigners.

The Shogunate had become 'effete', in Mitford's opinion, the 'mere slave' of the Emperor.[2] Japan's earlier rulers, he felt, would not have hesitated in the face of the challenge of dealing with the Western powers, but would 'proudly have taken upon themselves the responsibility of giving the answer in one sense or the other' – they would either have engaged with Westerners or got them out of Japan.[3] But Iemochi had only been twelve when he became Shogun and never had the chance to become an effective leader, dying at the age of twenty, of beriberi, a disease which afflicted the upper classes in Japan. They ate polished rice which had had its husks taken off, removing the thiamine (vitamin B1), which we need to stay healthy. Ordinary people, who ate the husks, were spared this disease. The death occurred on 29 August, but was not officially announced until 28 September six days before Mitford's arrival in the country. Japan was therefore nominally in mourning when Mitford landed – he was told that Iemochi's officers could not shave or wash for twenty-one days, 'so we hasten to get over our interviews before their Excellencies become too dirty. Luckily the weather is cool.'[4]

Iemochi's replacement, Tokugawa Yoshinobu, was much more able and was also older, being the same age as Mitford – they were both twenty-nine when he was officially proclaimed Shogun on 10 January 1867. He believed that a healthy Japan could only have one ruler – him – and, like Mitford, thought that the Shogunate had allowed its power to slip away through weakness.[5] He decided that a proper accommodation needed to be reached with the West, explaining to the Imperial Court:

> If we alone ... cling to outworn customs and refrain from international relations of a kind common to all countries, our action will be in conflict with the natural order of things. We will, I think, soon find ourselves in great difficulties.'[6]

This was putting it mildly. Potentially, Japan faced losing control of its affairs, as had happened to China. It needed to modernise to become stronger and to do that, it had to get assistance from the Western powers. The question was whether the Shogunate still had the strength to lead this move in the face of such violent internal opposition. Many in the outer domains thought not – they believed that Japan could only be made strong by becoming a modern, centralised state, legitimised by the ancient authority of the Emperor.

Yoshinobu was looking like a leader who had taken over when it was already too late for his regime. But he saw one last chance: persuading the Western powers to give him the support that would enable him to prevail against his enemies. Therefore, immediately upon being named Shogun, he invited the foreign Ministers to meet him in Osaka, promising to cut through all the negativity and misunderstandings of the past. It was the first time any such meeting had ever been suggested and looked like a fresh start. Parkes, however, wanted to be more sure of the situation before meeting him, and anyway did not want to look like he was at anyone's beck and call. It would be 'gratifying' to Yoshinobu, 'no doubt', he told the Foreign Office in London, to have 'foreign Ministers troop down the moment he signified to them that their presence at his Court would be acceptable'.[7]

Parkes' wish to delay meeting the Shogun was assisted by an event that came out of the blue: the death of Emperor Kōmei at the age of thirty-six on 30 January 1867. He had been suffering from smallpox, but it was a mild strain of the disease and not something he had been expected to die from. It seems possible that he had been poisoned to stop him forcing a disastrous show-down with the Western powers. We will never know the truth of this unless his remains are tested for poison. But as Satow put it, 'it is impossible to deny that his disappearance from the political scene, leaving as his successor a boy ... was most opportune'.[8]

Everything was now up in the air – there was a new Shogun, a new Emperor, fresh challenges from outside and chaos breaking out at home. But the Western diplomats only had a sketchy idea of what was going on. Once Mitford started to understand the events he was living through, he became a lot more engaged; he gradually discovered that he was about to play a part in the birth of a modern state.

The first significant step in this was when Parkes, unaware of Kōmei's death (it was not announced until 4 February), decided Mitford and Satow would go down to Kobe and Osaka. This was done in typical style, at very short notice – 'I ... am really bucketed about like a postboy' – to make the arrangements for a possible meeting between Parkes and the Shogun.[9] Gripes like this need to be taken with a pinch of salt – Mitford loved action and wanted to feel that he was participating in important affairs.

And to be fair to Parkes, he could only send them there when a Royal Navy vessel was going in that direction, commandeering a ship being an extravagance that had to be saved for emergencies. Indeed, Mitford and Satow had little room for complaint, as H.M.S. *Argus* was instructed to wait to transport them back to Yokohama when required. On top of this, Parkes asked Captain Courtenay to provide 'support ... to Mr. Mitford that is calculated to give him position in the eyes of the Japanese Authorities' and he told Mitford to insist on only speaking to the Governor of Osaka or someone of equal rank.[10] Parkes was very aware of the importance of appearances; if Mitford was treated like a senior figure by the ship's crew, the Japanese would probably follow suit. While Parkes was very concerned about Mitford's dignity, he was much less worried about his safety, instructing him to 'claim [the] liberty of moving about the town and of intercourse with native acquaintances' in order to gather intelligence, thus exposing him to the risk of a sudden random attack.[11] At the same time, Parkes told Courtenay to 'exercise a careful discretion' with respect to allowing his men to land in Osaka.[12] He did not want to risk any more British lives than he had to.

So, on 7 February, Mitford and Satow set sail from Yokohama for Kobe, a place that was even less substantial than Yokohama – no Westerners lived there yet and it was no more than a series of settlements clustered along the shore.[13] But it was in a beautiful setting, on a broad sweeping bay against the backdrop of the steeply rising Rokkō mountains. It also, like Yokohama, had a large deep-water harbour, and it served as the port for Osaka, Japan's main industrial centre and temporarily the seat of power.

Nowadays, the bullet train zips between Kobe and Osaka in thirteen minutes, but in those days, the journey took a lot longer. The thirty-five kilometres could be travelled by boat or overland. It was a toss-up which was more dangerous – if you went by sea, your boat had to negotiate a treacherous bar at the entrance to the Yodo river, which almost claimed Mitford's life a year later. Overland was probably safer and this is the way they went. The road was at least flat but as it approached Osaka it had been made zig-zag so that any invading force would be more exposed to flank fire from defenders waiting at the bends – something that meant there were more places for assassins to hide.

But Parkes' insistence that Mitford be treated as a VIP worked, the Government going to extraordinary lengths to ensure he and Satow travelled in safety. 'Besides a well appointed and mounted escort of ten men with two officers', Mitford reported to Parkes, 'a large force of infantry, probably not less than two thousand men ... had been stationed at all the villages and towns and at many points along the road: they all saluted us as we passed. Two resting places had been prepared at which we were received with every mark of respect and attention.'[14] Mitford was comfortable with all this fuss, but Satow felt differently, writing that he felt it gave them a 'novel and somewhat embarrassing sense of importance'.[15] Mitford recorded that 'not an offensive shout or gesture was noticeable', even when they went the wrong way and walked along streets where they were no soldiers to enforce good behaviour.[16] He concluded from this that either the Government's authority was more respected than in Edo, or that the people of Osaka were not so hostile to Westerners.

Mitford's description of Osaka fits it quite well now: 'almost exceptionally ugly, being entirely commercial and industrial'.[17] It was built on canals and because of this it was sometimes called 'the Venice of the East', a title Mitford thought was a 'sacrilege' because apart from the castle and a few temples there was 'not a building of any architectural pretensions in the place'.[18] But Mitford thought its people seemed 'well-fed and well clothed' and as there were few sword-carrying samurai around, it felt far less dangerous than Edo.[19] The main activity in Osaka was turning a profit, still the city's reputation (the traditional greeting in Osaka is 'Are you making any money?' – 'mō kari makka'). The upper classes of Edo thought trade was far beneath them and according to the rigid social structure of the time, merchants were ranked below both farmers and artisans because they did not produce anything. But Mitford believed this disdain of business was pure hypocrisy and that the samurai, while affecting to despise trade and merchants and only to respect arms and chivalry, the moment that the question of money comes forward, they show an amount of greed for gain that far outdoes the much talked of cupidity of the Chinese'.[20]

In Osaka, Westerners were such a novelty that the overwhelming emotion of its citizens was curiosity; the temple Mitford and Satow were staying in was mobbed by sightseers and (in true Osaka style) a fair was set up outside to profit from all the crowds. The pair were at least comfortable, the authorities having put Western-style furniture in the rooms and provided European wines.

Mitford's mission was to find out what the Shogun's Government planned to do about opening Osaka and Kobe to foreign trade, which had been promised for 1 January 1868. This was a near-obsession for Parkes who rated expanding British trade with Japan above everything else. Mitford also had to settle how the meeting with the Shogun would be arranged, which involved ensuring that Parkes was treated with sufficient respect. The danger was that the Japanese side would introduce subtle insults, or at least ways of showing they were superior; their etiquette was so complicated that this was easy enough to do. Nowhere can the rules relating to behaviour have been as precisely defined as they were in Tokugawa Japan. Writing later, Mitford commented that under the feudal system they had been 'fettered by the inexorable laws ... the complications of which must have been one of the most ingenious forms of torture ever devised'.[21] The remnants of this can still be seen in Japan today, where companies give long instruction manuals to new employees defining how they should behave when, for example, entering a lift while in the presence of a superior, or how they should hand over a business card to a customer. This said, Mitford rather admired the rituals of old Japan, at least as it applied to the warrior code; they were, after all, something that he could relate to, Eton, Oxford and the Foreign Office all having provided mild versions of something similar. And for someone like Mitford, in the comfortable knowledge that he was from the upper class in his own country, there was no obvious reason to complain too much about a system that organised the ranks so clearly.

We sense a touch of panic in Mitford when he found out that the Japanese intended to have Parkes only accompanied by his interpreter at the meeting with the Shogun, which would have meant that Satow would have been present, but Mitford himself would have missed out. He told the Governor that he believed that Parkes would not accept 'the separation of the Minister from his staff' and that he 'should be ill carrying out' his instructions if he 'did not call his attention to ... [these] objectionable arrangements'.[22] The Japanese side conceded the point.

More interesting to Satow in particular, who had been specifically tasked by Parkes to find out political information, Mitford was talking with powerful clan leaders, in particular those from Satsuma, in the southern part of Kyushu, who wanted to overthrow the Government. Mitford and Satow had to be circumspect because the Shogun's men, their 'guards', were watching their every move. When one of the Satsuma councillors came to meet them, Mitford gave the pretext that he had to give a present in return for kindness shown by his *daimyō* to some British sailors shipwrecked on the Satsuma Territory. This man had an intriguing request:

> When the Ministers come to Osaka ... the ... powerful Daimios [*daimyō*] will be at Kioto. Now should your Minister say ... that it is customary for Treaties to be made between Sovereigns only, and propose to make one with the Mikado [Emperor], the Daimios will lend him all their support, and this will be the death blow to the assumed Sovereign power of the Tycoon [Shogun].[23]

This was heady stuff for someone of Mitford's rank. He reported back to Parkes that he had maintained the official line: 'Great Britain does not interfere in the internal feuds and factions of foreign nations'.[24] However, it is reasonable to speculate that Mitford and Satow at least hinted that they would be sympathetic to *daimyō* overthrowing the Shogun and restoring the Emperor to the supreme position. Indeed, Satow claimed years later that around this time he had explicitly warned Saigō Takamori that the 'chance of a revolution' could be lost if the Western powers started supporting the Shogun, because it would strengthen his shaky regime.[25]

Mitford assumed that there would be widespread mourning at the death of the Emperor, and was surprised to find that this seemed to be absent; he told Parkes that in Kobe, at any rate, Kōmei's death did 'not appear to have produced any very sensible effect ... nor do the natives seem to think that it will interfere with the transaction of public business'.[26] To the Japanese people, the Emperor was an invisible, semi-mythical figure – a 'thing of another world', as Mitford put it – not a human being with whom they had any emotional connection.[27] In fact, contrary to appearances, Kōmei was receiving more respect than was customary for deceased emperors. Mitford was told that official mourning would last fifty days – in the past, while mourning for a Shogun had been for that length of time, an Emperor had only got five, a difference which reflected their relative importance. In addition to the fifty days mourning, there was also the killjoy banning of festivities for a year, which was the main effect of the death on ordinary people.

Kōmei's successor was his fourteen-year-old son Mutsuhito, who is now known as Emperor Meiji and usually considered the greatest Emperor in Japanese history. The fact that he was a child was seen as no impediment to his reigning because the emperors had traditionally had no real function other than being themselves. Indeed, Meiji's four immediate predecessors had all acceded to the throne before they were eighteen. At the time, there was almost no information about him. In a report to the Foreign Secretary, Parkes speculated that one of the few concrete facts they knew about him was significant. Meiji had been vaccinated against smallpox, a practice his father had rejected out of hand as unacceptably Western and new-fangled. To Parkes, this was an encouraging sign of 'a mark of some liberality in his own mind, or in the minds of those who surround him'.[28] It was a good thing to pick up on, because it symbolised the gulf between father and son which was, in fact, that between old and new Japan. Mitford was less optimistic about the new Emperor, passing on to Parkes what he had heard in Osaka – that he was an 'intelligent and generous minded youth', whose natural inclinations and talents were being 'warped' by the Shogun,

> who for selfish reasons keeps from him all useful knowledge and especially all that may tend to enlighten him upon foreign politics. Any one capable of teaching him is carefully removed from his court, and though there are many liberals among his nobles ... these have been repressed or imprisoned, and a bigoted conservatism or prejudice and ignorance is the only passport to favour.[29]

Normally, Parkes would have made a fuss about the postponing of the meeting with the Shogun because delay was a commonly used tactic by Japanese negotiators who wanted to avoid a meeting altogether, but on this occasion he was very happy to wait until the situation was clearer before committing himself.

At the same time, he was concerned that his great rival, Léon Roches, the French Minister, would get in before him and conclude a deal which gave exclusive rights to France. Their rivalry was personal, almost childish. According to Mitford, they hated one another and were 'as jealous as a couple of women'.[30] He records that one day Parkes entered his room 'like a whirlwind', saying:

> What do you think that fellow Roches has just told me? He is going to have a *mission militaire* out from France to drill the Shogun's army! Never mind! I'll be even with him. I'll have a *mission navale*![31]

Mitford later wrote: 'Who could have foretold that the foundation of the marvellously successful Japanese army and navy should have had its origin in the jealousy of the English and French Ministers?'[32] This sounds good, but is not really true. In his memoir, Roches claimed that it was 'in order not to hurt English feelings', that he had asked the Government to approach Parkes for the naval mission, which is also unlikely to be true – a selfless desire to help out the British was not evident in anything else he did.[33] The most likely explanation is that Roches knew that Parkes would not accept France training both the Shogun's army and navy, so he backed down over the navy.

Mitford had an ambivalent attitude to France and the French. Much of his childhood had been spent there, his hard-up father finding it easier to keep up appearances there than in Britain. They had spent the season – winter and spring – in Paris, in the ultra-fashionable area around the Madeleine church. As a child, Mitford had played in the gardens of the Tuileries Palace where he had sometimes seen King Louis Philippe walking along the palace's terrace.[34] At the time, Mitford viewed him with awe, but later saw him as a 'none-too-reliable old man', whose Court 'seems to have been the shoddiest affair that could be imagined'.[35] The Terror (1793–94) was still within living memory when Mitford was a child, and he wrote of often listening, 'my hair almost on end, to men and women telling how they had seen their nearest and dearest led off in the tumbrils'.[36] These stories helped form his political philosophy: he instinctively felt that power should reside in a state's traditional masters, as it did in Britain, and that revolutions of the people would inevitably lead to disaster. In French terms, this made him a 'Legitimist', believing that the executions of Louis XVI and Marie Antoinette had been murder and that France's kings should be their direct heirs, not Louis Philippe, or worse, Napoleon's descendant, Napoleon III, who was on the throne while Mitford was in Japan. Transferring the same logic to Japan meant that he saw the Emperor as the country's legitimate ruler; the Shogun could only be, at best, his chief minister, governing at the Emperor's pleasure.

Mitford's impeccable French did nothing to endear him to Roches, Mitford writing that he was treated by him with the 'wretched coldness' of which Roches was 'the high priest'.[37] However, in reality Roches was far from the chilly character Mitford makes him sound like here. He was a very unconventional diplomat; a 'handsome swashbuckler ... far more a picturesque Spahi [French calvary officer] than a diplomatist' in Mitford's words.[38] In his early twenties, he had gone to North

Africa, where he fell in love with Khadidja, a noble Algerian girl. The affair was perilous in the extreme; women were forbidden from being alone in the company of a man who was not related to them and any liaison with non-Muslims was absolutely out of the question. Undeterred, Roches learned Arabic, dressed as a local, and pretended to convert to Islam. However, Khadidja was forced to marry against her will, although Roches still continued to see her in secret. Her husband discovered this and took her to a remote area which was outside the control of France. Roches laid siege to the town she was in, Aïn Madhi, but unfortunately she died during the blockade.[39] In his memoir, Roches explained that he had been motivated by 'the desire to acquire new favours in the love of Khadidja, who, like all lettered Muslim women, professes the greatest admiration for courageous men'.[40]

As may be guessed from this, Roches had little patience with dreary diplomatic protocol. He preferred backdoor '*politique personelle*' to following instructions from his own Foreign Ministry, believing that he could achieve success for France with his charm and force of personality. Roches saw a great opportunity for France to provide military support for Yoshinobu's regime in return for special trading privileges – a 'whole network of schemes for the establishment of French monopolies', as Mitford put it.[41] If anyone was going to keep the Shogun in power, it would be Roches.

*

After nine days in Osaka, Mitford and Satow returned to Yokohama, arriving back there on 24 February – Mitford's thirtieth birthday. Aside from having had his usual sea-sickness ('we had awful rough times at sea') he was happy on that day.[42] He had had 'the double pleasure' of enjoying himself and getting through all his business satisfactorily, for which he 'got a slap on the back from Sir H. Parkes' who was 'delighted'.[43] Parkes commended to the Foreign Secretary the 'good judgment that has been shown by Mr. Mitford in the management of this delicate expedition'.[44]

One of Parkes' few virtues as a boss was that he was generous with his praise of his subordinates to his own superiors.

Mitford did not have to wait long to be setting off for Osaka again, leaving on 10 April, in order to check that arrangements were in place for Parkes' visit – he would depart five days later. Parkes made it clear that he would not meet with Yoshinobu unless it was promised that Osaka and Kobe would be opened to foreign trade on 1 January 1868, as previously agreed, and sites found there for foreign settlements. This was all granted without any difficulty, and a new atmosphere prevailed, the Shogun having given instructions to his officials that they were to be as friendly as possible.

On 29 April, Parkes, Mitford and Satow set out for Osaka Castle for the audience. The building was a 'stupendous monument of feudalism', as Mitford put it, more than twelve kilometres in circumference – only slightly smaller than Edo Castle.[45] It was protected by walls of huge granite stones, one nearly fifteen metres long ('The wonder is how such blocks of granite were lifted into their places').[46] Mitford thought it was a 'noble structure … very plain and simple, featureless with the exception of the curved roofs of the great towers, its very simplicity adding to its grandeur'.[47] The residence inside the castle was sumptuous, its walls lined with paintings from the celebrated Kano school. While they were waiting for the meeting, Mitford must have had a very careful look around, because he gave his father a detailed description afterwards, although it was one which could have applied to almost any wealthy residence in Japan:

> The interior of the palace is of its kind quite magnificent. The walls are covered with gold leaf decorated with paintings of trees, flowers, birds and beasts. The hangings were the finest rush mats hung up by gilt hooks from which are suspended huge silken tassels, in tricolour, orange, red and black …
>
> The upper panels are amply carved after the highest style of Japanese art, and the carvings are painted and gilt: each panel is different. Peacocks, cranes, groups of azaleas and other flowers are the kind of subjects chosen. The upright and crop beams are of plain unpolished wood and fastened with metal bolts … The ceilings are

in squares carved, gilt and painted, and the designs are richly lacquered in black and gold.[48]

Although the decorations were brightly coloured, they were not gaudy, Mitford thought; being two hundred years old at the time, they had been 'softened and subdued by the patina of time'.[49] He was lucky he had the chance to see it because the castle was largely destroyed the following year; then, following a familiar pattern, it was partly reconstructed in the 1920s; bombed in 1945 and rebuilt in the 1990s. What stands today is a concrete reproduction. It is the symbol of Osaka, a city whose origins date back more than two thousand years, but which has virtually no pre-twentieth century buildings left standing in it.

The British party arrived in full state, preceded by a mounted escort, and followed by a detachment of the infantry guard. The Shogun signalled his desire to be friendly in numerous ways, going well beyond what was originally agreed. They were allowed to remain on horseback beyond the point where all Japanese, whatever their rank, had to dismount and, as Parkes had requested, European court manners were followed, with chairs arranged around a table in the European style, for their comfort.

His appearance was elegantly stage-managed: 'two ... tall sliding screens ... were slowly and noiselessly drawn aside', wrote Mitford,

and that long-drawn "hush" caused by the drawing-in of breath which announces the coming of a great personage thrilled all through the whole palace like the most delicate *pianissimo* of a huge orchestra; for a second or two the Tycoon [Shogun], motionless as a statue, stood framed in the opening between the screens.[50]

Originally, nothing more than the briefest exchange of courtesies had been envisaged by the Japanese side – Mitford had been told that Parkes should 'deliver his sovereign's message and after receiving the Tycoon's answer will retire'.[51] But Yoshinobu had different ideas and, dropping all formality and any pretence about the situation, spoke frankly about all the difficulties which had stopped proper interaction between Japanese and foreigners and saying he wanted all this to change. They chatted for about an hour and a half before Yoshinobu asked to see their escort, which gave him a display of lance and sword exercise. As a keen horseman himself (Mitford found out that he was an 'indefatigable rider and dreads no weather'), he was fascinated by the horses belonging to the British, Gulf Arabs, imported from India.[52] He thought them greatly superior to his own, which Mitford agreed with, considering Japanese horses to be 'about as mean a breed of the genus horse as exists anywhere'.[53] Yoshinobu casually invited them to stay to dinner, at which he stood up to propose Queen Victoria's health – the first time this had been done by anyone of rank in Japan. But what was most remarkable about the dinner was how relaxed it was: the Shogun, Mitford wrote, 'frequently urged us to throw off all ceremony, and so we did. It was really a very merry party.'[54] After dinner he gave them gifts; Mitford got some crape, a pipe and a tobacco-pouch of silk embroidered by ladies of the household.

He sent them home and was livid with his father when he heard that he was casually giving them away: 'They were a present to me ... and I would not part with them for any money.'[55] Given how prone to disasters Japan was, it was clearly safer for Mitford's treasures to be at his father's house, but only if they were properly taken care of there. Unfortunately, his family, not knowing much about them, was largely unimpressed by them and treated them as being of little value. Part of the problem was their sheer quantity; Mitford realised two years into his stay in Japan that his father's house 'must now be full to overflowing' with objects he had sent over from China and Japan.[56] At the same time, friends and family were constantly asking him to acquire specific things for them, which were invariably impossible to obtain. Aunt Fannie asked for a box with card counters. 'I have hunted', Mitford told his father, 'I may say Japan over, for her. Such a thing in Japanese lacquer does not exist, I believe.'[57] About other requests he wrote, 'You might as well wish for diamonds as the old porcelain of Japan. And as for bronzes, I have seen none for sale that are above the Moderator Lamp class in art.'[58] 'Good lacquer is as rare as rubies.'[59] Acquiring beautiful things had been much easier in China – it was like one big curio shop – and this is where Mitford had really been bitten by the collector's bug. In Japan, fine pieces were not readily available because the wealthy did not go into shops. Rather, they would request items be brought to them by a merchant-agent and Mitford had to use this system – which involved being introduced to the right people – to get good quality items.

Mitford struggled to educate his family; about some yellow bowls that he suspected were not being treated with due respect, he told his father they 'were the personal property of the Emperor of China and have on the bottom, instead of a dynastic mark, the name of the particular hall of the palace for which they were made and in which they were kept.'[60] About a Chinese cistern that he had received unflattering comments about, he told them,

> it is really just *ce qu'il y a de plus beau* [the most beautiful thing]. The fact is that you none of you (pardon me!) know anything about Oriental porcelain which has its history and its interests. My cistern is a piece of Imperial tribute of the reign of … [Emperor Chenghua] who reigned from 1465 to 1488 A.D. [actually 1464 to 1487].'[61]

Yoshinobu's generosity continued as they admired some portraits of poets. He insisted on having one of them taken down and given to Parkes as a gift. Parkes said that it would be a pity to break the set, whereupon the Shogun said that 'when he looked on the vacant space it would give him pleasure to think that the picture that had once filled it was in the possession of the British Minister.'[62] Parkes, not an easy man to win over, completely succumbed to this charm offensive, telling the Foreign Office that Yoshinobu was 'the most superior Japanese' he had ever met and that he felt 'quite disposed to give him all the support' he could.[63] Mitford was also impressed. Writing with the benefit of hindsight he commented, 'He was a great noble if ever there was one. The pity of it was that he was an anachronism.'[64]

The Shogun's charm and bearing was matched by his looks: Hollywood could hardly have chosen someone who so looked the part. Although he was very short by Western standards, he was athletic: 'His frame is well-knit and does justice to his great bodily activity'. His mouth was 'very firm, but he has a gentle and very winning expression. Indeed, Mitford continued, he was 'the handsomest man, according to our ideas, that I saw during all the years that I was in Japan'.[65] As this comment suggests, he had a faintly Western air about him. He looked magnificent dressed as a European, posing for a photograph in a French uniform presented to him by Roches. His look would have served him well from about 1870 onwards when Western clothes came into vogue and the Emperor made an adapted Western uniform his standard wear – Yoshinobu was only very slightly ahead of his time. As it was, at a subsequent formal reception, he had to wear Japanese court dress which, according to Mitford, was 'absolutely grotesque' and

> really baffles description. The cap is a sort of inverted lacquer box tied on under the chin with black strings. The robes of the costume are of a hempen material of red colours, and the trousers are made a full yard too long for the wearer, so he has to shuffle about in the most absurd manner.[66]

Mitford was, however, aware enough that he was applying his Western values here to add that were the Japanese 'to give a description of us, they might fairly have a laugh at our cocked hats which must to their eyes be absurdity itself'.[67] He was not to know when he wrote this that the Japanese would shortly adopt the cocked hat, making it the 'coveted privilege of every Japanese official' in Meiji Japan, as he put it later.[68]

While they were in Osaka, Mitford and Satow wanted to explore the city, but they found that the street that their lodgings were in was shut at each end by bolted wooden gates, at which guards were stationed twenty-four hours a day. If they wished to travel around the city, they had to be followed by these men. This was very annoying until they discovered a gap in one of the walls, after which they went all over the city at night, accompanied only by Satow's Japanese servant, Noguchi. Satow wrote: 'The sense of a certain peril … combined with a sort of truant schoolboy feeling, rendered these explorations into the night life of Japan very enjoyable.'[69] He writes of how one evening they managed to get to the pleasure quarter and entered a room of 'bepowdered and berouged' girls who screamed in terror at the sight of them.[70] The owner begged the Englishmen to leave, telling them that a crowd might collect and he would get into trouble if there was any disturbance.

Osaka was an intense experience for Mitford and Satow – the days were full of official work, with Parkes ensuring that they were kept very busy. But the evenings were also full – of visits to temples, theatres, shops and entertainment places. The feeling of safety when they were moving around was a nice change; Satow wrote that 'although the crowds which we attracted were enormous on no occasion were we in any way insulted or annoyed … We were objects of curiosity and nothing more.'[71] Everything seemed set fair, Mitford telling his father: 'We are all in high hopes that this really is the beginning of a new state of affairs in Japan, and that our intercourse will now be free and friendly.'[72]

*

Around this time, Mitford was facing a choice about his future. It had been decided that he should return to Britain in five months, but he was now desperate to stay in Japan, enjoying a life of action compared to that he had experienced while working at a desk job at the Foreign Office in London. 'In these out of the way places', he told his father, 'there is something to be done – an object in one's work – and it appears to be more worth the living to live a man's life than to be copying all day and calling fine ladies' carriages all night.' He listed out why he did not want to return to Britain at this point:

- Reason 1: The Japan and China seas are awfully stormy in September, and I cannot get over seasickness.
- Reason 2: I leave a hot climate to face a London winter without any intermediate preparation.

- Reason 3: I arrive in London at the dullest time of the year.
- Reason 4: I miss the opening of Osaka and Hiogo [Kobe] to foreign trade which will be the last political event of any importance in Japan, and in which having been an actor in the early act, I don't want to be kicked out before the play is over, and when there is still something to do.[73]

Fortunately, Parkes was anxious to keep Mitford, telling the Foreign Office that he was his 'principal aide' and he 'should be much pressed for assistance without him' and so his return was put off.[74]

Although Mitford wanted to stay in Japan, he was still blowing hot and cold over how he felt about the country. On a good day, just before the meeting with the Shogun, he was writing 'I have grown to like Japan very much … by degrees Japan seems to exercise a sort of fascination upon everybody.'[75] However, in July, he had regressed to this:

> In everything I prefer China to Japan, which I look upon as the most overpraised country I ever saw. It is charming for a fortnight, so long as black teeth, public bathing and other peculiarities are novel. After that the country gradually sinks in one's estimation, and as for the people, my contempt for them is boundless.[76]

It is noticeable that he was more positive about Japan in spring and autumn. Although he had experienced more extreme climates in Russia and China, somehow the heat and cold were worse in Japan. Writing in July, he complained that it was 'very hot, very rainy and damp. I have not seen the sun for a week. The heat at Peking was intense, far more violent than here, but it was always dry.'[77] In the winter, he was writing:

> I don't know that I ever felt cold more than in Japan. It is not that the mercury stands low … but the cold has certain piercing and nipping qualities which are worse by far than the hard frost of St. Petersburg or Peking, and I believe much more unwholesome into the bargain.[78]

Mitford knew he was in Japan at an interesting time, although he was thinking that it would only stay that way until the opening to foreign trade of Osaka and Kobe on 1 January 1868. He thought that the structure of the Government would change, but that the Shogunate would basically survive; probably the Emperor would be restored to the supreme position, with the Shogun and chief *daimyō* serving as his ministers and everything would quickly settle down after that. 'What a blind prophet!', he later wrote – he did not realise that everything was about to be turned upside-down.[79]

4

AN ADVENTUROUS JOURNEY

July – August 1867

ℭ

AFTER HIS RETURN to Edo, Mitford did not have to wait long to be on his travels again. Parkes never liked sitting in the Legation, especially when the summer heat made it unbearable. Rather he would spend 'all day plotting and scheming to get up a sensation', in the words of Dr Willis.[1] Mitford told his father that 'the expedition promises to be enjoyable' – he enjoyed any kind of travelling, even if it was with Parkes – 'but, oh!', 'the vomiting that I look forward to and the heat and the discomfort of being on board ship'.[2]

The first part of their journey took them north to Hakodate on Ezo (now Hokkaido), a voyage of four days. It was Japan's wild frontier – almost unexplored by Westerners or the Japanese themselves beyond the southernmost part. Its climate was tough; it would have been pleasantly cool in the summer, but it had long, harsh winters. Ezo was the home of indigenous people called Ainu who had a distinct language and culture which would be systematically suppressed after Ezo became incorporated into Japan in 1869. Like nearly all Victorian travellers, Mitford saw aboriginal people as a curiosity and was keen to observe them, rather than interact with them as fellow human beings.[3] Satow recorded that their women were extremely ugly; they tattoo all round the mouth so that it looks four times its real size, their hair is dirty, unkempt and hangs in loose masses over their shoulders, or is tied up with a filthy rag ... But the men are handsome, or rather have a striking appearance to people who admire beards and moustaches. Their eyes and noses are also good, and they are covered with thick black hair on the legs and breast, not quite so bad as bears.[4]

Parkes had no interest in the people and was, as ever, focused on the business in hand, in this case, how the coal mines there could be developed and a breakwater built to allow foreign ships to dock to load the coal.

The dominant foreign power in Ezo was Russia. Britain was worried that it would stealthily take advantage of instability in Japan to steal territory in the north – it was only a little over ten years earlier that Britain and France had fought the Crimean War to prevent Russian expansion in Europe. The British believed that if there was commercial activity in Ezo, it would be easier to keep an eye on the Russians, in addition to the profits that could be made.

Unlike most British people, Mitford was sympathetic to Russia, having spent six months there, in 1863–1864, as third secretary at the Embassy in St Petersburg. He had been entranced by the extravagance of the wealthy there. 'It is idle', Mitford wrote in old age, 'to expatiate upon the grandeur and luxury of these great palaces'.[5] He added, 'The Russian noble has in perfection the greatest of all the qualities which go to make up the character of a *grand seigneur*'.[6] The Tsar, he believed, was a 'born king of men. His was a royalty about which there could be no doubt.'[7] To most of Mitford's peers, there would have been something decidedly middle class about this starry-eyed view of Russian nobility. He was also ignoring the suffering of Russian peasants that made such lifestyles possible. His attitude to Japan was different; there he saw with his own eyes the way people at the bottom suffered, and condemned the injustices they had to live with.

*

Parkes, Mitford and Satow sailed down the west coast of Honshu to see if they could arrange for ports there to be opened to foreign trade, or at least allow foreign ships to take refuge in if the weather was bad or they were in distress. They stopped in Niigata, now a major trading centre, but at the time difficult for ships to use because there was a treacherous bar at the entrance to its harbour. Nevertheless, it seemed like it might be possible to open the port to the West and turn an island in the river there into a secure foreign settlement. The three men landed on it and, determined to see it properly, Parkes scrambled to the top of a shed, 'much to the horror', according to Satow, 'of Mitford and myself, who were so orientalized by this time … that we longed to see our chief conduct himself with the impassive dignity of a Japanese gentleman'.[8]

We can imagine Mitford rolling his eyes at this behaviour, but he left no written comment on the episode. He was not as disapproving of Parkes as Satow, although it would have been easy enough for him to look down on him. After all, unlike Parkes (and indeed Satow), Mitford had an illustrious ancestry; perhaps this is the point at which we ought to take a closer look at his background. In his memoir he starts with a semi-apology for boasting about his family line: 'Of course it was not good taste in Ajax to brag so loudly of being the great-grandson of Jupiter', before going on to do something similar himself.[9]

He tells us about an interesting ancestor on his mother's side, John Ashburnham, who attended on Charles I at his execution on 30 January 1649. It was cold, and the King did not want to be seen to be shivering, and for people to misinterpret that as fear, so he wore a second shirt. Ashburnham was given that shirt, deeply stained with royal blood, and kept it as a precious memento. Later, Mitford's grandmother, returning from a trip, could not find it and asked the housekeeper where it was. 'Quite safe, Mylady', she replied, 'but it was so stained that I have had it washed.'[10]

His most distinguished ancestor was his great-grandfather, William Mitford (1744–1827), who raised his father, Henry (1804–1883), to whom the letters were written that were the main source for this book. William was the first Mitford to become a famous author, writing the monumental *History of Greece*, published in five volumes between 1784 and 1818. In his day, he was considered by many to be in the same league as Edward Gibbon, and Lord Byron thought him 'perhaps the best of all modern historians altogether'.[11] William lived in an inspiring place, a house called Exbury, which looked out on to the Solent. As we are discussing other Mitfords, we now need to call our subject by his given name – Bertie, pronounced 'Bartie' – although even to his father, he signed his letters 'A.B. Mitford'. Bertie described how from the drawing-room at Exbury, you could see 'the great battleships with their bellying sails – men-of-war of the pattern of Nelson's days – the stately wooden walls of old England, the huge West Indiamen travelling to and from Southampton, "sailing between worlds and worlds with steady wing"'.[12] There is always the suspicion with Bertie that he has added romantic flourishes, but in this case, he was not exaggerating. The vista still stretches across green fields down to the water, with the Isle of Wight beyond. If it were not for the mobile phone masts, it would be almost exactly the same.

The nearby church has a prominent memorial to William Mitford, who was its founder. It tells us that he was 'descended from the ancient family of Mitford, in the County of Northumberland'; there is nothing about his writing, which is what set him apart. But it was the bloodline that the Mitfords took seriously.

William was not the best person to bring up a young boy, being only interested in his writing and his garden, but Henry would have had plenty of intellectual stimulation there. He grew up to become highly cultured, although he was never in the league of his grandfather or son. Attempting to eulogise his father many years later, Bertie struggled slightly, mentioning the 'many accomplishments – music, painting, languages', and adding that he was 'wonderfully well-read in the old memoirs of the seventeenth and eighteenth centuries, and quite an authority on historic French portraits'.[13] Henry's working life was only four years long: he entered the Foreign Office from Oxford, as Bertie would, and was sent to Florence as an attaché. There, he fell in with a community of aristocratic ex-pats, some drawn by the arts and climate, others by the fact that the social conventions were looser than at home. Henry's congenial boss, the Minister, Lord Burghersh, was devoted to art and was a distinguished composer, writing operas that were performed in Florence. It is difficult to imagine that much diplomatic work got done at the British Legation in Tuscany, then an independent state. In Florence, Henry met Lady Georgina Ashburnham (1805–1882) who he married at around the same time he inherited Exbury from William. He left the Foreign Service, returned to England to live the life of a country gentleman, and never took paid employment again.

Henry and Georgina had seven children, but only three survived: twins, Percy and Henry, born in 1833, and Bertie, born just before Queen Victoria came to the throne in 1837. His birthplace was a house on South Audley Street in Mayfair, behind what is now the Dorchester Hotel. It was (and still is) an exceptionally prestigious area; the building opposite was the residence of the Duke of Cambridge, the King's brother. Bertie's parents would have been in London because it was the 'season', but Henry still owned Exbury at the time. However, when Bertie was just a year old, it had become, as he put it later, 'like diamond tiaras and ropes of pearls ..., a costly luxury'.[14] The house was let and the family, like so many others in a similar predicament, moved to the continent. The first place they went to was Frankfurt-am-Main, where Lady Georgina started an affair with Francis Molyneux (1805–1886), secretary to the British Legation there. Henry suspected nothing for three years; indeed during this time he and Molyneux were friends, often spending time together. In 1841, Henry went on a trip to Dresden with the thought that they might move there. This would have stopped Georgina seeing Molyneux, so she asked her maid to pack her things, kissed her children a tearful goodbye, and went off with her lover.

At the time, divorce was a hideously expensive, humiliating and rare process. Between 1700 and 1857, there were just 314 completed divorces in England and Wales – but Henry decided to try to obtain one. Normally, the only acceptable grounds for a divorce were the wife's adultery and it was necessary for the husband to prove this. The witnesses were almost always servants and the public loved reading reports of their testimonies in the newspapers. In the Mitfords' case, their own servants were frustratingly discreet, telling the court that Molyneux often visited the house 'whether or not Mr. Mitford was at home', but not offering any thoughts as to what Georgina and Molyneux did when Mr Mitford was not there. However, staff at the Hyde Park Hotel testified that a couple calling themselves 'Mr. and Mrs. Murray' (later found to be Georgina and Molyneux) had taken an apartment in the hotel and a housemaid said that there was 'the occupation of one of the beds by two persons. There was a bed in the dressing-room, but that had not been slept in.'[15] Corroborated by other staff at the hotel, this was enough – a special Act of Parliament was passed which received the royal assent on 23 March 1842, and the divorce was final. Georgina married Molyneux and they went to live together in Italy. Because of her adultery, Georgina automatically lost custody of her children and Henry seems to have made sure that she was cut off from them completely.

Mitford left a very air-brushed version of his upbringing in his memoir with nothing about the divorce in it. In its 798 pages, aside from discussion of her lineage, there is only this brief mention of his mother:

> Among others who occupied villas [in Florence] were my grandparents, Lord and Lady Ashburnham, and it was there that my father and mother made acquaintance. They were married in February, 1828.[16]

It looks like Mitford never let her back into his life; his great-grandson tells us that when his first child was born, Georgina, living in London by now, found out about it from a newspaper.

Parkes' background was very different. His father was the owner of an iron-founding enterprise, his mother the daughter of a bookseller. His paternal grandfather was an Anglican clergyman and his grandmother, a vicar's daughter. 'Respectable' was the word the Victorians would have used to describe this kind of family – certainly more respectable than Mitford's – but it reeked of middle-class effort which would have been looked down upon by much of the aristocracy. The influence of his background can be seen in the way Parkes conducted himself, filling every minute with useful activity. For him there was always intelligence that needed gathering, officials to be met, reports to be written, and trading concessions to be squeezed out, which entailed bustling around from first light until late at night. Time off was no less strenuous. Not long after returning from the trip to the west coast of Japan he, in Mitford's words, 'dragged Lady P. to the top of Fujiyama in spite of the snow and the cold which seems to have been excessive'.[17] October, when they went, is a marginal time to climb the mountain (nowadays, the official climbing season finishes at the end of August) and getting up to the top was very much harder than it is today.[18] Because there was a taboo against women climbing the sacred mountain, Fanny Parkes was probably the first woman to make it to the top.

Parkes was unusual in having a British wife and children with him in Japan. He had met Fanny during a trip back to England in November 1855. They had had a whirlwind romance; a friend described what happened on the day they met:

> Fanny had in other cases been hard to please, critical, sensitive, reserved. Yet in a few hours on that day it seemed as if her heart opened and let the stranger freely in. The surrender on the other side was no less rapid and complete, and their friends had to be startled and a little critical over the hasty love-making and engagement.[19]

However, their haste was necessary because Parkes would be returning to China in six weeks and one can imagine Parkes, never one to take longer over a task than necessary, liking the fact that their courtship had to be quick. The wedding took place on 1 January 1856 and they left for China on the 9th. They went on to have five daughters and two sons, Dr Willis delivering at least two of them. He thought the marriage was unhappy:

Lady Parkes appears of a melancholy disposition and I fancy there is not much domestic happiness in Sir Harry's nature. He is a bustling pushing man and I believe has objects of desire dearer to him than home or family ... He would be, I am quite sure, unmoved if an earthquake swallowed up wife and family, so absorbed is he in the game of self.[20]

This last accusation at least is untrue. In 1879, Parkes rushed back to England on hearing that Fanny was gravely ill, unfortunately arriving four days after she had died. He told a friend,

I left Japan by the first opportunity after receiving the earliest warning that her illness was attended with danger. I lost not an hour ... but I arrived too late to hear her last wishes and injunctions, to smooth her pillow, and to close her eyes ... She hoped to the last that I should have reached in time. I have now six children [their eldest daughter had died in 1872] to take charge of, and feebly indeed shall I replace her in that charge, while the Legation will have lost the bright and good spirit to which it owed entirely whatever attraction it possessed.[21]

What Parkes and Mitford had in common was great courage in facing danger. Both believed that they should never show any fear – in Parkes' case, it seems that he simply did not feel it, but with Mitford, he probably learned this at Eton, which was a rough place to go to school. Lord Robert Cecil (later the Prime Minister, Lord Salisbury), who was a pupil there from 1840 to 1845, told his father, 'I am bullied from morning to night without ceasing.'[22] Sexual activity, much of it forced, seems to have been rampant; Charles Simeon, the evangelical divine, said that he would rather take the life of a son than expose him to the vice that he had seen at Eton.[23]

Mitford took the bullying as a given, in spite of being subjected to 'methods of torture curious and ingenious'. He wrote of witnessing fights nearly as bad as the one that had resulted in the death of Lord Shaftsbury's younger brother in 1825 but, 'savage as it may seem to say so', disagreed with them being outlawed. He thought that his old headmaster was right when he said, 'If two boys have a quarrel I would rather see them fight it out ...

grudge-bearing is dreadful and has no end.'[24] His experiences at Eton meant that the constant threat of violence and sudden attack that was a fact of life for Westerners in Japan, was not completely new to him. In fact, when he grew a bit older, he positively liked fighting; at Oxford he spent a good deal of time boxing without gloves – he and his friends engaged a prizefighter from London to train them. Mitford believed that bare-knuckle fighting was actually safer than with gloves, although he admitted that there was 'unquestionably much ugly mauling'.[25]

In his memoir he makes it seem as if life at Eton was plain sailing but a letter from a teacher about him when he was fifteen suggests otherwise; his father was told that he had 'failed seriously' in the intermediate examinations, and that he was 'very weak'.[26] Mitford did not record things like this – it was not his way to dwell on the negative and he clearly recovered.

The only remotely snobbish comments Mitford made about Parkes' origins were about his lack of education. He remarked that his weakness as a diplomat was a lack of French – it was a sign of the priorities of the time that this language was considered more important to diplomats than the language of the country they were in. He also felt that while Parkes was an 'admirable oral interpreter' of Chinese, his knowledge of the language suffered from his lack of a classical education.[27] He noted that the great scholars of Japanese had 'brought the training and literature of the West to their studies of the East', while anyone without it (which, by implication meant Parkes) was a 'mere parrot' who, 'however clever', was 'held in little more esteem than a head waiter'.[28]

*

From Niigata, Parkes, Mitford and Satow went to the island of Sado to look at the mines there, and then carried on to the port of Nanao, on the Noto Peninsula. It had an immense natural harbour that had none of the problems of Niigata's port and Parkes was optimistic that it could be opened for British shipping, probably in tandem with Niigata. Unfortunately, Nanao never lived up to its potential – Satow estimated its population at around 9,000 and it is not much more than this now. Its problem is that it is too remote to be useful – even today it takes an hour or so along a windy single-track line to get by train to the nearest big city, Kanazawa. Parkes would have been better off concentrating on the two ports that were near Japan's main population centres: Yokohama and Kobe, which along with Nagasaki, would be the only ones that British merchants managed to make profits from trading in.

Nanao was in the Kaga domain, which was the richest, aside from the Shogun's own lands, in the country. Although foreign trade could potentially have been profitable for its *daimyō*, it would have been accompanied by all kinds of difficulties: he would have opened himself up to attacks from anti-foreign zealots and from the Shogunate, which would have been unhappy about him making independent arrangements with a foreign power. The *daimyō* did not lower himself to meeting with Parkes but, after keeping him waiting for two days, two of his councillors saw him on 9 August. Parkes expected better than this, and was seething when he met the emissaries, who, in Satow's words, 'sat talking, or rather being talked to, by Sir Harry for five mortal hours'.[29] Mitford wrote that Parkes 'used every endeavour to impress upon the Kaga representatives the desirability of entering into friendly relations with foreigners', although it would surely have been obvious that the men did not have the authorisation to make this happen.[30] Nonetheless, when they opposed him, Mitford said that Parkes gave them the 'roughest edge of his tongue, which in his case meant a good deal'. Mitford thought that Parkes' outbursts were counterproductive with the Japanese: 'Bluster does not succeed, but that was a lesson which our chief, with all his great qualities, never learned'.[31]

According to Mitford's memoir, since the Kaga officials were so unfriendly, Parkes declared that he would send Mitford and Satow overland to Osaka, upon which the meeting 'broke up with a little less than a show of politeness'.[32] Parkes had decided to risk the lives of his two most valuable men in a fit of pique, making them take a 300 kilometre trip through territory that no Westerner had entered before. The Japanese side was desperate to prevent this because had they been killed, it would have created terrible difficulties. Government officials pleaded with Parkes to change his mind, telling him that the Shogun did not have control over the area they would pass through and could not take any responsibility for Mitford and Satow's safety. Parkes was unmoved by this argument and Mitford did not blame him, writing, 'it was just the sort of trip that he himself would have delighted in, for where his own life was concerned he was always as big a gambler as the ace of spades'.[33]

According to Mitford's later account, Parkes was challenged about sending the pair on this journey by Admiral Keppel, Commander of the China station (which included Japan), and the only British person around who Parkes had to treat as an equal. According to Mitford, Parkes tried to make out to Keppel that it was their 'own foolhardiness which prompted the idea', to which Mitford replied that they were 'quite willing to obey his orders … as a question of duty', but they would certainly not have thought of undertaking the journey 'for a whim', which would not have been fair to their people at home.[34] At this, Parkes only laughed.

Probably Mitford and Satow could have refused to take the trip, but it looks like they wanted to go. No doubt, one reason they were so willing was because they were desperate to get away from Parkes – Satow had written in his diary earlier in the journey, 'How much jollier to travel in Japan by oneself than to play second fiddle to one's chief, eh!'[35] But they were both excited about the adventure of visiting a swathe of Japan which was completely unknown to outsiders.

It was the Shogun's officials that really wanted to stop them going – and if they could not be dissuaded, were insisting that they must accompany them. This was the last thing Mitford and Satow wanted because it was obvious that their real intention would be to spy on them, and they probably would have been of little use if they had been attacked. On top of this, Parkes wanted Mitford and Satow to gather as much intelligence as possible along the way, and they knew the locals would have been guarded if the Shogun's men had been with them. But the

Shogun's men replied that if anything happened, they would be blamed and forced to perform *hara-kiri*, a piece of emotional blackmail that was invariably used on these occasions. Eventually they were given a receipt which stated that Satow and Mitford were fully intact at the time they left them and thereby washed their hands of them.

So, Mitford and Satow set out, on 10 August, for their eleven-day trip with twenty guards from the Kaga domain, 'whether for show or for protection might be reckoned uncertain'.[36] Unde-sired they may have been, these guards had their uses, clearing people out of the way and forcing the locals they went past to crouch down and take off their hats to them, as they would have for a *daimyō* procession. Mitford and Satow were expected to ride in palanquins, which were beautiful, but agony, being too small for them and the motion 'very uncomfortable, painful to the back and stomach' according to Satow.[37] However, being in them made it easier to go through populated areas, enabling them to hide from the gaze of the hordes of spectators. When they left villages, they got out and walked, jumping back in 'with the modesty of brides' when they entered another settlement.[38] It would not have been as bad if they had felt confident in their appearance, but they were in rough travelling clothes and felt embarrassingly underdressed to be the star attraction.

The scenery on the journey was beautiful, 'here a lagoon, there a long stretch of seashore, and, above all, … the towering moun-tains of Echiu, … veritable "hills whose heads touch heaven"'.[39] Both Mitford and Satow seem to have relished the journey although it must have been excruciatingly uncomfortable. While the Sea of Japan coast was bitterly cold in the winter, it was bak-ing hot in the summer and very humid. The roads were terrible, especially after rain when they became a quagmire. The two men would also have been bitten to death, the wet heat being a per-fect breeding ground for mosquitoes, along with myriad other insects. In addition, much of the country they were travelling through was mountainous, so a good deal of the journey would have been stumbling and sliding up and down mountain passes. Parts of it would have been agonisingly slow – on a similar trip,

Isabella Bird wrote of taking eleven hours just to cover eighteen miles.[40] But the Japanese had some wonderful ways of overcoming natural barriers and Mitford describes the remarkable way they crossed a river on a different trip. Fording it on horseback was impossible so, they were sat with their saddle on a square board and were hoisted on to the shoulders of four 'coolies', who strode across the river. For the horses, the grooms stripped their clothes off and guided them across to the other side.

There was also the inconvenience of having to negotiate their way through guard houses; ordinary Japanese were not allowed to go through them without a special pass and the penalty if they were caught going round them was crucifixion. Five years later, when the system had gone and travelling had become easier, Mitford expressed nostalgia for the old ways:

> The guard-house is swept away now, together with the other encumbrances and annoyances of the obsolete Government, and men may come and go as they list. It is more convenient to be sure; but there was a quaintness and picturesqueness about the old customs … Now, even the old costume of the country is slowly but surely disappearing; and when the railroad shall be an accomplished fact, travelling in Japan will have lost its charm. Four years ago we were still in the middle-ages; we have leapt at a bound into the nineteenth century – out of poetry into plain, useful prose.[41]

On their arrival at Kanazawa, the seat of the Kaga *daimyō*, they were treated with painful politeness. An emissary came to them to express the hope they were not suffering from the heat and to rejoice at their arrival. Mitford told them that they had not felt hot (obviously a lie), that they were deeply grateful for the hospitality and kindness shown them, and would like to call on the *daimyō* in person. The emissary explained that the *daimyō* was sick – the standard Japanese excuse for avoiding anything at all difficult. Satow thought that the truth was that their meeting him would have involved 'far too important and complicated decisions on questions of etiquette for it to be lightly contemplated'.[42] When the emissary told them that the *daimyō* had commanded that an entertainment be staged for them, Mitford excelled himself and invented a flowery speech from Parkes expressing the desire for eternal friendship with the *daimyō* and people of Kaga, which gave great satisfaction. Doctors were also brought in, as the *daimyō* was sure that they must somehow be suffering from the heat. As the doctors were all trained in Chinese cures, in which, as Mitford put it, 'acupuncture and the burning with moxa held a high but painful place', both Mitford and Satow said that they were absolutely fine.[43] After a magnificent dinner, the Englishmen attempted to return to the topic of opening Nanao to foreign trade. They managed to make more progress than Parkes had, the following evening being told that some trade with the West could take place there, although in the end, nothing came of it.

On leaving Kaga, another receipt was written, absolving that domain of any responsibility for their safety and they entered Echizen, which is now Fukui prefecture. Here the *daimyō* was opposed to any contact with Westerners, and his feelings 'were reflected in the conduct of his people', who stared at them as if they were 'gorillas'.[44]

Their journey continued without incident until they reached Kusatsu on 20 August, which is on the east side of Lake Biwa, twenty-six kilometres from Kyoto. Here they got into an argument with government officials about the route they would take to Osaka. They wanted to go the shortest way, which would have been through the town of Ōtsu, at the end of the lake. The officials were very anxious that they not go there because it was close to the Imperial capital of Kyoto, which would be defiled should a foreigner go near. They used ingenuity in making their arguments, offering to let them visit the temple of Ishiyama, which had been barred to Parkes and was an attractive prospect for men of Mitford and Satow's interests; it was not only a beautiful place in itself, but it had many historical and literary connections, being where Murasaki Shikibu is supposed to have started writing *The Tale of Genji*, Japan's most celebrated novel, under a full moon in the summer of 1004. It was also suggested that they might travel via Uji – another appealing proposition as it was famous for producing the finest tea in Japan. However, Mitford and Satow remained absolutely determined to take the shortest route through Ōtsu, which as diplomats, they had the legal right to do.

The argument continued until Mitford said that if the officials would write a formal letter explaining why they should not go through Ōtsu, they would desist. Three times they came back with drafts that stated Mitford and Satow had not got government permission to go there, which they rejected as they did not need it. Eventually the officials wrote that there had been complications as a result of Parkes' passing through in May and therefore begged them as a favour to go via Uji. Having won a small victory, Mitford said they would comply, although they were annoyed at the fact that when they made the detour to Ishiyama temple, they were not allowed in. Two days later, Noguchi, Satow's attendant, overheard men talking of their disappointment at missing the foreigners in Ōtsu. Four hundred men had been lying in wait to kill Mitford and Satow there. There was something almost Biblical about their deliverance.

Ōtsu, which even now is not very big, seems to have been an unlucky place for foreign visitors. Nicholas II of Russia, when he was the Tsesarevich was attacked there by one of his escort policemen, Tsuda Sanzō, in 1891. Tsuda swung at the Tsesarevich's face with a saber and then tried again, the second blow being parried by Nicholas' cousin, Prince George, with his cane, which saved his life. Nicholas went back to Russia with a nine-centimetre scar on the right side of his forehead.

Mitford and Satow got back to Osaka in one piece on 22 August. Mitford did not mention the perils they had encountered in a letter to his father, simply saying that they had been on a 'most beautiful journey right through the heart of Japan'.[45] There was not a word of complaint about what must have been one of the most uncomfortable and dangerous trips imaginable. However, as usual, Osaka, which was surely more comfortable than what he had come from, brought out Mitford's negativity: 'Anything like the heat of this most odious and stinking place I never felt. The mosquitoes, too, must be experienced to be believed.'[46]

When they saw their colleagues, Mitford and Satow were full of their adventures, but their thunder was stolen by an incident in Nagasaki, in which two British sailors had been hacked to pieces by samurai while they had been lying in a drunken sleep. Parkes knew he had to demand justice for these men as strongly as possible – had he failed to do so, he would have sent a message that attacks on British subjects were not taken seriously. The trouble was they did not know who had committed the crime. There was only one slender piece of evidence: a steamer from Tosa, an important domain in Shikoku, was seen departing soon afterwards and based on this, Parkes decided that the criminals had to be from there and took Satow to Tosa in order to conduct a fruitless investigation there.

Mitford returned by sea to Edo and his lodgings at Monryōin, which in late summer, with cooling breezes coming off the bay, was very pleasant if, without his 'playfellow' Satow, 'rather dull'. He had to resort to socialising with a fellow diplomat, Max von Brandt, who was a 'very clever agreeable man', but unfortunately he was 'a Prussian, and people do crow so loud Unter den Linden these years'.[47] At the time, the British image of the Prussians was of ultra-conservative, humourless militarists and it looks like to Mitford, Brandt somewhat fitted the stereotype, even though Mitford was fluent in German and adored German culture.

Mitford could not completely relax at Monryōin – his cockle shell alarm system went off one night, when he was woken by some crunching. He gave Lin Fu his sword and revolver and went out with a rifle. That seemed to be enough to scare away the men who had come to kill him. On another day he found the headless body of a samurai outside his gate, who must have been killed according to the rules of a Japanese vendetta, which made revenge legal if it was officially registered. Although travelling was dangerous, staying at home could be even more traumatic.

THE BIRTH OF THE NEW JAPAN

October 1867 – March 1868

ಐ

Miya-sama, Miya-sama 宮さま宮さま	Your Highness, Your Highness,
On-uma no mae ni 御馬の前に	In front of your noble horse
Pira-pira suru no wa ぴらぴらするのは	the thing that is fluttering
Nan jai na 何じゃいな	is what?
Toko tonyare tonyare na トコトンヤレトンヤレナ	[the sound of drums]

THESE ARE WORDS from the most famous Japanese song out-side Japan, thanks to Gilbert & Sullivan using it in *The Mikado*. 'Mr. Mitford', W.S. Gilbert reminisced years later,

> very kindly offered to assist us in the production, and it was at one of the rehearsals at which he was present that I ... asked him if he could suggest an effective Japanese air with native words that would suit the Mikado's entrance. He at once suggested "Miyo [Miya] Sama," and Sir Arthur Sullivan, who jumped at the idea, took down the notes as Mr. Mitford hummed them, and I took down the words from his dictation.[1]

Mitford was a good musician, once being described as perhaps the finest amateur cornet player of his day.[2] He successfully passed on both the words and tune to Gilbert and Sullivan; where the words are different from the original, this was surely deliberate. The first line of the original is 'Miya-san, Miya-san', which would translate as something like 'Mr. Prince, Mr. Prince'. One of the charms of the song is that the writer is innocent and unworldly as well as being a bit tongue in cheek. But Mitford took princes seriously and replaced 'san' with the more respectful 'sama', which fits the tune just as well.

The question that Gilbert and Sullivan left in the air in *The Mikado* is answered in the second verse:

Are wa chōteki seibatsu seyo tono

It is the sign to punish the enemies of the Emperor:

あれは朝敵征伐せよとの
nishiki no mihata jiya

the noble banner of silken brocade

錦の御旗ぢや
shiranaika
知らないか
Toko tonyare tonyare na

Don't you know that?

トコトンヤレトンヤレナ

The purpose of the song was to rally forces against the 'enemies of the Emperor'. But who in Japan would be an enemy to a fifteen-year-old hidden away in Kyoto with no power whatever?

*

Mitford was bored. He was stuck in Edo 'vegetating as usual after a trip [to Japan's west coast] and clearing up the accumulation of rubbishy papers which a long absence generates'.[3] There was no shortage of things going on – machinations were raging in Kyoto and Osaka for the future of Japan – but unfortunately Mitford did not know about them and had to rely on unreliable rumours. On 14 October, he was writing that the Shogun had resigned – which was untrue – and two weeks later he was saying that it was unlikely to happen, when it was about to. He viewed the possibility in terms of his own convenience: 'I hope there is no likelihood of our business being interrupted by an internal crisis which at this moment would be particularly unfortunate.'[4] In fact, there was not much immediate disruption to Mitford's life when the Shogun really did resign in November, the event having remarkably little impact, even though it was an abrupt ending for a dynasty that had lasted more than 260 years. Parkes thought that as a result, there was a 'fair chance of the unworkable Government of Japan being replaced by an intelligible system. The great question as to which of the two so called sovereigns should give way – the Mikado [Emperor] or the Tycoon [Shogun] – appears to have been solved'.[5] Parkes did not realise that the Shogun's resignation was tactical and that a large part of the country was ready to fight for him to hold on to power. He was also not taking into account the obvious fact that a child – Emperor Meiji – was very unlikely to be assuming control of Japan.

As sometimes happens with political people when an event of huge significance is taking place, the British got somewhat side-tracked on two issues of secondary importance which distracted them from seeing the big picture. The first was the ongoing battle to find the murderers of the two seamen in Nagasaki, which for Parkes had become a personal obsession. The investigation brought out the worst in everybody, the British side tenaciously following dead ends (it later emerged that the killers were not from Tosa, as Parkes was determined to prove), while the Japanese were foot-dragging and creating endless obstacles. For Mitford, the episode made him temporarily give up on Japan:

> The … government are full of professions of anxiety to discover and punish the guilty parties, but when it comes to the point, they always refuse to take the most obvious steps to ensure success. Their feebleness and imbecility are beyond all belief. They will stick to their old ways of doing things, and as these are chiefly remarkable

for their consistency in failing to attain their object, we naturally
wish to see more stringent and active measures adopted. Certainly
Chinese and Japanese quasi-statesmen are the most provoking people on the face of the earth to have to deal with – especially the
Japanese, for their vanity is so inordinate that they will always think
their mode of action best.[6]

The other major British concern was that the opening of Osaka
and Kobe to foreign trade, which had been fixed for 1 January
1868, would go ahead – Parkes was determined that the Japanese
would not renege on this, regardless of what state the country
was in. Consequently, Satow and Mitford set off for Kobe and
Osaka at the end of November, to report back on the preparations for the opening of the ports. While they were there, they
tried to gauge the mood in that part of the country. Mitford told
his father:

> You may perhaps read of a crisis of great danger in Japan. Don't
> believe a word of it. Here we are in the hotbed of Japanese politics
> [Osaka] and the town is as quiet and dull as London on Sunday.
> The Tycoon has effected a great change, it is true, but it will be, I
> believe, for the advantage of foreigners and, at any rate, will not
> affect their safety.[7]

It was not only Westerners who were reading events in this way;
a samurai noted that Kyoto was calm and that 'people showed no
surprise' at the Shogun's resignation.[8]

Mitford came upon a street demonstration in Osaka on 13
December, which in other countries in a time of similar unrest,
such as in the Paris Commune of 1871, might have been terrifying. But Japan's version was fluffy and tame, Mitford describing
the demonstrators as 'happy fanatics', who were 'dancing along
the streets dressed in holiday garb' and 'shouting till they must
have been hoarse' '*Ii ja nai ka, ii ja nai ka*', which means something like 'It's not bad, is it?'[9] They had the essential gentleness of
the Japanese spirit, combined perhaps with a typically Japanese
willingness to basically comply with the wishes of those in authority over them. These 'protestors' were supporting the Emperor's

expected resumption of power but Mitford did not realise this; he was told that it was in honour of miraculous showers of paper inscribed with the names of gods, and from that, constructed a story that those gods, 'the founders of mankind', had left Edo 'in disgust at the state of political affairs, and the showers ... stopped here'.[10] Mitford was cynical about this at the time, but in *Memories*, he took a different view, arguing that to the 'simple folk', 'the showers meant 'the sacred traditions of a glorious past, and upon these is based a heroism before which the world has bowed its head in admiration [probably a reference to the victory over Russia in 1905]'.[11]

Mitford's main task was to find somewhere to house a new British Legation in Kobe. He had arranged to take buildings that had been occupied a few months earlier by what he called the Prime Minister – Itakura Iga no Kami, the chief of the Shogun's governing council. This person was someone who had Mitford's full approval: 'gentlemanlike and clever' who 'floors his champagne and cherry brandy like a man'.[12]

Unfortunately, as Mitford told Parkes, the premises had fallen into ruin in just a few months,

> the completeness of which would be incredible to any one unacquainted with the flimsy nature of Japanese houses. The ceilings have for the most part fallen in, and the roofs will have to be almost entirely renewed even in the main house, while the outhouses are little more than tumbledown posts and planks. However, the house appears to me for many reasons to be the most suitable place for the Legation, and I trust that by the time you arrive, should you delay your departure from Yokohama until the 16th [December] instant, part of the buildings will be rendered habitable.[13]

Consequently, as he complained to his father, 'My whole day is taken up with builders, governors, stovefitters and such incongruous people'.[14] Fortunately, there was probably no better country in the world to be in this situation. As Mitford had noticed in Yokohama, 'every third man seems to be more or less of a carpenter' so the work could be completed very quickly.[15] Parkes uncharacteristically gave Mitford a bit of breathing space, delaying his arrival until the 21st, telling the Foreign Office that as the situation seemed so calm in Osaka and Kobe, there was no reason for him to leave earlier.

The residence was big but uncomfortable, made ('built' seems to be too strong a word) of wood and paper, with nothing to keep out the winter chill. To his father, Mitford wondered, 'Shall I ever be comfortable again …? It will be very strange.'[16] Parkes never complained of discomfort – what bothered him was how secure the building would be and whether it would impress the locals with British power. He achieved the two aims by taking fifty men from the tenth regiment with him, explaining to the Foreign Office that they were 'both … a measure of precaution and for political effect'.[17]

Mitford also had to find a place for Parkes in Osaka, which had settled into effectively being the capital of Japan, being where the ex-Shogun was based, and close to Kyoto, where the Emperor was. He chose a huge old residence, immediately behind the castle – which also needed repair and the construction of a temporary barracks for the guards – again, work that would be done very quickly. As the castle would be the focus of any fighting, its vicinity was not the safest place in Japan, but at least it might offer a ringside seat on the action.

Intelligence was essential and Mitford and Satow prowled Osaka to get it, under the close observation of government spies. Mitford could now operate on his own, able to carry on conversation in Japanese unaided which, Satow thought, was 'remarkable proof' of his linguistic powers.[18] They climbed over the Legation walls at night in order to escape their watchers. In his memoir, Mitford emphasised how resourceful and scrappy they were: 'like a couple of boys breaking out to rob a neighbour's apple-orchard, we contrived to keep our chief posted as to what was going on; practical, but hardly very dignified'.[19] They discovered that there was a gradual massing of troops on both sides – 'We are in a terrible crisis,' Mitford told his father on 29 December, 'for the country is on the eve of a civil war. How soon it may break out, none can tell.'[20] But for the moment, everything was quiet and – as usual – Mitford and Satow went out to the entertainment district. There they found an 'entire absence of fear or dislike' on the part of Osaka women, according to Satow. 'Curiosity … triumphed over every other feeling', but as the women's teeth were dyed black, a sign of their being older, he thought they 'probably felt immune from attempts at flirtation'.[21]

Parkes need not have worried about the ports of Osaka and Kobe not being opened on 1 January – on 20 December the young Itō Hirobumi, who would go on to become Japan's first prime minister, told Mitford that it had to happen in order to keep the foreigners quiet while the plans for transforming the country went on. Their opening was accompanied by cannon salutes and came after a week of feasting in Kobe to celebrate, with processions of people in red silk crape and carts to transport earth to raise the site of the proposed foreign settlement, according to Satow.[22] (Unfortunately, they did not raise the site of the Osaka settlement enough, Mitford reporting that during the rainy season that year, it was under four feet of water.)[23] The locals were happy because they thought the foreign trade would bring the area prosperity. Indeed, Mitford found a new acceptance of Westerners, telling his father 'the Japanese have learned a lesson or two, and they know that it is impossible for them to talk as of yore of turning out foreigners and recurring to their old isolation.'[24]

On 7 January, Mitford and Satow went into the streets of the city to see what was going on. They saw big guns that had been set up to defend the approaches to Osaka castle and heard the Shogun's forces vowing that they would die for their master. Some had Western rifles, others, the spears and swords that the Japanese had used for centuries. They were a striking sight, wearing traditional armour with brightly coloured surcoats on top. On their heads they had, in Mitford's words, 'hideous masks of lacquer and iron, fringed with portentous whiskers and moustachios, crested helmets with wigs from which long streamers of horsehair floated to their waists'.[25] It was the last hurrah of the old Japan. To Mitford's sadness, at the loss of tradition, and worryingly for the rest of East Asia, the country would soon get forces that looked and behaved like modern fighters.

On that day, Yoshinobu abandoned Kyoto, which was a crucial development because Meiji was now in the hands of his enemies. These men could say that they were fighting for the young Emperor, who was the legitimate ruler of Japan, and so any forces which opposed them, were the Emperor's enemies, as *Miya-san, Miya-san* so memorably asserted. The Emperor's forces had the best slogans, but the Shogun and his allies still controlled most of the rest of the country, including, for the moment, Osaka.

At this moment of high drama, Mitford found himself embroiled in a personal crisis. His father was demanding that he go back to England, going so far as to threaten to speak to the Foreign Office to persuade them to force him to return. Mitford sent him a long, conciliatory letter, urging him to understand that he had hated his desk work in London and that Japan represented an opportunity to make something of himself. He closed his appeal like this:

> I consider this to be one of those chances which do not occur to a man twice in his life … If I go home, all my work here will have been thrown away and will not have advanced me one jot. I have had a successful career here so far, and if I am allowed to stay on for a while longer, I am determined to win credit for myself, and when I do go back to you at the end of a short time, you will be all the more glad to see me that I have endeavoured to do my best in the world. This may be a momentous crisis in my life. I entreat you not to shirk what I know will be very painful to you. Depend upon it, it must be for my advantage to go into the more active branch of the profession. I should be miserable at an F.O. desk after the work I have been doing in the East, and I should go home a thoroughly disappointed man.[26]

One argument Mitford used was that as he was a younger son, he could not expect to inherit enough money to live on and therefore had to pursue a career: 'Younger sons must work and fight and toil,' he wrote.[27] The only alternatives for men in Mitford's position were marrying a wealthy wife – which he would manage – or inheriting a fortune from a rich, childless relative – which he would also manage. But he was not to know that things would work out so well for him. For now he had to plan how he could secure his future by his own efforts.

Mitford's appeal to his father worked; when he received his approval he responded, 'You know I never run into ecstasies in letters, but I feel none the less all the sacrifice you have made and all your generosity.'[28] At the same time, it depressed him that his father could not get more excited about his successes in Japan and see something positive in his being there:

> You hardly seem to care whether I earn praise or blame ... You can-not think what a pleasure it would be to me to read a cheerful letter from you now and then, but you will look at the blackest side of things, which is not good for you and is very painful to me.[29]

Mitford's two older brothers were very different to him. Percy was responsible but dull, having married well, to the Hon. Emily Marion Tatton Egerton, the daughter of a fantastically wealthy MP, who had been raised to the peerage. He had joined the Scots Guards, and then at twenty-five moved to the Foreign Office, where he worked for sixteen years. Henry, on the other hand, was 'fallen', according to Bertie; we do not find out exactly what this entailed, apart from huge debts, which at the time could land people in prison. He spoke French, German, Italian and Hindi, but he seemed incapable of holding down a job, and having lost his reputation as a gentleman in Britain, was finding it impossible to gain a respectable position there. Their father was convinced that Henry should go to the Far East to find work because Bertie would be able to introduce him to people there, but this was an idea Bertie was dead against: 'I am certain that the life of one of the open ports of China and Japan is the very worst temptation into which a man inclined to be unsteady could fall. To bring him here would be ... like applying a match to gunpowder.'[30] Henry married a German wife in 1871 and went to live in Germany, something Bertie had suggested, as it was cheaper than Britain, and he would be able to manage on his allowance there. He remained there, dying in Bad Godesberg in 1910.

It looks like Bertie was the closest of the brothers to their father, being the one that he confided in. We sense that he was proud of Bertie, but at the same time was uneasy about his adventurous spirit; probably at the bottom of all his concerns was the fear that he might get himself killed. Also he would have been thinking that as he was now in his thirties, he should be settling down and getting married. Bertie, for his part, respected his father but did not want to emulate him – he wanted to make much more of his life than his father had.

The existence of the three brothers should have been fairly comfortable, although keeping up a position as a 'gentleman' was not cheap anywhere. They received an allowance from their father, which was probably around £1,000 a year. Bertie earned a salary of £400 on top of this, and added to it with various money-making schemes; we see him asking his father to try to sell some objects he had sent back from either China or Japan for £500. He also 'made a small speculation here with £200 which will, I think, be profitable. At any rate I cannot lose by it.'[31] He hoped to have made £1000 on top of his regular income by the time he returned home. 'As for hoarding money', he explained to his father, 'it is the last of my ideas or wishes. All I want is enough to fit myself out on reaching England and that I shall have.'[32]

*

Mitford watched Yoshinobu enter Osaka Castle, after his retreat from Kyoto. In spite of his diminished status, all the Japanese onlookers went down on their knees and touched their foreheads to the ground. He seemed 'worn and dejected, looking neither to the right nor to the left, his head wrapped in a black cloth'.[33] On 8 January, Parkes requested a meeting with him, but was refused in spite of the fact that he was seeing Roches in the castle at the time. Parkes stormed in accompanied by Mitford and Satow, and after an angry exchange with Roches, they saw the ex-Shogun together. The iron etiquette which governed such meetings had disintegrated completely. Yoshinobu claimed to have left Kyoto from patriotic motives, anxious that civil war might have been waged in the sacred city, almost in the presence of the Emperor. He told them that he thought that the Emperor nominally ruled, but that the men beneath him did nothing but quarrel and had no idea how to govern.

That evening, Admiral Keppel invited Mitford to sleep on board his flagship, the *Rodney* which was anchored off Kobe. It was stormy and getting dark, and Mitford was nervous about going there by boat in bad weather. But Keppel dismissed his concerns as the ignorant worries of a landsman, telling Mitford that he 'did not know what a steam-launch could do'.[34] So they set off, towing a second boat. But as they reached the mouth of the Yodo river, a gale began to blow strongly and it was now dark. Mitford milked the drama to the full in his memoir:

> The wind was howling like Bedlam; the sea was terrific; now and then there was a rift in the clouds, and we could see the mockery of the wicked moon shining luridly through the ugly green waves which towered over us, hungry to swallow us up.[35]

They had to cast adrift the boat they were towing and concentrate on saving themselves. The Admiral told Mitford he had never seen 'death so near', which considering the adventures that Mitford knew he had had, was a frightening thought.[36] They finally managed to get alongside a French ship, the *Laplace*, but could only hang on to it – it would have been too dangerous for them to have tried to get on board. They ended up sitting for five hours, up to their waists in freezing water, while the French crew lowered sardines, biscuits and mulled claret down to them, Mitford wryly noting that the wine was 'most acceptable'.[37] Eventually there came a slight lull in the storm and they managed to get to another French ship, the *Sylvia*, which hoisted them up, one by one, into safety and the 'joy of sleep between hot blankets, after a steaming and strong glass of grog'.[38] When they reached Kobe the following afternoon, they heard that the American Commander-in-Chief, Admiral Bell, and all his boat's crew had been drowned. It had been yet another narrow escape for Mitford.

Two days later, another storm was raging and unbelievably he was going to return to Osaka by steam-launch again. He had a life-belt on this time – not much help in January – but managed to get as far as Osaka in safety and entered its waterways. However, as they neared the castle, they noticed that one of the bridges was crowded with a hostile mob which was preparing to drop a huge stone on their boat, thus dashing the fondly-held theory that Osaka was a safe city for foreigners. Fortunately, the coxswain managed to avoid it.

On 27 January, Mitford saw the sky filled with flames in the direction of Kyoto and heard that there had been fighting in Fushimi, south of the city – the first battle of what became known as the Boshin War, which would continue for over a year. It seemed as if the Shogun's troops would win easily – they outnumbered their enemies by three to one. But the Emperor's forces were better armed and helped by defections, won the crucial victory. Facing defeat, Yoshinobu escaped in disguise on an American ship and fled to Edo, which he could still control.

After hearing of all the bloodshed, Mitford reflected on the responsibility that the Western powers had to take for it:

> And all this misery has come on the country simply in order that a few European merchants can be enriched! For there is no concealing the fact that the advent of foreigners was the beginning of the trouble ... They are now impoverished, hungry, paying ruinous prices for everything. They have the horrors of a civil war to face, and they have gained absolutely nothing. They have only to show for their money the arms with which they are about to massacre one another. I have seen the so-called march of Western civilization both in China and Japan, and I have seen it a curse to both nations.[39]

These were his thoughts at the time, but he would completely change his mind. When a stable, effective government was established with relatively little bloodshed – around 3,500 killed in total – things looked very different. Mitford claimed credit for the West for helping make it happen, writing that the 'repressive might' of the Shoguns had been weakening for centuries, but it was contact with Western powers that rendered 'still more odious a feudality which men felt to be out of date'.[40] He even claimed credit for himself and Satow for the way a constitutional government was formed, saying 'we could ... recognize the reflection of hints which ... Satow and I had given'.[41] Japanese commentators have tended to attach less importance to the influence from overseas than Mitford. Probably the West's greatest contribution was to unify the Japanese to face the challenge it posed; as the historian Tokutomi Sōhō put it, 'The concept "foreign nations" brought forth the concept "Japanese nation".'[42]

Whatever their role may have been, the foreign representatives had no part to play in this fighting and instead had to get out of the way. On 30 January they were told that the ex-Shogun's forces could no longer guarantee their safety in Osaka and promised to arrange boats to transport them to Kobe, from where they would be able to board their ships if necessary. At 2.30 the following morning they were woken to be told they had to leave immediately; Mitford described the scene of 'fighting for boats which were not forthcoming in the general panic and such a row?!'[43] Like many others, Mitford had to abandon his larger possessions, including a beautiful cabinet which 'used to shine in the morning sun like semitransparent gold'.[44] He was so devastated at losing it that he gave up on collecting for a while. It took nearly a year, but Mitford would be partly compensated for his losses by the Japanese Government. He told his father he had lost about £250 worth of items, but as he was by far the largest loser, he did not like to send in the full claim. Rather, he asked for £130, which was closer to what other members of the Legation were claiming.[45]

Most of the British Legation travelled by water to Kobe, but Mitford was ordered to ride in charge of the mounted escort because there were not enough boats to transport the horses. It was a hellish journey: a snowstorm was raging, they did not know the exact direction they were going and their horses were slipping on the ice. On the way, they came to a river that they needed boats to cross. They saw several hundred soldiers who were in the same position. Mitford had no idea whether they would be friendly to foreigners or not, but he approached the commander of the troops on his own. He casually lit a cigar and, addressing him with the 'utmost ceremony', told him who they were and what they were doing.[46] To his relief, the man responded in a civil way, apologising for holding them up and Mitford said he was sorry for disturbing his soldiers. In the chaos of war and freezing conditions, Mitford and this commander managed the delicate quadrille of the Japanese etiquette fit for such potentially tricky situations. Mitford was to be rewarded for his trouble; the commander ordered the ferry boat to take his party across, and when he caught up with them again later, gave orders for his troops to present arms to Mitford's men and escort them into Kobe. 'It had been a bitter ride,' Mitford later wrote, 'and I doubt whether a more shivering lot of men and horses, starved with cold and hunger, faced the mangers that night'.[47] If Mitford was hinting at the nativity story, it was appropriate, because many would have to make do with very uncomfortable accommodation. The Ministers were all right in the old Custom House but Mitford ended up in a 'shanty' that was a Kobe version of a 'fifth-rate Margate lodging house'.[48]

Having struggled to Kobe, the foreign representatives received a message from the Imperial forces saying that they regretted the foreign Ministers leaving Osaka, because they could have guaranteed their safety there. This fact became more relevant when they discovered that Kobe was more dangerous than Osaka. On 4 February, the Legation staffs were going about their business, busy with the extra work the situation had created. They were in the recently-created foreign settlement, which at this point was small – about 400 metres wide and 600 long; the only buildings standing there were the new Custom House, a bonded warehouse, and the British Consulate, all in one corner, on the waterfront. It was a fine day, and most people were outside. Some of them stopped to look at the sight of several hundred Japanese troops marching towards Osaka. They turned out to be from the violently anti-foreign Bizen domain (now south-east Okayama prefecture). Suddenly, the soldiers stood opposite them and fired six or seven volleys straight at them. Most of the foreign representation, including all the Western Ministers, was in clear view and completely exposed; Parkes explained that they 'could only seek safety by endeavouring to gain the cover of the Custom-house and other buildings at the opposite corner of the square, and to do this they had to cross the large open space under the fire of their assailants'.[49]

Fortunately, the Bizen men did not understand the sights on their rifles, which had been recently imported from America and nobody was killed, while the building behind them was riddled with bullets. Had they been good shots, they could have wiped out a large part of the diplomatic corps at one blow. Mitford commented that if they were bad marksmen, they were 'mighty runners', all of them managing to escape from the foreign Lega-tion guards, apart from one old coolie.[50]

The only injury the guards managed to inflict was on an old woman who was shot in the leg. Dr Willis went to treat her, but it turned out that she was *eta*, the lowest social class in Japan, whose presence, it was believed, would pollute even the poorest house of any other class. Mitford wrote that the Japanese ser-vants strongly protested at her 'being treated as a human being' and said that the Legation would be permanently defiled if she was brought into it.[51] Dr Willis nonetheless insisted on treating her as any other patient.

It would be nice to be able to say of Mitford that he was offended by the existence of an outcast class, but he did not write anything against the system – rather, he went out of his way to emphasise what outcasts they were, describing them as 'despised', 'shunned', 'polluted', 'accursed', 'squalid' and 'degraded'.[52] He saw the *eta* as a point of interest and, deciding that as no account of Japa-nese society would be complete without some mention of them, included the seventeenth-century story of the doomed love of one of the Shogun's retainers and an *eta* girl in *Tales of Old Japan*. In his defence, we might say that he was not imposing his Western values on the country, but he gave his opinions about other things. *Eta* (now known as *burakumin*) gained equal legal status with other Japanese in 1871, but they are still said to be discriminated against in some parts of the country, particularly in marriage, where fami-lies want to know if a potential partner has *burakumin* blood.

The anti-Shogun forces were consolidating their power in western Japan. On 8 February, a notice was presented to the foreign ministers stating that the Emperor would 'henceforward exercise the supreme authority in all the internal and external affairs of the country. Consequently the title of Emperor must be substituted for that of Tycoon under which the Treaties have been made.'[53]

This announcement was a blow for Roches, who had declared that he would never represent France to anyone other than the Shogun. He got no sympathy from the other Ministers, who had resented his closeness to Yoshinobu and all the special favours he had gained for France through it. This feeling got stronger after Mitford discovered that the Imperial Court had ordered the Shogun to invite the Foreign Ministers to an audience of the Emperor in Kyoto – Roches had advised Yoshinobu that this should be kept secret, believing that if the foreign Ministers had direct contact with the Emperor, it would fatally undermine Yoshinobu's position. Mitford described Roches' actions as 'vain and foolish'. Vain, because another invitation would be issued, and foolish because 'it was bound to break the eleventh commandment [Thou shalt not get found out]'.[54]

Now that Yoshinobu had abandoned the area around Kyoto and Osaka, the fighting moved to Edo. Reports of it were sketchy and the diplomats had little idea what was happening. Mitford, who liked to be in the thick of the action, even if it meant being in peril, did not like it: 'Anything like the dullness of the last fortnight here I never knew.'[55] Such was his liking for action that later in the year, he was sorry to miss out on a trip with Dr Willis to the front (Willis had been asked to help with the wounded among the Imperial forces), which would surely have been full of horrifying sights, writing: 'He will have a most interesting journey on which I should much have liked to have accompanied him.'[56]

Under the new regime, there were many signs of a warmer attitude to foreigners. Mitford believed the change was 'not from goodwill towards us but from fear', but nonetheless was grateful for it.[57] The *daimyō* of Aizu, in the north, had said just a few years earlier that when the first foreigner set foot in Osaka, he would come down with his men and kill him. But when Mitford met him in Osaka, he 'found him a most placid amiable gentleman of middle age', with whom he exchanged gifts.[58] The secret of Mitford's success with people like this was his careful following of Japanese customs; most Westerners found the ritual exchange of presents tiresome and empty of meaning, but Mitford took the trouble to do it. The Japanese still like nothing better than a foreigner who takes care to follow their ways.

An important sign of the improved position of Westerners was the way the Emperor's Government dealt with the man who had ordered the troops to fire on the foreign diplomats, Taki Zenzaburō. Two of the Emperor's leading advisors came to meet with the foreign Ministers to discuss the punishment. Parkes advocated clemency, believing it would encourage a warmer feeling towards foreigners among ordinary Japanese, but the majority thought that Taki should be ordered to perform *hara-kiri*. Mitford agreed with them, thinking that mercy would have been mistaken for weakness.

So that the foreign Legations would be satisfied that the punishment was genuinely carried out and that no substitute was made, witnesses were invited from all of them, and Satow and Mitford represented the British. Both of them were entranced by it; Mitford liked the way that the Japanese could manage seamier, unpleasant things (prostitution is another example) in a carefully prescribed, refined way. Satow thought that it was 'a most decent and decorous ceremony', and 'far more respectable' than what Britain produced 'for the entertainment of the public in the front of Newgate prison'.[59] The *hara-kiri* can hardly be compared to a British public hanging as it was not an execution, but it was usually not suicide either, death coming when the second chopped off the head. Mitford translated it as 'self-immolation by disembowelling', but 'performance' seems the best way to describe it – the players followed a detailed if unwritten script, taking meticulous care to play their parts correctly. It was most like something out of the theatre.

Mitford probably wrote and re-wrote his account of the *hara-kiri* many times, wanting to not only describe all the details accurately, but also capture the atmosphere. He made good use of it, sending it to the *Cornhill Magazine*, which published it in 1869, and including it in *Tales of Old Japan*.[60] It became a classic; one of the best-known pieces of writing by a Westerner about the Japan of that time.

He starts it as if he was describing a pleasant evening gathering: 'The courtyard of the temple presented a most picturesque sight; it was crowded with soldiers standing about in knots round large fires, which threw a dim flickering light over the heavy eaves and quaint gable-ends of the sacred buildings.'

The witnesses were shown into an inner room, where they had to wait while the preparations were made. They were asked if they wished to say anything to Taki, and they said not. They were then invited into the main hall of the temple where the ceremony was to be performed. Mitford takes up the description:

It was an imposing scene. A large hall with a high roof supported by dark pillars of wood. From the ceiling hung a profusion of those huge gilt lamps and ornaments peculiar to Buddhist Temples. In front of the high altar, where the floor, covered with beautiful white mats, is raised some three or four inches from the ground, was laid a rug of scarlet felt. Tall candles placed at regular intervals gave out a dim mysterious light, just sufficient to let all the proceedings be seen. The seven Japanese [witnesses] took their places on the left of the raised floor, the seven foreigners on the right. No other person was present.

After an interval of a few moments of anxious suspense, Taki Zenzaburō, a stalwart man, thirty-two years of age, with a noble air, walked into the hall attired in his dress of ceremony, with the peculiar hempen-cloth wings which are worn on great occasions. He was accompanied by a *kaishaku* and three officers who wore the *jimbaori* or war surcoat with gold-tissue facings. The word *kaishaku*, it should be observed, is one to which our word *executioner* is no equivalent term. The office is that of a gentleman: in many cases it is performed by a kinsman or friend of the condemned, and the relation between them is rather that of principal and second than that of victim and executioner. In this instance the *kaishaku* was a pupil of Taki Zenzaburō, and was selected by the friends of the latter from among their own number for his skill in swordsmanship.

With the *kaishaku* on his left hand, Taki Zenzaburō advanced slowly towards the Japanese witnesses, and the two bowed before them, then drawing near to the foreigners they saluted us in the same way, perhaps even with more deference: in each case the salutation was ceremoniously returned. Slowly, and with great dignity, the condemned man mounted on to the raised floor, prostrated himself before the high altar twice, and seated himself on the felt carpet with his back to the high altar, the *kaishaku* crouching on his left-hand side. One of the three attendant officers then came forward, bearing a stand of the kind used in temples for offerings, on which, wrapped in paper lay the *waki-zashi*, the short sword or dirk of the Japanese, nine inches and a half in length, with a point and an edge as sharp as a razor's. This he handed, prostrating himself, to the condemned man who received it reverently, raising it to his head with both hands, and placed it in front of himself.

After another profound obeisance, Taki Zenzaburō, in a voice which betrayed just so much emotion and hesitation as might be expected from a man who is making a painful confession, but with no sign of either in his face or manner spoke as follows:

I, and I alone, unwarrantably gave the order to fire on the foreigners at Kōbé, and again as they tried to escape. For this crime I disembowel myself, and I beg you who are present to do me the honour of witnessing this act.

Bowing once more the speaker allowed his upper garments to slip down to his girdle, and remained naked to the waist. Carefully, according to custom he tucked his sleeves under his knees to prevent himself from falling backwards; for a noble Japanese gentleman should die falling forwards. Deliberately, with a steady hand, he took the dirk that lay before him; he looked at it wistfully, almost affectionately; for a moment he seemed to collect his thoughts for the last time, and then stabbing himself deeply below the waist on the left-hand side he drew the dirk slowly across to the right side, and, turning it in the wound gave slight cut upwards. During this sickeningly painful operation he never moved a muscle of his face. When he drew out the dirk, he leant forward and stretched out his neck; an expression of pain for the first time crossed his face, but he uttered no sound. At that moment the *kaishaku*, who, still crouching by his side, had been keenly watching his every movement, sprang to his feet, poised his sword for a second in the air; there was a flash – a heavy, ugly thud, a crashing fall; with one blow the head had been severed from the body.

A dead silence followed, broken only by the hideous noise of the blood throbbing out of the inert heap before us, which but a moment before had been a brave and chivalrous man.[61]

Death over dishonour was at the heart of Mitford's beliefs and he had the highest respect for the combination of courage and adherence to tradition that the *hara-kiri* demanded. He wrote of being 'filled with admiration at the firm and manly bearing' of Taki, and of 'the nerve with which the *kaishaku* performed his last duty to his master'.[62] He believed that these showed the power of education, the samurai being trained to look upon the *hara-kiri* as a ceremony that he may have to perform some day, either as the principal or the second. 'If the hour comes he is prepared for it and will bravely face an ordeal which early training has robbed of half its horrors. In what other country in the world does a man learn that the last tribute of affection which he may have to pay to his best friend may be to act as his executioner?'[63]

We sense the glow of satisfaction Mitford felt about being in the first group of Westerners to witness the ceremony. He thought it important to educate the British about the *hara-kiri* and described the act in terms that Victorian upper class Englishmen would relate to, indeed something that could almost have been part of their own gentleman's code. But many in both Britain, and even in Japan, thought it was a horrific relic from the dark ages. A newspaper article in the *Japan Times* argued that it was disgraceful for Christians – Mitford and Satow – to have attended the ceremony.[64] There were voices speaking out against the *hara-kiri* in Japan, but they were few. Mitford writes of a motion in Parliament being introduced to outlaw it in 1869. Out of 209 members, 200 voted against it with only three in favour. The proposer of the motion was murdered shortly after the debate took place, which shows how dangerous it was even to suggest such a thing.[65]

One Japanese opponent of the *hara-kiri* was Yoshinobu, who argued that it was a barbarous custom that was out of date. This was a convenient belief for him to have held, because many expected him to go through it himself after his defeat in Osaka, instead of fleeing to Edo.[66] In *Tales of Old Japan*, Mitford describes a member of the Second Council telling him,

> Sir, the only way for you now to retrieve the honour of the family of Tokugawa is to disembowel yourself; and to prove to you that I am sincere and disinterested in what I say, I am here ready to disembowel myself with you.[67]

At this, the ex-Shogun flew into a rage and said he would not listen to such nonsense, leaving the room. However, the retainer, to prove his honesty, went to another part of the Castle and solemnly performed the *hara-kiri*. Mitford adds no comment to his telling of this story – it went without saying that he thought Yoshinobu should have done the same as his retainer. Most people agreed that he was a coward; a mocking rhyme, which has a nice ring to it in English, did the rounds in Edo: 'He came back in flight, afraid to fight, leaving his men behind.'[68]

Taki's *hara-kiri* was a turning point both for Mitford and Japan. It made Mitford respect the country in a way he had not done before; while he would still complain about specific things, he stopped writing contemptuously about the nation as a whole. Before it, he had seen the Japanese as cowardly, telling his father,

> As for their boasted valour, that seems a very doubtful matter. Their attacks on foreigners have all been sneaking ambushes ... I do not believe in any single Japanese facing an armed foreigner. They always let a man pass in peace and rush out on him from behind when he least expects it.[69]

After this *hara-kiri*, Mitford stopped thinking that they lacked courage. Among the Japanese, it changed the attitude towards attacks on Westerners. The Emperor had personally given the order for this *hara-kiri*, showing for the first time his desire to protect foreigners in Japan. This did not turn Japan into a safe country overnight – fanatics could say that the Emperor was being guided by evil advisers – but it was the start of its becoming so. In many ways this *hara-kiri* fulfilled what Mitford thought was one of the great strengths of the act, that of drawing a line under a conflict: something that 'might have involved a war and cost hundreds of lives' he wrote, could be 'wiped out by one'.[70]

6

KYOTO

February-March 1868

ぞ

語れ、月遠き都の哀れをも
見るらんものを夜な夜なの空
Speak to me, oh moon,
Of the distant capital,
To whose woeful plight
You nightly now bear witness
On your journey' cross the sky.[1]

THUS THE POET Shinkei (1406–1475) pined for Kyoto. The city was the literary and artistic centre of the country and to be exiled from it was a torment for him. Even today, if Tokyo is the brain of Japan, Kyoto is its heart. Following the fighting in January 1868, the city also had a claim to be its capital again, at least of the part of the country the Emperor's forces controlled, although the Shogun was still master of Edo and northern Japan.

Kyoto had, after all, been home to the emperors for more than a thousand years, although they had been so completely hidden away that many Westerners believed their existence was a myth. Their rare audiences were given from behind a curtain and everything possible was done to ensure that they were seen by as few people as possible, and certainly not by the profane eyes of foreigners. But the times were changing and agonised discussions were going on as to whether Meiji might give an audience to the Western Ministers. Would this be a desecration, or a helpful boost to a regime whose survival was in the balance?

Mitford was unaware of these developments, only thinking that he might be able to someday have a look around the city, 'as we seem to be breaking down every prejudice and barrier which used to lock us in'.[2] He had no idea that he and Parkes were about to break down the biggest barrier of all.

Kyoto was probably the most dangerous place in the country for foreigners, as their presence in the 'Holy of Holies of Japan', as Mitford called it, would be considered most offensive.[3] He cannot have forgotten the four hundred men that had gathered in Ōtsu to murder him and Satow for straying too close to it just eight months earlier. But if it was a choice between safety and making history, Mitford would not hesitate to choose the risky option.

The initial breakthrough came in February 1868, when Dr Willis, who had so impressed the Japanese with his Western medical techniques, was invited to the city to treat injured soldiers there. Mitford would have gone with him, but he had fallen ill, laid low by his nightmare journeys between Kobe and Osaka the month before. He was trapped in Kobe in a typically uncomfortable place: 'Such a room to be stuck in! No fireplace, but a brazier of charcoal; no windows or fitting doors, nothing but paper slides; no bed but a quilt spread on the mats.'[4]

This meant that Satow and Willis beat Mitford to Kyoto, which seems to have seriously upset Mitford who had set his heart on being the first Englishman in the city; 'foolish but I think excusable'.[5] Mitford made an uncharacteristic snipe at Satow, writing that he raved 'about a porcelain made there called Kiomizu ware – blue and white. I think the specimens he has brought back great trash'.[6] Perhaps this suggests that underneath all his admiration of Satow, Mitford felt that he was slightly lacking in refinement. But then again, Mitford tended to think nobody could judge Chinese and Japanese art as well as him and he often complained about other people's taste: 'Anything as trashy,' he told his father', as the things that are brought to this Legation and bought with avidity by our guests who almost fight over them you never saw. They call them "curios" and when one man has bought an object of the greatest rarity and is triumphing over his competitors, the dealer will produce six out of his pocket exactly identical and offer them at a reduction if he takes the lot.[7]

In March, the Emperor's ministers sent another request to Willis to go back to the city and this time Mitford was well enough to go with him. Willis was a good travelling companion; a genial Ulsterman who was also an outstanding doctor. He was a giant, even by British standards; at 6ft. 3in. tall, he towered over any Japanese he met. Many years later, Satow paid this tribute to him:

> Those who have had the fortune to profit by his medical or surgical aid, feel that no man could be more tender or sympathetic towards a patient ... [In the 1860s] a doctor had frequently to encounter personal risks ...; he exposed himself freely, in order to succour the wounded ... Big men are big-hearted, and he was no exception.[8]

The Government wanted him to see what he could do for the retired *daimyō* of Tosa, an important domain in Shikoku. Such men were known as *inkyo* and Mitford understood their true position, writing that they were 'by no means "ex" or "retired" ... They abdicate the title and the nominal rule of their Provinces in favour of a son real or adopted, but the iron hand remains theirs.'[9]

For a change, they had a fairly comfortable journey, travelling most of the way from Osaka to Kyoto in a small pleasure boat, of the kind people enjoyed hot summer nights on, with 'a lacquer box full of rice and fish enough for a regiment'.[10] The boat took them to Fushimi, now a southern suburb of Kyoto, which had been the site of the crucial battle at the end of January. Mitford wrote that there was little sign of the warfare there, barring the part of the town that had been destroyed by fire, but as fires were so common in Japan, a burnt-down area was hardly worth mentioning. On their arrival, they were met by a guard of Tosa men, which Mitford had fun describing:

[L]ittle ugly fellows with helmets covered with masses of black or white horsehair which fell in tangled locks over their shoulders. The object being to look savage they were a success [but] from any other point of view they would have been a decided failure for they appeared like imitation goblins out of a bad dream or out of the opening scenes of a Pantomime.'[11]

But they did at least ensure Mitford and Willis' safety, which counted for something.

The *inkyo's* palace was immense and they had to walk through interminable maze-like passages to reach his apartments. To his father, Mitford recounted the scene:

We found the old 'Viveur' lying on the mats in the midst [of] a pile of quilt and coverlets covered with the finest purple crape. At his head was his wife, an old black toothed and shaven browed lady, ministering to his wants and behind his bedding with her hands inside the bed clothes to keep them warm was his last and favourite concubine, such a pretty little creature with teeth and brows as nature made them, who at first was much abashed at the sight of the hideous and inauspicious foreigners.'[12]

The *inkyo* received them warmly and thanked them repeatedly for coming so quickly. Willis stayed to treat him – patching him up, Mitford wrote later, to live for several more years 'rendering good service to the state'.[13] Meanwhile, Mitford left to talk to leading men in the new Foreign Office. While he was in conversation with them, news came that eleven Frenchmen had been murdered at Sakai, a port south of Osaka. Some had been shot at point blank while others were beaten to death with iron-hooked poles. There seemed to have been no provocation or reason for the attack beyond blind hatred.

The perpetrators were Tosa men, and as Mitford and Willis were staying in the Tosa residence, this meant that they were at the centre of the drama. In his memoir, Mitford made out that the incident placed him and Willis in great danger, writing darkly that there would have been two or three hundred men debating whether to kill them almost within earshot.[14]

He was not above adding a little extra to the mix to keep his readers entertained and admiring him for the dangers he had faced. In fact, their safety was guaranteed by the *inkyo* himself who, along with the senior Foreign Office official who was there, unambiguously condemned the murders. Mitford took down a statement from the *inkyo*, in which he said, 'The act of violence which my retainers have committed has caused me to be deeply ashamed' and he expressed the desire that only Tosa and not the whole of Japan be punished for it.[15] Mitford judged that the *inkyo* was sincere, telling Parkes, 'the assurances ... they would bring every guilty man to justice were very satisfactory, as affording a proof that the crime was not encouraged or countenanced by the military class, who regarded it as the act of a set of lawless ruffians'.[16] The fact that Parkes and Roches were happy to accept Mitford's assessment meant that there would be no wider punishment, which could have dangerously escalated the situation. This was one of the most important things that Mitford did during his time in Japan.

The twenty men deemed responsible for the attack were all ordered to perform *hara-kiri* and a party of Frenchmen from the ship the victims had come from, had to witness this. Watching twenty men go through the same gruesome and elaborate ceremony was hard, and once they reached eleven (the same number as the men who were murdered) the commander could bear it no longer and asked them to stop. As Satow pointed out, they were all equally guilty, so this made it look more like revenge than justice.[17]

Mitford took the opportunity to look around Kyoto, which disappointed him. While its situation left 'nothing to be desired', as a capital, the city certainly was 'mean'. Kiyomizu-dera, one of its highlights, was no more than a 'lovely spot with all the graces of hill and trees and water', and the Shogun's residence there, Nijō Castle, was a 'poor place as castles go'.[18] In the whole city, 'there seems not to be a striking edifice of any kind'.[19] Like Edo, Kyoto did not match up to his idea of a capital city, not having any of the grand buildings of the ones that he knew, like London and Paris. Kyoto's attractions are of a different nature: modest, restrained buildings surrounded by exquisite, intimate gardens. To be fair to Mitford, he did half-heartedly acknowledge this, writing that there were 'some fine and ancient Temples, but these do not stand out'.[20] Today, when you exit Kyoto station and walk towards the centre of the city, there is nothing that suggests you are anywhere special aside from hordes of tourists. But today's visitors have their guidebooks informing them they are in one of the world's most enchanting cities. Mitford had nothing to tell him that he had not been cheated, that the place had not been mythologised, built up into something almost magical when in reality it was ordinary. Satow agreed with Mitford's assessment. He thought the houses were 'badly built', and that Nijō Castle, 'hardly deserves the name'.[21] Mitford never completely warmed to the place. In his memoir, he wrote that it was 'but a dull, grey city – if the truth must be told, rather shabby; for the grand shrines which are the glory of its sanctity are hidden away, screened from the profane eyes in those lovely groves which were the first temples of the gods'.[22]

Part of what put Mitford off on his first trip there was that he had to be surrounded by annoying guards wherever he went, although these were certainly necessary as he was shortly to discover. He was, however, taken with Gion, then, as now, the part of the city where the highest class of entertainment was available. He went to one of the most famous teahouses there, where geisha were employed to gracefully serve and entertain guests. Mitford thought them beautiful, 'if they only would be persuaded not to paint quite so much and above all not to gild their lips'.[23] Initially they avoided him, but eventually the prettiest came to sit beside him and things gradually relaxed. He liked the fact that unlike in the West, where you were expected to eat courses as they were served, in Japan, you could nibble and sip continuously over what, in this case, turned out to be a seven-hour dinner.

However, the greatest excitement Kyoto could offer was not to be found in the entertainment areas, nor in the city's great buildings. It was the ultimate unattainable goal for almost anybody, Japanese or Western: to see the 'Son of Heaven' as Mitford called him. After fierce debates behind the scenes, Emperor Meiji was informed that it was the usual practice for monarchs in other countries to give audiences to foreign Ministers and was asked to do the same. Japan would not give up on its traditions completely – they would be kept as short as possible and conducted from behind a screen so that the Emperor would not actually be seen by foreign eyes. Nevertheless, it is remarkable that Meiji agreed, because his father had absolutely refused to accept the presence of Westerners in Japan. In a society where respect for parents held a high place, this Emperor was going against everything his father had held dear. Perhaps, as has been suggested, the court women who had brought him up had been less conservative and were the stronger influence on him. Whatever the explanation, even as a boy, he was showing that he would be a new kind of monarch.

On 9 March, an invitation was issued to all the foreign representatives, but only the British, French and Dutch accepted; the Americans, Italians and Prussians decided that their duty was to be in Yokohama to ensure the safety of their citizens there in the civil war.

The three audiences were fixed for 23 March and it would be the French first, followed by the Dutch, and then the British. At about two o'clock in the afternoon, the Emperor entered the Hall of State Ceremonies, carrying the imperial sword and jewel and sat behind the screen of state, with senior officials standing behind him and outside. Roches was escorted into the imperial presence; he bowed at the screen and the Emperor's voice could just be heard saying 'We are pleased to learn that the Emperor of your country is well. We hope that the relations between our two countries in the future will be ever more cordial, lasting and unchanging.'[24] Roches was only expected to give the set response, but he always had to be a bit different and added a prayer for the prosperity of Japan and for divine protection for the Emperor. He left, and the Dutch Minister went in for his audience. However, when it came to the British turn, they were not there.

In retrospect, it proved to have been unwise for their Legation to be accommodated some distance from the Palace – they had to travel around five kilometres to reach it. They were staying at the magnificent Chion-in temple, in the two guest houses there, which had been built in 1639. The walls and sliding doors were decorated with paintings from the Kano school. The previous day Parkes had been to see senior officials and it was all smiles as they talked over the arrangements, including their security. Mitford was so confident that everything would be all right that he left his revolver at home.

The British processed to the palace in great state. First came the Inspector of the Legation Escort, who rode alongside a Japanese officer named Nakai Hiroshi, from the Satsuma clan.[25] Then came the British mounted escort and Japanese troops, followed by Parkes, Satow and Gotō Shōjirō a high-ranking official in the Foreign Office. These were followed by a guard of infantry, both British and Japanese. Mitford's horse had gone lame, so he travelled in a palanquin near the back.

Suddenly, when they reached a turning, two men came out of nowhere and started wildly attacking the procession with swords, running down the line to kill or injure as many men as they could.[26] Nakai bravely jumped off his horse and engaged one of them in desperate combat. However, he was not dressed for fighting and his feet got entangled in his loose trousers and he fell on his back. His attacker tried to cut off his head, but he managed to parry the blow and stab the man in the breast. Then Gotō hit the assailant on the shoulder with his sword and Nakai cut off his head.

The other attacker, after slashing many of the escort, charged at Satow, wounding his horse near Satow's knee and clipping off part of the horse's nose. Satow had moved up to protect Parkes, an obvious target in his magnificent ceremonial uniform. Mitford himself was far from the action and from inside his palanquin could not see what was going on. At first he thought that the disturbance had been caused by restive horses. It was only when he heard 'Kill him! Stop him! Cut him down!' and saw the Inspector of the Escort come cantering down the street, firing his pistol, that he realised what was happening. He jumped out of his palanquin, drew his sword and ran to the front, seeing man after man from the mounted escort with blood streaming from his wounds. He found Parkes standing with the headless body of one of the attackers at his feet. He was, of course, completely unruffled; his comment was 'Sensation diplomacy this, Mitford.'[27] Mitford had watched as one of the attackers rushed into a house, being pursued by three officers and Mitford now ran back to him. He was cornered, having been shot in the jaw and received other wounds; 'covered with mud, and clotted with gore so that his features were hardly human, he glared at me with the stricken eyes of a man who sees his slayer before him'.[28] Rather than kill him, Mitford was anxious to keep him alive – in order to question him – and so had to protect him from the uninjured members of the escort who wanted to exact revenge.

This is essentially how Mitford described what happened to his father at the time, but his account in *Memories* has a very significant variation on this. There he writes,

> I saw the murderer coming at me, by this time himself wounded, but not seriously, and full of fight ... I knew enough of Japanese swordsmanship to be aware that it was no use to try and avoid his blow, so I rushed in underneath his guard and wrenched the bleeding sword out of his grip.[29]

Neither Satow's, nor Parkes' accounts say anything about Mitford tackling one of the assailants single-handed, or even assisting with bringing him down – and this is the case with ten other witness statements from the Legation guard.[30] It looks like Mitford simply invented this act of bravery. Perhaps by the time *Memories* was published, in 1915, Mitford felt that there was virtually nobody left, apart from Satow, to contradict it, and Satow would not have done that to an old friend. And to be fair to Mitford, he certainly behaved creditably, if not heroically – Parkes singled him out, along with Satow and Willis, for praise in his report to the Foreign Secretary.

Mitford reflected later that it was remarkable how many men just two attackers managed to injure before they could be stopped – they wounded a total of thirteen: 'It ... shows how much mischief a man may do if he does not try to save his own skin.'[31] However, a large part of the reason they were so successful was the fact that the men protecting them did not fight back very well. The Japanese guards almost all ran away and only returned when it was safe to do so and the British Legation guard did not do very much to save the situation either. Their problem was they were carrying lances, which looked magnificent, but were not practical weapons in a narrow street. In fact, it was the quick actions of the Japanese officials, Nakai and Gotō that did most to ensure that nobody was killed. Probably they were motivated by the thought of the dire consequences for them if the British Minister had died. You fight hard if you know that the price of failure will probably be having to perform the *hara-kiri*. Their courage was recognised in Britain, the two men being presented with swords of honour from Queen Victoria in recognition of the gallantry with which they had protected her Minister. For Mitford, Gotō's most impressive bravery was not saving Parkes' life but standing up to him; he admired the fact that he was 'quite able to hold his own against our rather peppery chief' in spite of being subjected to him at full fury. Mitford considered him one of the 'three or four ablest men who engineered the revolution', but he is largely forgotten now.[32] When Mitford returned to Japan in 1906, he visited Gotō's grave and reflected that he 'was one of the first of the leaders … to hold out his hand to the strangers from the West and he remained their consistent friend to the end.'[33]

There was difficulty finding men to carry the wounded, and Mitford needed the point of his sword to force two shopkeepers to carry the assailant that was still alive in his palanquin – they considered it to be the work of *eta* and thought they would be polluted by doing it. The British Legation's base in Kyoto, the Chion-in,

> was turned into a ghastly hospital. Our wounded men, bleeding as if their life must ebb out, lay patiently in the verandah waiting their turn of the assistance of the Doctors who stripped to their shirts, seemed almost to multiply themselves, so quiet and skilful were they. Shirts and sheets were being torn up into bandages, buckets of bloody water were being emptied and refilled – everything one touched or saw was bloody.[34]

Parkes decided that he could not now go to the Court to have his audience, although it is easy to imagine him having carried on regardless. Mitford made his priority interrogating the prisoner, who he thought was probably dying. He was 'a most hideous fellow with fierce, rolling black eyes and the hair on his large head, which as a priest he shaved all over, beginning to grow'.[35] He said that his name was Ichikawa Samurō and that he lived at the temple of Jōrenji, near Osaka. He said that he had simply set out to kill foreigners and nobody other than him and his accomplice knew of the plan. He had never seen a Westerner before. He added, 'I repent of my crime. It was a sudden thought on the part of both of us. I had no previous hatred to foreigners.'[36] Mitford thus established the crucial fact that the assailants were not in the employ of a *daimyō*, or part of an organised plot to kill Westerners. However, the following morning, Ichikawa was questioned further by a Japanese officer who pretended to be a hater of foreigners and by praising his deed, got out of him the names of three further accomplices who had been waiting in a house further down the street to continue the attack should they only partially succeed, although in the event, they did nothing. Mitford found himself sympathising with his prisoner, unlike other members of the Legation who only wanted to see the man dead. Mitford took him some rice and soup, gave him some tobacco for his pipe and sat down for a simple chat with him. Ichikawa was grateful and kept saying over and over that if he had known what decent people foreigners were, he would never have attacked them. He deeply regretted his actions and now wanted only to die.

The incident created consternation in the Emperor's court. The fear was that Britain, which was much the most powerful of the Western powers in the area, would become hostile to their precarious regime. The Emperor sent high officials of state dressed in court robes to express their deep regret at what had happened. In the past, it would have been necessary for Parkes to insist on punishment and reparation but not in this case: the officials assured him that the wounded would be compensated and should any of them die, provision would be made for their fami-

lies. More importantly, they begged Parkes to understand that
the wicked act of a couple of men should not stand in the way of
friendly relations between the Emperor and Britain. Parkes had
no problem with this – it was obvious that the Emperor's Government had had nothing to do with the attack. Indeed, he was
generous enough to tell the head of foreign affairs that he 'considered a graver outrage had been committed' upon the Emperor
than himself, as it had been the Emperor's wish that they should
visit him.[37] Ichikawa was denied the privilege of *hara-kiri* and
was beheaded as a common criminal. Further, the Emperor's
Government decreed that anyone attacking foreigners would
be deprived of their swords, stripped of their rank as a samurai,
executed in a similar way and that their heads would be exposed
at the execution ground, as was Ichikawa's. Mitford believed this
was 'an immense point gained in our relations with Japan'.[38]
He made the most of the incident, sending a graphic account of
it to *The Times*, which printed it. This was the first time he had
appeared in print. Unfortunately, it was under the byline 'from a
correspondent', but it was a start that he would build on.

Nothing was left to chance with the new arrangements for
the audience with the Emperor. Three was a lucky number in
Japan, so the date chosen, 26 March, which was the 3rd of the
3rd month in the Japanese calendar, was an exceptionally auspicious day. From early morning the courtyard of Chion-in was
full of Japanese soldiers with 'plumed lances and arrayed in the
panoply of medieval warfare', in Mitford's description. He added
that even those who were 'more or less "blasé" about such sights'
were 'struck with the surprising picturesqueness of the scene'.[39]
Two powerful figures, the *inkyo* of Uwajima and the *daimyō* of
Hizen (in what is now Saga and Nagasaki prefectures), came
in person to conduct the delegation to the palace, and their
immense retinues added to the splendour. Unfortunately on the
British side, only two of the mounted escort were able to ride.
Special care was taken at all the corners, and crowds turned out
to watch the extraordinary procession.

On their arrival, Mitford was struck by the simplicity of the
Emperor's Palace, something that still surprises visitors, used to

associating monarchy with places like the Palace of Versailles or Windsor Castle. It had no fortifications and was surrounded with plain whitewashed walls. Inside, Mitford observed that there was no decoration at all, but 'with all its simplicity it is not without a certain grandeur of its own'.[40] Although it covers a large area, it is one of the less notable sights of Kyoto, Nijō Castle, or even a temple like Chion-in, being more striking. Mitford took up the theme in a letter to his father:

> Gold, silver, jewels, there were none. The only costly article worn were swords of great price. The regalia were represented by … two wooden lions … which, from their great age, are as traditions of the Court, the motto of which should be *simplex munditiis* [simple elegance]. It is very grand, solemn and imposing … The emblems of real strength … [need] no advertisements of precious stones and metals.[41]

The British party was treated with the highest respect. They were allowed to dismount at the Inner Gate, usually only the right of Princes of the Blood, and made their way through successive courtyards to a waiting room where Prince Yamashina, the Emperor's cousin, came to receive them. The Emperor was eating lunch so they were given sweets and *kasutera* – a sponge cake that had been introduced centuries before by the Portuguese, while they waited for him to finish. No doubt the officials thought that being foreigners, they would appreciate something foreign.

The Court was a remnant of the medieval age; Mitford expressed regret when it started to look like its Western counterparts, but he nevertheless enjoyed poking fun at it in a letter to his father. The tall *tate-eboshi* hats were like 'those monstrous piles of hair' which were the fashion in the 1820s in Britain. The way members of the court wore their swords made them stick 'out behind like a monkey's tail'; their trousers were 'baggy and clumsy in make'. However, the shoes exceeded 'all the rest in grotesqueness'. They were huge black lacquer clogs,

> worn in crossing the courtyards and so constructed that the wearer shuffles and shambles about in them with a sort of uncertainty and

inefficiency that make his misdirected efforts the very parody and
reductio ad absurdum of walking.

However, all this was capped by the 'music':

> As we were waiting ... there suddenly arose a hideous din [like] the
> *concordia discors* [discordant harmony] of a hundred cats waiting for
> their mates on distant gutters – if all the children of all the charity
> schools in Christendom could be clubbed together, each armed with
> a comb and a bit of paper, and backed by a posse of Drummers, say
> one Drummer to every fifty children – if each child were told to play
> as loud as it could on its comb without reference to the doings of its
> fellows, and if the drummers had *carte blanche* to fall to when they
> pleased, the result would be a something akin to the wild hubbub
> that alternately stunned us and punished our nerves.[42]

Unfortunately, while they were waiting it started to rain tor-
rentially, meaning they had to splash through courtyards almost
ankle-deep with wet sand to reach the audience hall. Only Parkes
and Mitford could enter because no one else at the Legation had
been presented at the British court. It must have been miserable
for Satow to miss out on this momentous occasion for such a
trivial reason and this rule was subsequently dropped.

When Parkes and Mitford went into the hall, they were
greeted by an unprecedented sight: the Emperor leaning against
a high chair, under a canopy supported by four pillars covered in
black lacquer and draped with white silk. It was the first time a
Japanese Emperor had ever given an audience like this without a
curtain. Mitford did not understate the significance of this:

> [A]ll of a sudden the veil of the temple has been rent, the holy of
> holies has been thrown open, and the God-King has descended
> from the elevation of his spiritual throne to the commonplace of
> Imperial Sovereignty ... [T]he whole web of bigotry and folly, in
> which the Japanese have wrapped themselves for centuries has been
> destroyed.[43]

Two princes were kneeling behind Meiji to prompt him should
it be necessary and in front of him knelt other princes. All the

great men of Japan were standing in rows, including many of the *daimyō*. Mitford described the Emperor like this:

> He's a remarkably high bred looking youth, as indeed he has every
> right to be … He is about sixteen years of age [he was fifteen] but tall
> of his years. He has a bright eye, good features and a clear complex-
> ion. He is dressed in a white coat with long padded scarlet trousers
> trailing like a lady's train. His head-dress is the same as that of his
> courtiers. His teeth are blackened; his eyebrows shaved and painted
> in high up on his forehead; his lips are stained red. Poor Mikado!
> What a victim to tradition. And yet in spite of all this grotesque
> disfigurement, the Son of Heaven contrives to look dignified.[44]

Mitford was entranced by royalty and was ready to admire the
Emperor. Meiji did so little at this stage that it was easy for
observers to see what they wanted to in him. Frank Japanese
descriptions of him are rare – he was viewed as sacred – but
Yokoi Shōnan, a member of the new Government, told his family that while his looks were 'average', 'he makes a most imposing figure'.[45] Anna Brassey, who saw him in 1873, thought he
was 'a young, not very good-looking man, with rather a sullen
expression'.[46] The impression from the earliest photograph taken
of Meiji is indeed this, but the awkward teenager changed into a
much more impressive-looking figure in his twenties. It was certainly a problem that he spoke so quietly, and his strange manner
of walking, thought perhaps to be from sitting on his knees so
much, or from having been brought up by court ladies, attracted
comment.

The Emperor addressed Parkes and Mitford, speaking barely
above a whisper, after which his words were repeated by a prince
and then translated thus:

> I hope that your Sovereign enjoys good health. I trust that the
> intercourse between our respective countries will become more and
> more friendly and be permanently established. I regret deeply that
> an unfortunate affair which took place as you were proceeding to
> the Palace on the 23rd has delayed this ceremony. It gives me great
> pleasure therefore to see you here today.[47]

The young dandy: Mitford at the age of twenty-three, 8 September 1860, photographed by Camille Silvy. National Portrait Gallery, London.

2

Portrait of Mitford by Samuel Laurence, drawn in 1865, just before he went to China.

3

Probably taken in the garden of Hongakuin/Hongakuji temple in Osaka on 11 February 1867, just before Mitford's thirtieth birthday. Mitford is standing second from the right – Lin Fu is to the right of him. Satow is seated bottom left; behind him is his 'boy', Yasu, who did odd jobs for him, and next to him is Satow's devoted servant Noguchi, a samurai, hence his two swords. Mitford and Satow were unusual in being photographed with their servants, especially in such an equal way.

4

The reason 'the sun shone so brightly' on Mitford's days in Japan. Ernest Satow, on leave in Paris in 1869.

5　　　　　　　　**6**

The big-hearted doctor at the British Legation, William Willis.

The fiery Sir Harry Parkes.

Emperor Meiji, at the age of nineteen, photographed in May 1872 by Uchida Kuichi.

The last Shogun, Tokugawa Yoshinobu, who so impressed the Westerners but could not save his dynasty.

Mitford's friend and one of the key figures of the early Meiji period, Kido Takayoshi. 'Tall and handsome', thought Mitford, 'a man of singularly winning manners and sweetest temper, an accomplished scholar, he was a born leader of men'.

The young Itō Hirobumi in 1863, who changed from anti-foreign fanatic into helpmate of Mitford and Satow and later, the Meiji era's greatest statesman.

'Sir Harry Parkes and suite, in the vestibule of the palace at Osaca, going to visit the Tycoon.' Illustration and caption from the *Illustrated London News*, 10 August 1867. Both A. B. Mitford and Ernest Satow attended and are included in the 'suite'.

A woodblock image from *Tales of Old Japan*, showing a Buddhist sermon being given. Mitford is sitting at the back with two companions.

The first in the series *One Hundred Famous Views of Edo* by Ando Hiroshige, *Sunshine on Snow in Nihonbashi*. Edo looks peaceful and untroubled in this print. Online collection of the Brooklyn Museum, New York.

Yokohama Hon-chō and the Miyozaki Pleasure Quarter by Utagawa Sadahide, 1860. This is a sanitised view of the Yokohama that Mitford saw on arrival in 1866. The print shows how delineated the town was; at the top is the crowded Japanese part; in the foreground, the more spaced-out Western area. On the left are the pleasure quarters, connected by a path lined with tea-houses. Metropolitan Museum of Art, New York.

Batsford House from Mitford's garden. Photograph by the author.

'The Nobleman of the Garden' – an affectionate caricature of Mitford in his late sixties by Sir Leslie Ward, published in *Vanity Fair*, 16 June 1904.

Not, as Mitford admitted, terribly exciting, but the symbolism was everything. The meeting was a dramatic fresh start and suggested that relations with Japan would now be on a better footing. There was the same heady feeling that had prevailed after they had met the Shogun for the first time. In this case, Meiji made far less effort than Yoshinobu, but he did what he had to do to bring the foreigners round to recognising the new regime and, in the case of the British, stop the attack on them turning them into enemies.

On 27 March, the British party left Kyoto, with eight litters of their wounded. It was a very slow procession to reach Fushimi to catch the boat to Osaka, which they reached the following day. The scene was sombre, but inside Mitford was ecstatic at having been present at such a significant moment in Japanese history. A sign of this is the extraordinarily long letter – 2,750 words – he wrote his father describing it, not sparing him any detail.

Everybody apart from Mitford went on to Yokohama, which was the main base for commercial activity, still at the heart of Parkes' concerns. Mitford would stay in Osaka, to maintain Britain's relations with the Emperor's Government, which was based there for the moment. It was a heavy responsibility and after the high of Kyoto, he would be brought back to earth with a nasty bump.

· 7

OSAKA

March-July 1868

೮

MITFORD WAS NOW largely accepting Japan the way it was. He was revelling in the fact that he was there at such an exciting time and was proud of all the firsts he had notched up: first Westerner to see a Japanese Emperor, first to witness a *hara-kiri*, first to visit so many places. These things had made the Japan experience key to his sense of his own importance – he now had an emotional stake in the country, having stored enough memories to later be able to endlessly reminisce about the unrepeatable experiences he had had there. Indeed, he was already being revered for having seen Meiji: 'I am quite a Lion as the man who saw the Son of Heaven and heard him speak', he boasted to Parkes. 'To every Japanese that comes, and they are not a few, I have to rehearse the scene.'[1]

Unfortunately, having achieved this new level of contentment with Japan, he was plunged into another difficult phase. Now living in Osaka, he had been left to represent all the Western powers to the new Government single-handed – business that would normally have occupied whole Consulates of staff. Many lives would hang on how successfully he managed his negotiations with the Emperor's officials. He was also fighting for his own future. If he acquitted himself well, he knew he could gain a successful career in the diplomatic service. Osaka would make or break him.

Edo was still under the control of the ex-Shogun, but its castle would shortly be surrendered to the Imperial forces and it was gradually looking certain that they would eventually gain control of the whole country. *Daimyō* who could read the writing on the wall were voluntarily giving up their lands to the Emperor, something that was necessary if Japan was to establish a central government and a national revenue. Mitford hugely admired their actions seeing them as nobly fulfilling their obligations to the nation. He translated their long declaration (which he quoted in full in *Memories* because it was a document which 'made history'), in a way that mirrored its epoch-making nature: 'The Heaven and Earth belong to the Emperor ... It is his to give and his to take away; of our own selves we cannot hold a foot of land, we cannot take a single man.'[2] Japan was on the way to becoming a unified nation and the diplomats could give up on Yoshinobu and focus their attention on the Emperor and his ministers.

Osaka, which Mitford had characterised as a dreary commercial place, had received a new lease of life, as it was now the base for the Emperor's Government. Its importance was sealed by an extraordinary event – a visit by Meiji himself. Mitford claimed to his father that it was the first Imperial progress for a thousand years, which was probably true. It was taken in painfully slow stages, the journey of around forty kilometres being spread over three days, from 14 to 16 April. Meiji was carried in a closed palanquin, with reverential crowds kneeling along the way. The journalist John Black believed that the escort had at least 10,000 men in it, and a quarter of Osaka was barricaded for the visit.[3] Mitford saw great danger in curious Westerners getting too close, issuing the following warning: 'Should Europeans unacquainted with the language and customs of this country trespass too near the precincts of the Court, they may most unwittingly give offence and lay themselves open to great personal danger.'[4]

Three days after he had arrived in Osaka, Meiji showed his face to ordinary people and became probably the first Japanese Emperor to see the sea, when he reviewed part of his fleet in the manner of a European monarch. The crowds were immense, Black writing that 'masses of people, such as had probably never before been gathered in Osaka' turned out to see him.[5] Mitford watched him from the French man-of-war, the *Dupleix*. He thought that the Emperor should have gone out onto the sea himself and speculated that as it was like glass on that day, 'he must have been reassured and perhaps next time will do a little more than merely look on from the shore'.[6] The following day, Mitford was invited to a lunch on the *Dupleix* for the Emperor's uncle and Commander-in-Chief, and a number of important *daimyō*. Most of them had never been to sea before and Mitford wrote that the ship made some 'capital prestige' by firing its big guns 'which astonished them not a little'. 'I must say', he added, 'it is very interesting to see the gradual wakening up of this wonderful old Court of the Mikado which has been sleeping like a Beauty in the Wood for so many centuries'.[7]

What Mitford really meant was that the Court was starting to behave along European lines, which included the Emperor performing public duties. One of these would be another audience at which Parkes would present his credentials from Queen Victoria – this time there could be no question of Meiji going back to being hidden by a curtain. These credentials were important because they recognised the Emperor, not the Shogun, as the Sovereign of Japan. Parkes was pleased with himself for being the first foreign Minister to obtain them, having requested them in November the previous year in anticipation of the Emperor becoming the supreme ruler. He arranged to put on a naval display for Meiji, to impress on 'the mind of the young Mikado … a just sense of the rank and dignity of the Queen and also of the power' of Britain.[8] Satow, often keen to denigrate Parkes, thought that the purpose of the ships was to 'assist in glorifying' him.[9] The British party was big: Parkes, Mitford and his staff; Admiral Keppel and the officers commanding his ships, along with 160 marines. The Emperor was evidently nervous; when Parkes tried to give him the letter from Queen Victoria, he seemed 'bashful or timid', in Satow's description, and needed to be assisted.[10] He also forgot his speech; after being prompted, he got out one sentence, upon which an official gave up on his managing the whole thing and read out the full translation. One has to feel sorry for this fifteen-year-old, who must have felt over-whelmed by the expectation and responsibility that was now on his shoulders.

Mitford was also feeling overwhelmed; his time in Osaka was, he told his memoir, 'the hardest-worked' of his life, at it 'from early dawn till night'.[11] It was also probably one of the most dangerous – he does not mention any guards, suggesting that his only security was the revolver he kept with him all the time.

He had found a place to live near what had become the office from which Japan's foreign affairs were being conducted. His only concession to the West was a table and chair and other-wise he lived in simple Japanese style without a bed; his sleeping area was enclosed by two screens, and he laid down on a quilt on the mats. This would have seemed an impossible hardship to Westerners who customarily took the kitchen sink with them when travelling to the East, knowing they would never have to carry a stick of it – an army of coolies was always on hand to transport their bulky Victorian furniture. But the calamities Mitford had encountered, starting with the Yokohama fire, had reduced his personal possessions to very little. He had learned the hard way the virtues of living without clutter. Indeed, he was proud of the fact that he was adaptable enough to live like this and he enjoyed his garden, 'not much larger than a good-sized dining-table', but 'a little gem in its way, with a miniature Mount Fuji, a shrine to Inari sama, a forest, a waterfall plashing into a lake, in which were several fan-tailed gold-fish'.[12]

Mitford immersed himself in his local neighbourhood and this is probably when he became really fluent in Japanese. He must have been a local celebrity, being the only Westerner in the city. He got all his meals from a nearby cook shop and opposite him lived a swordsmith, Kusano Yoshiaki, whom he became friendly with. Mitford was fascinated by the fact that this man had a conscience about being in a trade that resulted in deaths and so in order to atone for this, he believed he should do what he could to alleviate suffering in the world, which he did to such an extent that he impoverished himself. The man was also, accord-ing to Mitford, honest in a trade that was customarily dishonest; most swordsmiths would counterfeit the mark of a famous maker of old on swords, but he did not do this. Mitford admired his simple labour, 'the clank' of his 'hammer and anvil' being audible from 'daybreak to sundown'.[13] Japanese swords were the best in the world; Mitford was told that the sharpest blades in expert hands could cut through three human bodies laid on top of each other at a single blow.

Apart from his interaction with his servants and neighbours, Mitford had virtually no social life; his 'playfellow', Vice-Consul Robertson – 'a very good fellow, and so *on vivotte*' – lived down the river, so he only rarely met up with him.[14] 'On vivotte' is French slang for 'gets along by hook or by crook', which summed up what life was like for an official in an isolated post. Mitford also occasionally saw his French counterpart in Osaka, Captain du Petit Thouars, who was living on the *Dupleix*. Du Petit Thouars was as friendly as Roches had been hostile and was, Mitford thought, 'in all things a most thorough and loyal gentleman'.[15] The two agreed that the rivalry between Parkes and Roches had been absurd and made a pact that they would work together, du Petit Thouars informing Mitford of any naval developments, while Mitford would tell du Petit Thouars what was happening on shore.

The pair were entertained by the *inkyo* of Uwajima (in present-day Ehime prefecture in Shikoku) and Higashikuze, Minister for Foreign Affairs, being taken out for a ride in Osaka; 'Fancy such a gallop through the streets and fields six months ago', he told Parkes.[16] Uwajima (Westerners referred to *inkyo* and *daimyō* by their domain name), who became head of the Foreign Office in 1868, was always sympathetic to the Western view. Mitford saw him as a 'great gentleman, one for whom foreigners conceived the highest respect. Blessed with the kindliest disposition, [he was] always courteous, always hospitable'.[17] His position should have been weak; he was not born into the Uwajima dynasty but because it had found itself without an heir, he had been plucked out to be adopted by the family at the age of twelve, thanks to being a distant relation. As Mitford observed, by European standards, the succession rules were 'extremely lax' – the crucial thing was to have some kind of male heir, otherwise the death of a *daimyō* meant the domain was forfeited to the state.[18] On top of this, his domain was small, with a population of only about 100,000 people. But driving ambition; a passionate interest in the West and a determination that Japan should adopt its technology, along with having played a part in overthrowing the Shogunate, turned him into one of the most influential figures in the Meiji Restoration.

Mitford liked Uwajima so much he asked his father to get a gold signet ring made for him, 'by the best artist', with his crest – a bird pecking at a bamboo.[19] This kind of gift-giving often got out of hand, Mitford receiving precious gifts and then somehow having to reciprocate. The *daimyō* of Aizu gave him a valuable sword, whereupon Mitford gave him a 'very handsome' revolver in return.[20] For another *daimyō*, he asked his father to buy three gold hunting watches costing £120 – more than a quarter of his annual salary. Mitford lamented that Japanese gentlemen were 'expensive friends to associate with, and economy rather puts a limit to the influence I might otherwise gain in the country'.[21] What made matters worse for him was that in order to stop gifts such as these being used as bribes, men in Mitford's position could not keep them without the approval of the Foreign Secretary, which could only be requested in exceptional circumstances.

However, Mitford now had real power for the first time in his life. He was representing the world's biggest empire to the new Japanese Government at a time when Britain's support or opposition could have determined its survival. On top of that, he was effectively representing France, as well as the other Western powers about issues, like the safety of foreigners in Japan and the future of Christianity in the country, which they cared deeply about. Of course, Parkes was determined to remain in charge, but it took at least a week for him to receive a reply to a letter to Parkes, so he often had to make his own decisions and predictably we see for the first time him having serious clashes with his boss.

The roots of their conflict were in their different approaches to Japan. Parkes was hard-headed, only won over by concrete results and always suspicious of Japanese intentions. Mitford was a romantic, believing that there was now real goodwill towards the West in the Government, but that it would take time for them drop the old hostility; he thought they would be much more likely to do this if they were gently coaxed rather than forced. He expressed it like this to Parkes:

> I cannot help thinking that a great deal [of the trouble they were having] must be ascribed to the newness of the situation in which these people find themselves. Government is a difficult piece of machinery to set in motion, and with a little patience at first, we may perhaps make what figure we like out of the moist clay.[22]

In the short term, Parkes would prove to be right – the new regime was no real friend of the West, just more pragmatic than the old Shogun's Government. But in the longer run, Mitford was correct; Britain and Japan would become very close, eventually, in 1902, forming an alliance.

Mitford's new found assertiveness with Parkes was probably partly bred out of frustration at his working situation. The diplomatic service was bureaucratic and operated on the assumption that there was always a number of men available to do the endless copying of reports and despatches that was necessary. All Mitford's reports had to be sent to the Foreign Office in London as well as to Parkes and as there was nobody apart from him who could write in English, he had to make the copies. There was also nobody to translate communications with Japanese Ministers, so he had to do this and again send copies to Parkes and London. He had two Japanese secretaries, but they knew no English so they were only of use for the Japanese work. 'I am my own copyist, translator and interpreter', he told his father, 'and I am at it all day one way or other.'[23] The huge effort he had made to learn Japanese was a double-edged sword – he would never have had so much put on his shoulders if he had been like a normal British diplomat in that era and not bothered with the language. To make things worse, the British Treasury in its usual stingy style refused to pay for his secretaries; Parkes wrote on his behalf requesting the money, but the Treasury said that if

Mitford had done good service he would be promoted and that would be his reward. Parkes also requested £200 – half Mitford's annual salary – to recompense Mitford for the money he had spent learning Japanese, but this was also refused. There was the feeling that it was somehow immoral for someone to go into the diplomatic service to make money – like members of Parliament, who received no income, it was felt they would be compromised if they worked for pay. Mitford did not see it this way, writing,

> I think myself that the public makes a false economy in not paying its servants more highly in these countries. We are worse paid than the meanest clerks in merchants' houses who run no risk and live at their ease and in comfort. Whereas we are exposed to every sort of danger and hardship and are so poor that we can barely keep up our position as gentlemen.[24]

What made it more annoying was that the traders, who were 'such a set of snobs and ruffians', gave themselves the 'airs of Princes of the Blood', looking down upon the diplomats like him because their salaries were so low.[25] In addition, Mitford was having trouble getting even his meagre wages out of the Foreign Office. We see him writing in May 1868, 'I cannot make out that I have received any F.O. pay since September 30 1866', and asking his father to claim the money he was owed. He had not been able to do this himself because he had lost his first set of forms in the Yokohama fire and the second during the chaos in January. 'For the future', he reassured his father, I shall draw all my pay out here, and as I neither speculate nor gamble and live very carefully, I hope to be able to let a little nest egg accumulate.'[26]

Parkes agreed with Mitford that they were underpaid, and eventually managed to get him some extra money to help with the costs of his office in Osaka with the following persuasively-worded appeal to the Foreign Office:

> It is usual to allow an officer £100 a year who is competent to serve & does serve as an Interpreter, & I have certainly not known a case in which such a reward has ever been better deserved than it is by Mr. Mitford.[27]

Incidentally, Parkes would also plead for more money for himself, and in 1867 managed to get his salary raised from £3,000 to £4,000 a year (something in the order of £300,000 in today's money). In his letter of thanks, he was careful not to be too effusive: 'It has relieved me of some cause of anxiety for since I have been in Japan my pay has not covered the demands upon it.'[28]. To be fair, Ministers were expected to pay for their large household and entertaining out of their salaries, but even so, they seemed very well remunerated. Perhaps some of the pressure on Parkes to get more money came from his wife, who Dr Willis thought had a strong feeling of entitlement, mixed with stinginess: 'Lady Parkes … like many people that good fortune has done a great deal for, … thinks the Japan service was made for [her] special benefit. Besides she is always in a state of chronic difficulty with her servants. Fancy, Sir Harry gets £4,000 a year and the housemaid complained to me that she has to sleep without sheets.'[29]

The first issue Parkes and Mitford fought over was the publishing of a decree outlawing attacks on foreigners. The Government only planned to exhibit it in one place in each town or district, which Mitford agreed with, telling Parkes that 'to placard it at every little stationhouse would only be to vulgarize it', adding hopefully, 'I expect that you entertain the same views, and until I hear from you to the contrary shall be contented with its exhibition in the place set apart for such decrees.'[30] Parkes did not agree, believing that this meant the Government was not serious about enforcing it – he thought that they were half-hearted about the decree, more concerned about not upsetting anti-foreign elements than protecting foreigners. He pressured Mitford to make forceful efforts to get it widely disseminated. Mitford was sure this was a mistake; he knew that the Government was divided and feared that by pushing too hard, he would weaken Britain's friends and destroy the goodwill that had been built up. Nevertheless, we see him writing in an uncharacteristically strident style to Parkes, reassuring his boss that he was maintaining an appropriately tough attitude:

If the Kioto fools continue to be obstructive I should be glad to be authorized by you to tell them as you said to me "that you can yet return to the subject in a way that they will not like." In fact having been most moderate and conciliatory with them hitherto, I would be glad to be authorized to pitch into them should they continue obstructive.[31]

However, Mitford almost certainly never intended to 'pitch into them', because he was sure that a constructive attitude was more likely to produce results. That said, he later admitted that he had felt this way because most of the Japanese he talked to were cordial – the ones who were determined to make no concessions to foreigners would not meet him. He explained it like this in his memoir:

> The ministers with whom I had to deal were large-minded men with liberal views, but they … had to reckon with important personages, who, after being immured … in the mystic darkness of a prehistoric cloister, were no more fit to face the sunlight of the nineteenth century than those perhaps fabulous batrachians which have whitened for aeons untold, encased in the crevices of the limestone rock.[32]

The most talented man he encountered was probably Itō Hiro-bumi, the twenty-six-year-old Governor of Hyōgo (Kobe). He was setting out on a brilliant career and is now considered the Meiji era's greatest statesman. He spoke English, having travelled to England and studied at University College London.[33] He had been impressed by how advanced Britain was compared to Japan and was sure that Japan had to work with the West to become more powerful. 'We have come to study your strength', he explained on a later visit to California, 'so that, by wisely adopting your better ways, we may hereafter become stronger ourselves.'[34] However, before his stay in Britain, he was certainly someone who Mitford would have defined as 'immured in darkness'; he assassinated a classics scholar who he wrongly believed to be seeking ancient precedents for dethroning an emperor, making him probably the only murderer to become Japanese prime minister.[35] Also, he had been so hostile to foreigners being in Japan that in 1863, he had helped burn down the British Legation building. When they became friendly, Mitford would tease him about his arson; Itō never admitted to having been part of it with Mitford, but he did so elsewhere.[36] (Arson, incidentally, was considered the most heinous crime of all and was punishable by being burned to death. Mitford thought this was reasonable: 'cruel as it may seem to say so, it is not too severe a punishment considering the nature of their crime in this country where it involves such danger to life and property.'[37])

Itō published the decree outlawing attacks on foreigners in Kobe without authorisation from the Emperor's Government. He had to withdraw it, explaining to Mitford that he had exceeded his powers. Mitford was suspicious that his actions might have been part of a plan to only promulgate it in Kobe, where Westerners would have seen it, which would have made them think it had been published all over the country. Mitford adopted a condescending tone in reporting this to Parkes, telling him:

> I cannot help thinking that if we encourage or teach the Japanese to conduct their business on an unsound basis we shall have ourselves to thank if there is a return to that chicanery and duplicity from which we hope we have escaped.[38]

But Mitford believed that adopting a teacherly stance was worthwhile because he saw the Japanese as an 'improvement-seeking people ... with their eagerness to learn and profit by the experience of other nations'.[39]

Mitford did eventually get his way, with the law finally being fully published on 14 April. He took credit for this in his memoir, writing that after 'many an hour of debate ... I succeeded in getting the government to post the famous edict in every town, village and hamlet throughout the land'. He added slightly sourly, 'It was a triumph' for which Parkes (note) 'received great kudos'.[40] In a report to the Foreign Secretary, Parkes was less certain about Mitford's part, writing only that he thought the promulgation had been 'accelerated' by his exertions.[41] Nevertheless this was a signal success for Mitford, albeit one that had come at the price of a great deal of ill feeling with the Emperor's Government.

As the weather became hotter, the relationship got worse, with Mitford being ground down by near-daily, long, usually unproductive meetings with high-ranking officials. He hated the heat, which he thought was extra bad in Osaka and depressingly, he found himself saying the same things he had been saying about the Shogun's Government. He blamed the men around the Emperor, telling Parkes,

> [N]obody believes in the *Kugés* [court nobles] who for centuries have never been up to any higher flight than the composition of a slip of poetry. It was owing to the unfitness for power of the old *Kugés* that the *bakufu* [Shogun's Government] had its existence, and their descendants of today are no stronger.[42]

As usual, Mitford went to the other extreme, later extolling the *kuge*, writing that they were 'far removed from the poor, bigoted, monkish recluses that they had been represented to be' and that when the critical time came, 'there were found among them men ready and fit to take part in what developed into a great national movement'.[43] The truth is that some of the *kuge* were talented (Iwakura Tomomi, who became one of the Emperor's most trusted Ministers, is a stunning example of this), others were idiots. They were also divided; some were conservatives who hated Westerners, but others were modernisers who, while not necessarily liking foreigners, believed that Japan needed their help to industrialise. Mitford knew this, but was getting sick of being pushed hard by Parkes to get results, while conducting exasperating negotiations with officials who were intentionally stonewalling because they could not agree among themselves. He complained to Parkes:

> These younger men in the Government are beyond expression tiresome. There is a certain Machida Mimbu who makes me tingle to the tips of my fingers. A wretch who with all the pride of Old Japan combines the vanity and self-sufficiency of a smattering of English [he had visited Europe]. He is now a fixture at the F[oreign].

O[ffice]. and I have to endure him every time I go there. There is now not even the pretence of friendship for foreigners among the present Govt.[44]

Much of the bad feeling derived from a bitter dispute that arose over Christianity in the country. The religion had been banned since a brutal suppression which saw thousands of Japanese Christians tortured and killed between 1614 and 1650. In spite of this persecution, substantial pockets of 'hidden Christians' had held on to the faith through the generations, particularly in western Kyushu. One village called Urakami, near Nagasaki, had a population of around 4,000, which was all Christian. French missionaries discovered these Christians and encouraged them to come out of hiding in spite of the fact that the religion was still illegal in Japan.

This was interpreted by the Emperor's Government as a direct challenge to its authority and in April 1868, signboards were erected stating, 'The Christian heretical sect is strictly prohibited. Anyone arousing suspicion should be reported to the village office. A reward will be bestowed.'[45] On 14 June, 114 Christian leaders were imprisoned under harsh conditions and in the next months, more than 2,400 followed them. Around 500 recanted under extreme pressure, but the rest did not. A majority of the Emperor's Ministers argued that those who refused to submit should be executed.

British policy was to not interfere in Japan's domestic affairs and no British interest was at stake. But pressure from religious groups back home to come to the aid of the Japanese Christians meant that Parkes had to do something. He handed the problem to Mitford, telling him to do what he could to try to persuade the Government to back down. Mitford did his best, arguing that religious persecution in Europe had been disastrous and saying how bad for Japan's reputation it would be if any Christian was executed: 'Western nations, ignoring the difficulties by which the Government is beset, and the provocation which has aroused its anger, would see in such an act, an insult to the creed which they profess and a wanton shedding of blood.'[46]

Mitford was hampered by the fact that he had a good deal of sympathy with the Japanese position. He pointed out to Parkes that the Taiping Rebellion in China, which had finally been crushed in 1864 at the cost of around 20 million lives, had been founded on a few Christian tracts. Conceivably, the Kyushu Christians could spark a resurgence of armed opposition to the Government. Mitford also thought the missionaries who had found the hidden Christians and encouraged them to reveal themselves were irresponsible, telling Parkes they were 'fanatic bigots', who refused 'to recognise any other authority spiritual or civil than that of the Roman Catholic Priests'.[47] In his memoir, Mitford wrote, 'Interference with the laws and internal affairs of the country were meat and drink to the Franciscans' and quoted the Meiji statesman Kido Takayoshi saying: 'It seems to me that missionaries are men who are sent here to teach the people to disobey the laws of their country.'[48]

He also shared Japanese outrage that Pope Pius IX had given a French priest, Fr Bernard Petitjean, the 'ill-chosen title of Bishop of Japan,' which, he told Parkes, the Japanese he had spoken to regarded as 'thoroughly offensive to the pride of the nation'.[49] He would have recalled a similar British experience of the high-handed ways of Pius. In 1850, without any consultation with the British Government, he had issued a Papal Bull dividing England into twelve territorial bishoprics. The ensuing furore brought down the Government and the following year, Parliament retaliated by passing an act which forbade any Catholic bishop to use any episcopal title of any place in the country. In both Britain and Japan, the actions of the Catholic Church were seen as a direct challenge to their right to govern their own affairs.

In his low opinion of the Catholic Church, Mitford was being typically English and Parkes and Satow felt the same about its actions in Japan, in spite of the fact that the three men differed in their religious observance. At this point, Parkes was the most devout; at home his family regularly prayed together and he attended church services when possible. Satow had been brought up in a strict low-church household where family prayers had been said every morning and evening, a chapter of the Bible was read, along with a long prayer, and Sunday was entirely devoted to religious activity.[50] However, he had completely lost his faith in China and it would be many years before he regained it. Looking back after he had, he wrote, 'I became a complete ... infidel', adding that 'A worse school [than the 'East'] for a half-educated boy could not be found'.[51] A sign of how little Satow and Mitford were interested in religion is that when the English Episcopal Church in Yokohama was fundraising in the British community in 1868, neither of them contributed any money, while Parkes donated £60 and Dr Willis, £10.[52]

Indeed, in all his writings from and about Japan, Mitford never mentions going to religious services (other than Buddhist ones) there. He did attend church later in life, but this seems to have been mostly due to the influence of his devout wife – one of his sons-in-law called him a 'pagan'.[53] However, he seems to have changed right at the end of his life, when we see him revealing much more than a superficial faith: 'Christ represents the Birth of a new day, of a new civilisation dawning under the sign of the Cross ... a civilisation at which we must work for many a long day before it may be worthy to be called by His name. That said, he was still not impressed by the Catholic Church, writing of its followers being 'choked by the mephitic vapours of Roman dogma'.[54]

Whatever Mitford thought about the Church of England's teaching at this point, his innate conservatism and respect for tradition instinctively made him want to defend it. One of his few comments about British domestic politics made from Japan was about Gladstone's bill to disestablish the Church of Ireland (as Ireland was mostly Catholic, Gladstone thought it was wrong for the country to have a Protestant established church). 'I can't understand the country consenting to the disestablishment of the Irish Church', wrote Mitford; 'the English church must follow for in these things it is only the first step that is difficult, and when the English church is gone, God help the Crown and the country.'[55]

He had little time for missionaries, even when they acted within the law, believing that Japan did not need Christianity. He told Parkes:

> The Japanese claim a high degree of merit for their own faith, which for centuries has taught the people the duties of children and parents, husbands and wives, masters and servants, brothers and friends. This is the religion which the people understand; the mystic doctrines of the Fathers only bewilder them.[56]

In *Tales of Old Japan*, Mitford gives his readers a sympathetic description of Japanese beliefs and morals in three sermons that he translated. He is notable for never using the, at the time customary, negative terms when describing an Asian religion, like 'pagan' or 'idolatrous'.

After weeks of 'weary debates', Mitford managed to get an assurance that no Christians would be tortured or executed. Rather, they would be forcibly separated and dispersed to different parts of the country for three years, during which time they would be induced to recant. If they did not do so during those three years then they would be severely punished, Mitford could not ascertain how. It was a historic moment, being the first time the Japanese Government had taken into account the feelings of foreigners when making a domestic decision. From Mitford's point of view, he felt he had won the best deal available and he was pleased – 'It really was a great victory' he wrote later.[57] In his memoir, Mitford makes it seem as if he gained this success single-handed, but it was in fact the immense, and ultimately irresistible, pressure from the West that ensured that no Japanese Christians died for their faith at this time.

The issue continued to be a running sore in relations with the Western powers, because while Christians who did not recant were not killed, they were still subjected to some brutal treatment. Iwakura Tomomi, explained to the British Chargé d'affaires in 1871 that the Government was not in favour of persecution, but that the people were so strongly against Christianity that there would be a revolution if it was allowed.[58] However, in 1873, it was legalised, when the Government felt secure enough to withstand any backlash. It is a sign of how quickly Japan changed in the early Meiji years that it would move from threatening Christians with execution to tolerating the religion in the space of just four years.

Parkes must have been aware that Mitford's success had been based on ignoring some of his instructions, but he turned a blind eye to this when, at the end of July, Mitford was finally able to make his escape from the 'distant hole [Osaka]', being characteristically generous with his praise of him to Lord Stanley, the Foreign Secretary:

> I should … commend to your Lordship's special notice the excellent services he has rendered … in the isolated position which he occupied … [W]hen he was stationed alone at Osaka, he proved himself most useful in maintaining communications and promoting a friendly understanding between myself and the new Government. The great advance he has made in the Japanese language … particularly qualified him for these duties … and I should take this opportunity of particularly drawing your Lordship's attention to the industry and ability which Mr. Mitford must have devoted to his Japanese studies in order to obtain an amount of knowledge which so materially adds to his efficiency.[59]

For Mitford to have successfully managed relations with the Japanese Government on his own after less than two years in the country really was a remarkable achievement. Stanley was relieved that the problem of the Christians had been substantially resolved – a headache for him as the Government was heading towards an election at which they would be faced by the formidably devout William Gladstone. He would have been happy to make political capital by accusing the Prime Minister, Benjamin Disraeli, whose Jewish ancestry made him easy to portray as not caring about Christianity, of letting the Japanese Christians die. Stanley ordered that Mitford receive an extra £100 for his services in Osaka, but more important to him was the praise he got from Stanley, Mitford telling his father this was 'worth more than the money'.[60]

As luck would have it, Captain du Petit Thouars also had to return to Yokohama at the same time so Mitford could travel with him on the *Dupleix*. The ship was the 'perfection of comfort', the cook 'a genius' and du Petit Thouars, 'one of the most agreeable companions'. On top of that the sea, which always seemed to be rough when Mitford was sailing on it, was a 'dream of beauty, its countless smiles rippling under a cloudless sky'.[61] It was an augury of the calmer days that lay ahead for him.

8

TOKYO

October 1868 – January 1870

ℬ

WHEN MITFORD WENT back to the house at Monryōin in October, he found it in a state of ruin, as he must have expected. This no longer bothered him because he knew it could be quickly fixed up. But Edo itself was also in a poor state. When he had last been there, ten months earlier, it had been a bustling and vibrant place. Its prosperity had been based on its being the Shogun's capital and all the activity created by having the *daimyō* residences there. With the defeat of the Shogun and the dispersal of his apparatus of government, it had lost around a third of its population.[1] Mitford told his father it was 'a city of the dead', with its great buildings rotting: 'Grass grows in the streets and the palaces of the Daimios are wildernesses dotted with rotten tumbledown buildings.'[2] The civil war and heavy summer rains had taken their toll and even the castle was a wreck. To top it off, the bad weather had devastated the harvest, meaning there was widespread hunger there – Kido Takayoshi thought that the eyes of the people had 'the look of famine victims'.[3] Everything was damp, Mitford writing of the 'mire and slosh not to be described'. Anything metal was covered in rust; 'boots and shoes bore a rich crop of unwholesome fungus'; 'our crazy wood-and-paper built cottages ... smelt of mould' and the 'very people one met in the streets looked mildewed and sodden'.[4]

Mitford was treated to the sight of the Shogun's retainers (*hat-amoto*) in their fallen pride. They had been left behind when Yoshinobu fled the city and now had no income. In *Tales of Old Japan*, Mitford cast them as villains, writing that they had 'waxed fat and held high revel, and little cared they who groaned or who starved'.[5] They had been, he told his father,

> magnates before whom the baser had grovelled in the dust, not dar-ing to speak above a whisper: men who, as they rode in the streets, neither looked to the right nor to the left, and who would not con-descend to look ... at ... foreigners. It was beneath their dignity to notice anything.

He added that, 'Not five minutes ago, one of these very men interrupted me, begging me to purchase a small lacquer box for about £3.10! The mighty are fallen indeed.'[6]

In spite of its ramshackle state, Edo's status had risen immea-surably because it had been chosen over Osaka and Kyoto to become the nation's capital. Its position was sealed on 3 Septem-ber 1868 when it became Tokyo – 'Eastern Capital', although it would take a long time for the new name to catch on – British diplomats would continue to call the city Edo for years after-wards. It was not clear whether or not Emperor Meiji would be living there. After all, Kyoto was still Kyoto – 'Capital of Capitals' – and his leaving it would be breaking with more than a thousand years of tradition. Mitford usually supported keep-ing things like this the same, but in this case he thought it was a good idea for Meiji to move to Tokyo because it would help him look like the Emperor of the entire nation – Edo had been accustomed to thinking of the Shogun as its sovereign.[7] The city was seen as enemy territory by the new regime – its people were disappointed in Yoshinobu but were no friends of the Emper-or's Government. It urgently needed to establish its authority there. Tokyo was also much more appropriate for a capital than Kyoto in Mitford's opinion: 'Instead of being huddled away in wretched little houses in a small city ..., the grandees of the land will inhabit large and imposing palaces round the castle which is a far more fitting imperial residence than the sacred precincts' of Kyoto.[8] Mitford was beginning to see that while it lacked great buildings, Tokyo was a fine city in other ways. As Satow put it, it was

> one of the handsomest cities in the Far East … [I]ts position on the seashore, fringed with the pleasure gardens of the daimiôs, and the remarkable huge moats surrounding the castle, crowned with cyclopean walls … all contributed to produce an impression of greatness.[9]

For the diplomats, Tokyo had the huge advantage over Kyoto of being on the coast. They hated living in cities that had no access to the sea because if violence directed at Westerners started, quick escape was impossible – they would be 'like rats in a trap', as Mitford put it.[10] Beijing was another inland capital that made them nervous. But the best thing for the diplomats, as well as for Japanese officials, was that the endless travelling between Kyoto and Osaka and Edo/Tokyo could stop and they could settle in one place, a fixed and undisputed capital.

*

In spite of its bedraggled state, Mitford quickly felt at home in Tokyo: 'I did not like it the first year … but it is a place that grows upon one immensely, and then it gains so by comparison with the other Japanese cities.'[11] (He was probably thinking here of Osaka, which he never had a good word to say about.) After all his adventures in western Japan, it was boring but safe – a 'dull monotone' which was a 'new and … delicious sensation'.[12] Yokohama had also risen in Mitford's estimation. He had stopped there first after returning from Osaka at the end of August and found it pleasantly cool: 'quite an English climate' (the wet weather had kept the temperature down) and 'perfectly delightful'.[13] He had been shattered from his time in Osaka, and 'dreamt away' a fortnight there, 'listening to the hum of the insects and as lazy as you please' to recuperate.[14] A friend from England, F.O. Adams, 'the best of good fellows', had joined the Legation as first secretary (therefore ranking above Mitford), which meant that Mitford had someone he could chat to about home and family with.[15] 'Conceive', he told his father, 'what it is to me to be with an old friend. The only living soul that I have ever met since I have been in the East that had known you – or could talk of anything that really interested me.'[16] Letters like these suggest that Mitford suffered bouts of homesickness but we cannot be sure how truthful he was being. His father wanted him to return to England, so he felt under pressure to paint a picture of one who was sacrificing his present happiness for the sake of his future.

Mitford settled into a comfortable routine with his valet, two Japanese secretaries and his devoted Lin Fu, who went everywhere with him, although Mitford almost never mentions him – the custom among the British upper classes was to take servants as a given. All we find out about him from Mitford was that he was 'the handiest of men', 'as adaptable as moist clay' and able to cope with anything.[17] He also tells us he was a 'strict Confucian' and we learn from Satow that he was nicknamed 'the philosopher', which suggests that he was also a man of learning.[18] Mitford does not say which language he spoke to him in, but it would probably have been Chinese, enabling him to keep up that language.

If, as seems likely, Lin Fu spoke little Japanese or English he would have been dependent on Mitford for everything and he probably had no personal life at all, nor expected any. A photograph of them taken in 1867 shows Lin Fu standing a little behind Mitford, the top of his head only reaching to just above Mitford's shoulder. He has a calm, resigned expression and is wearing Chinese clothes – he had lost everything in the Yokohama fire, so Mitford must have had these clothes made for him in Japan, a sign that he was a considerate master.

Mitford noted that servants were treated differently in Japan to the West, believing that 'no feature' of Japanese society was 'more curious than the relations between master and man'. Assuming the servant was of the samurai class, the

master admits his servant to his intimate society ... He takes his
place at dinner with the utmost humility, and having done so, bears
his share of the conversation, addressing freely not only his master,
but even guests of the highest rank ... Yet, the moment the feast is
over, the man retires with the same profound obeisances and marks
of deference with which he entered, and immediately relapses into
the servitor; nor will he in any way presume upon the familiarity,
which ... disappears until occasion calls it forth again.[19]

Traces of this are still visible in Japan today, where it is common
to see groups of office workers of different levels of seniority getting raucously drunk together, safe in the knowledge that everybody will be at their desks the following morning as if nothing
had happened.

Mitford's household grew when Adams moved in with him,
adding a cook and his help, a coolie and a gardener. The garden was a 'never-ceasing amusement' to Mitford and in spite
of the fact that he was planning to leave soon, he was busy
improving it, under the directions of the gardener 'who rules
me with a rod of iron, a tyrant with spade and scissors. I must
say', he told his father, 'I never saw such an eye for planting
shrubs and dwarf fir trees so as to show them off to the greatest
advantage.'[20] Mitford 'nearly broke' his gardener's heart when
he decided he could no longer stand being bitten by the 'myri-
ads of mosquitoes' which 'used to live and love, bringing up
innumerable families' in his small pond. He filled it in, replac-
ing it with a bog garden with clumps of irises, breaking numerous rules of Japanese garden design in the process. But Mitford
wrote that 'even the greatest sticklers for precedent' among his
Japanese friends were 'enraptured at the beauty of an innova-
tion only pardonable in a barbarian'.[21] He named his second
daughter 'Iris', maybe to remind him of the happy times he had
spent looking at those flowers.

That Mitford could concern himself about such things is a sign
that he now had some spare time. In December, he described his
routine, which was now much more typical of the existence usual
among men in the diplomatic service at that time than his life
before:

I rise at seven after a cup of tea in bed, Eastern fashion – till nine I dress and dawdle. Then I have my official work and letters to write. This occupies me until twelve when I breakfast. At one I have a class of three Japanese whom I am teaching English. At about half past two I go out, returning at five. I then work at my translations for about two hours, after which dinner is ready, and at eight I work away again until 10 or eleven o'clock when I go to bed.[22]

Mitford does not say what the official work was, probably because in comparison with what he had been doing in Osaka, it was trivial – in the Foreign Office files we frequently see his handwriting in sets of dispatches written by other people, which suggests that copying them took up quite a lot of his time. Parkes was still hyperactive, but Mitford was now being allowed to work on what he cared most about – the translations, which would become *Tales of Old Japan*. Mitford could not see his future clearly, but, in combination with his fluent Japanese and Chinese, he was thinking this book could be the key to maximising the profit from his stay in the Far East. Being so calculating was frowned on by the upper classes in Britain, and even more so in Japan. But Mitford was skilled at giving the impression that he was above the rat race, appearing calm and unbothered about his position, while underneath carefully mapping out how he could become a great man – the worthy scion of the Mitford dynasty his older brothers could never be.

*

Emperor Meiji arrived in Tokyo on 26 November 1868, after a twenty-day overland journey, undertaken at walking pace, from Kyoto. His arrival was a momentous event – the first time in two thousand years a Japanese Emperor had visited the eastern provinces. Mitford joined the crowds who turned out to see the spectacle but he was not impressed, hating the fact that the escort was no longer dressed in the old way (in spite of the fact that he had complained about how ridiculous traditional dress was when he had visited the Emperor's palace in Kyoto):

> The procession was no great sight, for the Japanese have now thrown
> away their gorgeous old armour and dresses and made their soldiers
> wear a sort of mongrel European uniform which is more grotesquely
> absurd than anything you ever saw.[23]

Mitford wanted the Japanese to be Japanese and hated it when
they tried to be like Westerners. Some of them really were ridiculous; he saw one samurai who was wearing a red soldier's jacket
he had bought in Yokohama, over which he was wearing under-
wear, believing them to be trousers. To 'complete the comicality
of his appearance, his Japanese sword and dirk are stuck in a
shining leather belt', adding, 'how proud he seems of his bits of
foreign finery'.[24] The nobles of the Court, however, were dressed
in the traditional way and were 'very magnificent', and the chair
which carried Meiji was 'a sort of black lacquer palanquin sur-
mounted by a gold Phoenix and borne on the shoulders of about
sixty men in yellow silk robes cut after the ancient fashion of
the Court'. This was a 'grand sight'.[25] The Emperor himself was
completely hidden from view – either he or his court was not
yet ready for his face to be seen by the ordinary people of Tokyo.
He must have spent twenty days in a dark box.

Mitford's slightly jaded response to this spectacle was a sign
that he had got as much out of Japan as he was going to. He was
missing the adrenalin rushes from the action he had encountered
earlier, and life now felt humdrum. It was time to think of going
home. He told his father, 'I have no wish to stop and see the baby
country through its teething'.[26] His letters become trivial – mild
complaints about having to spend Christmas Day 1868 with the
Parkes family ('I could not well say no') and endless discussions
about what silk, swords, pieces of lacquer etc. he was going to get
for people at home.[27] The country had become much safer and
more settled, although Parkes would be lunged at with a sword
one more time, in the following September. Satow went off on
leave in February 1869, which made Mitford busier as he was
asked to do more dull translating and copying work by Parkes.
In Satow's absence, Parkes considered Mitford his best translator
of written Japanese (with the help of his Japanese secretaries) and

in June he yet again asked the Foreign Secretary for another £100 a year to recognise his extra duties. Money was still a sore point with Mitford; he never pointed it out in his letters, but it must have rankled that other than the Student Interpreters, he was the lowest paid man in either the diplomatic or consular service in the Legation – language specialists who did no diplomatic work were getting £100 more than him a year. He received plenty of praise for his translating but it did not 'bring anything solid' with it:

> Of course I don't want extra pay for the extra work, for I hold that every one ought to do his best for the service, especially in such a country as this, but I grumble sometimes when, after a hard day's work, I have to pay my men [his secretaries] their wages out of my own pocket.[28]

*

The gentle flow of Mitford's life was disturbed in the summer of 1869, with the news that Queen Victoria's second son, Alfred, Duke of Edinburgh, planned to visit Japan on his ship, the H.M.S. *Galatea*, as part of a tour around the world. This prospect threw the Emperor's ministers into a quandary and it took them two months to respond to Parkes' letter informing them of it. Clearly, they wanted good relations with Britain, but the question of whether the Emperor could receive a foreigner on anything approaching equal terms, was a fraught one. At the same time, if the Emperor refused to meet Alfred, or did so in a way that was lacking in respect, it could have had bad consequences for Japan. In the end, it was decided that the old ways had to be dispensed with and Parkes was informed that the Emperor was

> delighted beyond measure; and, although our country can offer but poor hospitality, His Majesty would be intensely pleased if your Prince would consent to take up his abode in the gardens of O Hama-go-ten, the seaside palace of His Majesty.'[29]

Japan's welcoming response was in contrast to that of the Imperial court in China which offered the Duke no official reception of any kind, much less one that involved their Emperor. Nevertheless, Parkes was well aware that the Japanese side was divided and that there was a danger that if the conservatives got the upper hand, they would revert to the bad old ways of treating foreigners as being inferior to their Japanese counterparts: '[I]f at the last moment I see anything derogatory in their arrangements' wrote Parkes, 'I can decline the reception'.[30] The practicalities of managing the visit were formidable, and Parkes had Mitford deal with them. Mitford made it seem as if he was unhappy about the visit: 'We … are looking forward with dread to the Duke of Edinburgh's arrival. How hot it will be! And what a bore, dancing attendance on him.'[31] But this needs to be taken with a grain of salt – it was *de rigueur* to roll the eyes at the thought of royalty, but Mitford was fascinated by it and relished the closeness the visit would bring him to Emperor Meiji and his court. He also hoped he could give the Duke 'a sight of Japanese country life and scenery which I think should be seen, as well as their city life', although disappointingly, his stay turned out to be too short to allow this and everybody wanted a piece of him.[32] But above all, the visit would be another 'first' he could add to his list – being witness to an unprecedented meeting between a Japanese Emperor and a Western prince.

Admittedly, making the arrangements was hard as there was a lot that could go wrong, the scheduling of the visit being very vague – Mitford only had an approximate idea of what day the Duke would arrive, how long he would stay, or what he wanted to do, and the Japanese side was similarly unclear about how it would receive him. Mitford told his father: If all goes well I shall not get the credit. If anything goes wrong upon me will fall the blame.'[33]

The main challenge was working out how to accommodate the Duke, the Japanese side having no experience of this at all. There was not a stick of European-style furniture in the Imperial residences, although Mitford did not see any problem in this, believing that Alfred would probably enjoy staying in Japanese-style accommodation, as he himself would have done. Parkes disagreed: Japanese aesthetics made a 'very pretty show' and were in 'perfect taste' but were 'wholly irreconcilable with our requirements'.[34] Unfortunately, the Japanese Government told him that it was impossible for them to provide any Western furniture so the British side had to procure some in Hong Kong. Mitford thought that what came had 'a strong flavour of Tottenham Court Road' which 'jarred piteously with the imaginative poetry of the Japanese artists'.[35]

At the beginning of August, Mitford moved to the place Alfred would stay in the Hama Goten garden so that he could closely supervise the arrangements. This pleasure garden had only come into the Emperor's possession the previous year, having belonged to the Shogun. It was the most comfortable place available to accommodate the Duke in the summer, with cooling breezes from Tokyo Bay taking the edge off the heat. Aside, that is, from the 'specially voracious and venomous species' of mosquito in the gardens.[36] Mitford did not think much of the Western-style house that was being put up for the Duke, although it would remain the main site for entertaining foreign guests until the 1880s. It was

> a great big clumsy uncomfortable building, for the Japanese can never succeed in making anything European. But the decoration inside is extremely striking. The walls covered with the wildest most fanciful pictures, a mass of colour and gold that would be fatal in the hands of a European artist, but some how or other these people have the knack of harmonizing the most outrageously gaudy colouring.[37]

Mitford's plans were almost wrecked by a devastating typhoon which struck on 20 August when he was at his house at Monryōin. It destroyed much of that building, the ground floor having been 'stripped as if by a knife' and the roof badly damaged, while strangely, the ceiling of the upper storey was intact. He told his father,

I am sitting ... among ... ruins[,] for the house ... suffered terribly.
As for the tiles they flew about as if they had taken to themselves
wings – and the garden is a wreck. I certainly never saw such a sight
in all my life.'[38]

Parkes' residence in Yokohama was in a similar state, which was
particularly unlucky because he had just finished repainting,
papering and decorating it ready for the Duke's arrival. Fortunately, the house built for the Duke was all right, although the
garden and trees had been 'knocked about terribly'.[39] Mitford
was now used to losing a house in a disaster and confined himself
to the thought that he would 'not be sorry' to see the back of
'all these strange sensations'.[40] The *Galatea* arrived in Yokohama
Bay on 24 August, but thankfully the Duke did not disembark
until the 31st, when all the arrangements were complete. Nothing was left to chance on the Japanese side. Prayers were offered
to Kanjin, the god of China, involving, according to Parkes, the
revival of an 'extremely ancient' ceremonial, dating from when
Japan's only foreign relations were with China and Korea. 'Kanjin', Parkes explained, 'is, therefore, the patron saint of foreigners, who are all united under his protection'.[41] The route Alfred
would travel along was cleaned and repaired, and prayers were
offered to the god of roads. Unfortunately, either the repairs or
the prayers did not work: the road was still very uneven and the
springs of the Duke's carriage broke twice between Yokohama
and Tokyo.

Rites of purification were also performed on Alfred himself,
what Mitford describes as 'a sweeping away of evil influences
with a sort of flapper with a hempen tassel'.[42] The purpose of
these was to prevent him, a foreigner, polluting the palace, but
Mitford does not seem to have realised this. Indeed nobody on
the British side complained and Parkes surely would have done
had he known. However, the acting American Minister, did
understand their purpose, telling President Johnson that they
had been done 'because in the eyes of the Japanese, all foreigners, whether of noble lineage or common, are alike impure as
animals', which undoubtedly had truth in it.[43]

At the same time, the Government bent over backwards to treat the Duke with utmost respect. All along the route from Yokohama he received the same honours that the Emperor himself did: the windows of upstairs rooms were sealed so that nobody could look down on him and as he went past, the crowds got down and touched the ground with their foreheads. No member of British royalty had ever received such deference anywhere. Security was tight, which would have been reassuring for the Duke who five months earlier had been shot in the back in Australia.

Mitford had to interpret for Alfred and Meiji, for which he had to be coached in the language of 'the people above the clouds', which was painfully polite and arcane. No doubt it was nerve-wracking for him, but the kind of thing they would say to each other could easily be predicted. The initial meeting was very formal. When the Duke's party was shown into the room, they saw the Emperor standing on a raised dais. Alfred took his place on another dais opposite him, with Mitford standing beside him. Everybody on the Japanese side was wearing the traditional court dress; 'living pictures out of the dark centuries', as Mitford described them.[44]

Only the 'usual commonplaces' were exchanged and Mitford's interpreting skills were not too stretched at this point.[45] Afterwards the Emperor invited the Duke to talk with him privately in the garden, which really was a big departure from how things had been done in the past. Parkes was concerned that the 'poor young Mikado suffers much from severe shyness and his ministers fear the prince will find him very uninteresting'.[46] However, judging by Mitford's report, they seem to have done all right. The Emperor told Alfred that as he had come such a long way, he begged him to stay long enough to repay the fatigue of the journey. Unfortunately, he would be disappointed, the Duke having already decided that he would stay in Tokyo just a week. Meiji also said that there would be many shortcomings in the reception and urged Alfred to express any wish that he had so that he could have the pleasure of gratifying it. The Duke replied that the reception had surpassed his expectations, and that he had long wished to come to Japan. He then congratulated the Emperor on the restoration of his authority. The Emperor said that his Government had 'received the greatest assistance from the advice and counsels of Sir Harry Parkes, and he was glad to take so important an occasion of acknowledging this debt of gratitude'.[47] Then the Duke gave the Emperor a diamond-mounted snuff-box, an item which Mitford thought second rate. The British must have been embarrassed by the fact that the Emperor was a lot more generous, presenting Alfred with a good selection of Japanese arts and crafts: lacquerware, a short sword, *netsuke*, bronzes, pottery and enamels.

Mitford knew that Meiji composed poetry and suggested to the Duke that he ask the Emperor for a poem written in his own hand which he could present to his mother on his return. Meiji consented, and the sentiments expressed in it were not ones she would have quibbled with:

世を治め
人をめぐまば
天地の
ともに久しく
あるべかりけり

If one governs the land
And benefits the people
Heaven and the earth
Will surely last together
For all eternity.[48]

Virtually nothing else in the Emperor's hand survives, his other poems having been copied out by expert calligraphers and then the originals destroyed. Therefore, the slip of paper containing these few words, now at the Royal Archives in Windsor Castle, is virtually unique. Parkes generously made sure that the Foreign Office knew whose idea it was – 'It was owing to a happy thought of Mitford's that the … [poem] was obtained'. Parkes believed it set an important precedent because a month later, Meiji sent a signed letter to the Emperor of Austria, the first time a Japanese Emperor had addressed a 'brother' monarch (other than the Emperor of China), signifying his wish to be included in the ranks of European royalty. It is 'not too much to say', Parkes wrote, that this 'was considerably facilitated by the autograph writing given by the Mikado to the Duke of Edinburgh.'[49]

The Japanese side was determined that the Duke would get a sampling of its culture, *nō* performances being specially put on for his benefit. Mitford thought that Westerners had never seen such a performance before, so it was yet another first for him. However, *nō* is probably the Japanese performing art that is the most difficult to appreciate for the uninitiated. It is slow (painfully slow to those who do not understand it) with graceful, prescribed movements, full of subtle meaning. Japan's other main dramatic form, *kabuki*, attracted audiences from every walk of life, holding the position of musicals in the present day. It had visual spectacles, vibrant costumes and was more fun, with its singing and dancing. It is now considered to be high art, but at the time, it was not respectable and nobody would have dreamt of letting a foreign prince see it.

Mitford did his best to make the *nō* interesting for the Duke, preparing a full explanation of the plays for him. Not wishing to waste a good thing, Mitford included these in *Tales of Old Japan*. But to the sailor Prince, who was not known for his appreciation of traditional arts in any language, the performance must have been hard work. Bernard Shaw thought that *nō* drama 'is no drama', while at the same time considering it the most interesting thing he saw in Japan.[50] Mitford certainly would have agreed with the first part of this:

> The beauty of the poetry – and it is very beautiful – is marred by the want of scenery and by the grotesque dresses and make-up. In the *Suit of Feathers*, for instance, the fairy wears a hideous mask and a wig of scarlet elf locks: the suit of feathers itself is left entirely to the imagination; and the heavenly dance is a series of whirls, stamps, and jumps, accompanied by unearthly yells and shrieks … The intoning of the recitative is unnatural and unintelligible, so much so that not even a highly educated Japanese could understand what is going on unless he were previously acquainted with the piece.[51]

Admiral Keppel was even less polite about the performance, writing that the movements of the actors were so exactly like those of a turkey cock with his tail spread out, 'that any one who has watched that bird … strutting about, needs no further description'.[52]

Mitford also had to help the Duke out with sundry other matters. He found two swords for him that cost £80, which he thought were authentic because they came with certificates. He considered himself an expert on swords, but Keppel thought he had probably been taken in. Alfred was tattooed, something which became a tradition among visiting British royalty, the future George V, among others, having one done when he visited in 1881.[53]

Mitford had to handle the situation when a number of valuables, including money, gold rings and a gold watch were stolen. He had engaged the servants for the Duke's visit, so felt responsible for the theft. His reaction suggests that he had really fallen under the influence of Japan, where people in a fix like this could be expected to offer to perform *hara-kiri* as the only means of redeeming their honour. Mitford did not quite go that far, but he did say that he guaranteed the servants' honesty with his life, and would undergo torture on the wheel if they were found guilty of the crime. Eventually, a lamp-trimmer he had recruited was discovered to be the culprit. All the goods were returned to their owners, and Mitford's offer of submitting to the wheel was forgotten.

*

Alfred's stay in Japan was a triumph for Mitford; both the making of the arrangements and the interpreting had been very public tests of his talents, and he had passed both, seemingly with ease. The Japanese Foreign Office was grateful for his efforts, expressing 'the profound obligations of the Japanese Government for the trouble you took in assisting them in the preparations made for the reception of His Royal Highness the Duke of Edinburgh and for your valuable cooperation during his stay at the Summer Palace' and asking him to accept a lacquer box as a gift.[54] Parkes managed to get the permission of the Foreign Secretary for Mitford to actually keep this present 'under the special circumstances of the case'.[55]

He was, however, relieved when it was over and he could return to working on *Tales of Old Japan*. In October, in order to get material for it, he took a journey which today could be done as a series of day trips from the capital, but at the time was an expedition: going south to Kamakura, then west to Hakone, before returning to Tokyo. He observed the lifestyles of people in the countryside and spoke to every kind of person he could, to gather traditional stories and any information that he might be able to use. He was accompanied by a Japanese secretary, a groom for the horses, Lin Fu, and three government employees charged with protecting him. In the past, they would have been mainly there to spy on him, but now they had 'changed their manner' and vied 'with one another in their obliging eagerness to please'.[56] Mitford observed 'country-folk' in 'picturesque groups', the women 'almost always tidy, and sometimes even smart'. The 'Japanese husbandman, … a hard-working and industrious soul, toiling early and late' for the rice crop of which he, 'poor man, may scarcely get a taste'. The 'unhappy inmates' of the village brothel, 'bedizening and painting themselves … and sitting down wearily at the open window to attract the attention of travellers'. One of those women was outside, tied hand and foot, having been 'beaten and ill-used', as a warning to the others – she had tried to escape.[57] He carefully observed the etiquette of ordinary people; his groom bumped into a friend and in spite of the fact that both were half-naked with 'their wonderfully tattooed limbs showing the lowness of their class', they bowed and prostrated themselves with 'more ceremonious greetings than would be exchanged between two western potentates'. Yet when they separated, Mitford heard his groom saying what a 'rogue, rascal, and villain' the man he had just parted from was.[58] There was also, of course, the scenery, Mitford regretting that it had never been done justice to by a 'gifted word-painter' like John Ruskin; he tried perhaps a bit too hard to fill the gap:

The shapes of the mountains, sometimes grand, sometimes fantastic; the marvellous gradations of the tree-colours from the exquisitely tender green of the feathering bamboo, slender and graceful, to the gloom of the sturdy pines and cryptomerias which spring from the more barren soil; the rocks streaked and patched with lichens and mosses, with many a rare fern and lycopod peeping out of chinks and crannies ... To me the memory of these places is like that of a beautiful dream of fairyland, vivid and bright, but utterly beyond the pale of description.[59]

On this trip Mitford caught up with Kido Takayoshi, one of the three principal leaders of the Meiji Restoration. He met him at the spa town of Miyanoshita – 'a sort of Japanese Tunbridge Wells'. Mitford describes a picnic at which he contributed 'sundry bottles of pale ale and porter', where they discussed politics and the 'application of European principles of government to Japan'. 'Of all subjects', Mitford wrote, 'this is the favourite'.[60] One suspects that the British loved boasting about the greatness of their parliamentary system, regardless of whether people from other countries wanted to hear about it or not, but Kido's diary backs up what Mitford said: 'He told me many new things about foreign lands; and the conversation lifted my spirits'.[61] When Mitford returned to Japan in 1906, he visited Kido's grave in Kyoto. 'Tall and handsome', Mitford reflected, 'a man of singularly winning manners and sweetest temper, an accomplished scholar, he was a born leader of men ... [T]he man who loves Japan will ... climb to the little enclosure on the heights [his tomb], and bestow a thought upon the noble heart which ceased to beat all too soon [he died at 43].'[62]

Mitford worked with his Japanese secretaries with the material he had collected to put it into English. It was painstaking labour and as the date of his departure loomed he had to turn on 'extra steam' in a frantic effort to finish the work on it that could only be done in Japan.[63] In order to round it out, he needed material about Europe and asked his father to send him a set of books for him to read on the voyage home. They give a sense of how – at heart – serious and scholarly he was: Henry Thomas Buckle's *History of Civilization in England*; Henry Hallam's *A*

View of the State of Europe during the Middle Ages and *The Constitutional History of England* and Thomas Macaulay's *The History of England from the Accession of James the Second*. Mitford needed them because he did not want to appear ignorant of the West in his book about Japan: 'I want to write something which shall show the contrast between the Japanese feudal system and that of Europe, and I don't want to write nonsense.'[64]

He could have stayed longer in Japan, but he felt very unwell and yearned to get back to England. Parkes asked for sick leave for him, which was generous; with Satow going to be away for another year, he would be left without his two most valuable men – a big gap in a Legation of only seven officers. Parkes unsuccessfully tried to get Mitford an extra £200 from the Treasury, which would have been very useful; because he was leaving early, returning home was expensive, the Foreign Office only giving him £75 – half his passage money. He took Lin Fu with him and the trip cost £275 in total (he travelled in a higher class of cabin than the Treasury allowed for), which is approaching £20,000 in today's values.

Two major feats of construction opened in 1869 which made Japan more accessible to the West: the transcontinental railroad across the United States and the Suez Canal. These developments, and the fact that Japan became safe for Westerners to visit, made it a prime destination for wealthy tourists. Before that, it was for adventurers only, but there were enough of these expecting to be shown round for Mitford to complain to his father: 'You can't think what a bore it is.'[65] As there were virtually no hotels, if visitors came with letters of introduction, the Legation staff had to put them up, sometimes for one, two, even three weeks. Tokyo, Mitford commented afterwards, 'was a show place, and we were obliged to show it for nothing ... it was a very heavy expense'.[66] But the biggest problem was the visitors not respecting Japanese customs, Mitford having to be constantly

on the look out against people committing some outrage against national feeling. Englishmen are always the most inconsiderate and tactless of travellers, and they are ten times more so when they think they have to do with barbarians who in fact might read them a lesson in good breeding.'[67]

The quickest route to Europe now was crossing the Pacific by ship, then across the United States overland (express trains could get from San Francisco to New York in six days), followed by another ship across the Atlantic. This meant the journey to London could be done in around thirty-six days, compared to fifty-three or so via the Suez Canal. Newspaper advertisements at the time made the train journey across the United States sound enticing:

> Passengers on the Pacific Railroad pass over the Sierra Nevada Mountains and Rocky Mountains, where some of the sublimest scenery on the American continent is to be seen. They also pass through the leading American cities. The trip is an uninterrupted pleasure across the entire American continent.[68]

For Mitford this route would also have been the most interesting way home because he had not been to America, although the main attraction of it for him was the prospect of visiting Honolulu: 'a great addition to my list of curious places visited'.[69] But there was no suitable vessel taking this route and he was desperate to leave: he wrote that he was so unwell on the day of his departure, New Year's Day, 1870, that he virtually had to be carried on to the ship by Dr Willis.

We never find out exactly what was wrong with Mitford – he seems to have been afflicted with some of the vaguely defined but debilitating ailments that were prevalent among Westerners in Japan and which often resulted in early deaths. He smoked constantly while he was working, but otherwise seemed to live healthily and he was still young. Parkes, after fifteen years as Minister there was diagnosed with 'blood impoverishment, nervous exhaustion, mental and physical strain, a disturbed liver, a troublesome cough, and frequent attacks of gout', but he served another thirteen years in Tokyo and two in Beijing, before dying at fifty-seven in 1885.[70] Unlike Parkes, Mitford took time out to relax and recover – he felt that he could afford to rest on his laurels for a while, something Parkes never allowed himself the luxury of doing. Mitford's sickness seems to have developed in November. At any other time, it would have skewered his plans, but on this occasion it suited him – he had wanted to leave around then anyway, and it gave him the excuse for leaving at the time of his choosing rather than when the Foreign Office wanted him to.

Mitford was departing from Japan without regrets and had the satisfaction of hearing the praise of everybody from the Foreign Secretary – 'Lord Clarendon's entire approval and satisfaction at the zeal and ability which you have displayed in discharge of the important duties which have been entrusted to you' – down, ringing in his ears.[71] He was, however, uncertain about how returning would make him feel, writing later, 'I wonder whether other men feel the same shyness about coming home'.[72] He warned his father in advance that he had changed: 'I am afraid, in many ways you will find that the very rough life which I have led for nearly three years will have altered me a good deal.'[73] He cannot have looked forward to the journey home, after all the traumas he had experienced on water and having heard all the horror stories of voyages in the China seas that had ended in tragedy. Indeed, soon after Mitford left Japan, it was blandly reported in a Kobe newspaper that the *Crofton*, 'on nearing some islands near Macao ... foundered, and the crew took to the boats and landed on an island where they were all murdered by the natives'.[74] But the disasters were not preventing ships coming to Japan. The sight presented by Yokohama harbour when Mitford left was very different to the one when he arrived – there were seventy merchant ships in the port, a threefold increase on what had been there in 1866. In addition, Britain was now less dominant. In 1865 64% of foreign ships entering Japanese ports had been British, but by 1870, the proportion had fallen to 42%.[75]

Mitford's journey was fairly trouble free, and he took it in easy stages, staying for a month in Singapore to recuperate, then going via the brand new Suez Canal, in which his boat smashed its screw, and on to Marseille. As a man had died from tuberculosis in the Red Sea, all its passengers were supposed to be quarantined, but Mitford, because he was carrying official despatches ('I took good care never to travel without a Foreign Office bag') had to be allowed off the boat.[76] From Marseille, he took a train to Paris, and finally London.

He felt like a 'pale and faded version of the prodigal son' on his arrival, but his old servant met him warmly at Victoria station, 'tears ... in his good, old, kind eyes' and he soon caught up with his father.[77] Mitford found that the 'Great Reaper had been merciful' in the five years he had been gone, sparing his nearest and dearest and everything was pretty well how he had left it. And, perhaps most important of all to him, he was back in time for the 'season' which in 1870 would be 'brilliant', with 'London ... at its gayest.'[78]

He was aware that he would find it strange being back knowing that Ambassadors and Ministers and even second secretaries found it hard suddenly not having people dancing attendance on them. (The last Governor of Hong Kong, Chris Patten, wrote of the shock of finding himself having to queue for a taxi at Heathrow Airport when he flew home after the handover to China.) But in Mitford's case, he would not have to wait long before some big opportunities opened up for him.

9

AFTER JAPAN

1870–1905

∞

MITFORD MUST SURELY have breathed a sigh of relief at making it back to Britain in one piece, having survived both one of the most dangerous overseas postings imaginable, and the journey back. He was now enjoying good health again and with plenty of wonderful stories to tell. If he had picked the right time to go to Japan, he had also chosen a good time to leave it – there would be no more really exciting events involving the Western diplomats there, and back in Europe the Japan boom was raging, meaning that everybody wanted to talk to him. Having left Britain a low-ranking diplomat, on his return he found himself a figure of some importance.

Mitford was able to pick up where he had left off with his most important connection, the Prince of Wales, who invited him to stay with him at Abergeldie Castle in Scotland for nearly a month. Queen Victoria sent for him to see her at nearby Balmoral. She was the only person Mitford admitted to being frightened of, but she was 'most gracious' and put him at his ease.[1] He was impressed by her knowledge of Japan, gained by reading Parkes' dispatches: 'I was able, of course, to tell her a good deal that was outside of what was contained in dispatches; but her knowledge of those was marvellous.' Talking about a recent massacre of Christians in China, she agreed with him that Westerners should not try to interfere with native people's religious beliefs:

'I am afraid' she told him, 'that sometimes the missionaries are rather injudicious.'[2]

Mitford's expertise about Japan was also valued by others. The Japanese Government wanted to start building railways and needed to raise capital overseas to do so. In August 1869, Itō Hirobumi had told Mitford they hoped to borrow £3 million, offering a ten-year lease of the mines on the island of Sado as a guarantee. In London, this seemed a very unsafe proposition because Japan was such an unknown quantity. Mitford was virtually the only person in Britain who knew the country as it had become after the Meiji Restoration. The banker Julius Beer tracked him down at his club and asked him the simple question, 'Was it safe to lend Japan money?' He told Beer that it was, but in the end Japan was only lent £1 million, a 'pitiful accommodation', Mitford thought, because the country surrendered the right to build the railway and the annual interest rate was 9% (plus 3% to the negotiators).[3] It was such a poor deal for the Japanese that Parkes feared they would never want to do business with British banks again.

Mitford was also debriefed by Lord Clarendon and Edmund Hammond, the Permanent Under-Secretary of State at the Foreign Office. Hammond oversaw the day-to-day running of the department and had a reputation for being omniscient. Mitford described him as an 'imposing figure, big and burly, with a rather quick, jerky, incise manner, which was apt to make men shy until they got to know him well'.[4]

In addition, Mitford gave evidence to a Parliamentary select committee which was looking into the diplomatic and consular service. He took the opportunity to complain about the lack of support for diplomats to learn languages; there was, he said, 'every inducement' not to make themselves masters of Chinese and Japanese because 'if a man studies those languages, it is a matter of great personal cost to himself' – the Foreign Office did not cover the expenses of it.[5] He said that he had earned £400 a year, but spent £800. When asked whether he thought he had been extravagant, he said that such expenditure was 'necessary … if you wish to keep up your position at all towards the natives'.[6]

From a twenty-first century perspective, it seems remarkable how much this entailed. In his last eight months in Japan, his staff had consisted of Lin Fu, a valet, a coolie and two Japanese secretaries for himself, and he had shared a gardener, a cook and his help with Adams (they ate together). Including Adams' own staff, the two men had employed twelve people. 'No one', according to Adams, 'in our position could keep house with a smaller establishment', and he affirmed that Mitford had needed all his £400 just for the essential expenses of running his household and office and keeping a horse.[7] At the same time, Mitford thought that the diplomatic service and the Foreign Office should remain the preserve of 'gentlemen' who could afford such positions, even if it meant that men like himself had to do menial tasks like copying despatches. Hammond, who also spoke to the committee, agreed with him, arguing that 'Nothing is so destructive to the harmony of an office … as to have a difference between the social classes of the men'.[8] He also thought that the upper classes were more likely to be discreet: 'Remember that there are no secrets here', he had told Mitford when he started; 'everybody is trusted, and you will find that nothing is hidden from you. But you must hold your tongue.'[9] The system worked. Twenty years later, Mitford was told by a financier that the British Foreign Office was the only one at which he had never been able to buy information.

He was held in high regard and the Foreign Secretary discussed with Hammond making him Secretary of the Legation in Beijing, one rank below that of Minister. Hammond said that he was in favour of the appointment, but was not sure about Mitford's health and he also knew confidentially that the Prince of Wales had his eye on Mitford for something (although nothing would come of that for many years).[10] Mitford did not want to go back to China and was anyway on a year's leave. While in Japan he had toyed with asking for Constantinople ('I feel sure that there must be a great field there for any one who will take the trouble of learning the language, and what an easy task after Chinese and Japanese') or Florence ('as I wish to study the silk question for which my stay in the East has given me a special interest').[11] In the end, he was offered a post in St Petersburg, which was known as being a particularly expensive place for a diplomat. Mitford had not particularly liked Russia, and it would have seemed tame compared to Japan. He refused it on the grounds that he could not afford it and was placed *en disponibilité* (on a leave of absence), but did not actually resign from the service until 1873. He was, in his own words, 'a gentleman at large'.[12]

However, he was far from idle, busily preparing *Tales of Old Japan* for publication. He had been determined to get published for some time, and while still in Japan he had asked his father to try to get a journal to take three articles: 'don't stick out for money – I want them in print – with my name attached – "translated by A.B. Mitford"'.[13] The *Cornhill Magazine*, a popular and highly-regarded literary journal, took them, publishing them in 1869. This was in spite of the fact that two of them do not sound very exciting: a pair of Japanese 'sermons', which were translations of talks made by a popular wandering preacher who went around teaching religious morals to ordinary people. But the Victorians were more interested in religion than we are (although one reviewer wrote that as the British were so 'overstocked' with sermons, they could hardly be pleased at being 'thrown a new and unexpected supply' from Japan).[14] Mitford gives a good description of listening to one of the sermons in the *Tales* with a cast of character types that would be familiar anywhere. In one corner, there was the lay clerk, 'armed with a huge pair of horn spectacles, through which he glared, goblin-like, at the people, as they came to have their names and the amount of their offerings to the temple registered'. The congregation was principally composed of 'old women, nuns with bald shiny pates and grotesque faces, a few petty tradesmen, and half-a-dozen chubby children, perfect little models of decorum and devoutness'. There was a lady richer than the others, 'nicely dressed, and attended by a female servant; she came in with a certain little consequential rustle, and displayed some coquetry … as she took her place, and, pulling out a dandy little pipe and tobacco-pouch, began to smoke.' He added that ashtrays and spittoons were handed around, 'so that half an hour which passed before the sermon began was agreeably spent'.[15]

The sermons were striking in that much of their message could have come from a Christian one: 'If a man loses a fowl or a dog, he knows how to reclaim it. If he loses his soul, he knows not how to reclaim it.'[16] Or, 'From this time forth repent and examine your own hearts.'[17] In the book Mitford does not point out the similarity, perhaps wary of being attacked by evangelical Christians, who would have been offended by any comparison with 'pagan' beliefs, but to his father, he compared them to the sermons of the famous evangelical preacher Charles Spurgeon.[18] Indeed, he seems to have deliberately made the sermons sound Biblical – he once wrote that before translating from Chinese or Japanese he made it a practice to read a little in the Bible, thinking it 'the best of all models for rendering an oriental language', so he was aiming at its style anyway.[19] The *Saturday Review* was suspicious of them, questioning whether a wandering preacher would have written his sermons down and thinking them too similar to British ones to be believable. They thought that Mitford had faked them.[20]

Mitford had now identified with Japan to the extent that he was concerned about what British people thought about it. He was countering one of the most potent charges against it: that its people had no religion, only superstition. It was certainly true that the Japanese were very superstitious, particularly about numbers, with great care being taken to choose auspicious times and dates for important events. Japan has not lost this completely – most couples are careful to avoid having their wedding on an unfavourable day, and the belief that four is unlucky, because it is a homonym of death, still has semi-official status, with Japanese hospitals not having room numbers with a four in them.

The third piece Mitford sent to the *Cornhill* was his account of the Taki *hara-kiri*. This must have been more interesting for the typical reader – it was not sensationalised, but it still had enough bloodshed to appeal to the Victorian love of the gruesome and was, above all, the first authentic account of the act in English. These three articles would all reappear in *Tales of Old*

Japan, which with its other descriptions of actual events, legends, ghost stories and fairy tales, was something of a jumble. The thread that binds the book is the attempt to reveal the Japanese spirit by portraying the people as they saw themselves. Mitford believed he understood them because he was sure that deep down, humans were the same wherever you went; a difficult view for most British people, who tended to believe that non-Europeans were almost a different species.

Mitford also saw the book as a way of preserving the feudal past that he had seen disappearing in front of his eyes while he had been there. He knew that it was rightly doomed, but he still saw it almost as a magical time that should not be forgotten. It would be a 'dull and sorry world without the glorious inheritance of the Middle Ages' he wrote elsewhere, adding that it was 'feudalism that gave birth to the spirit of chivalry, a spirit that still breathes in that loyal and self-denying patriotism which was the religion of the samurai, the religion of the Christian knight.'[21] His love for Britain was not based on its Empire or industrial might, but rather found its roots in a past that was long gone there, but which he had seen a very good version of in Japan. He was like many upper-class people in Britain who felt that industrialisation had wrecked both the landscape and the social structure of the country. He believed that the poor had been better off with the aristocracy governing their lives than rapacious factory owners. Of course, this was only true when the upper classes were benevolent to the lower – Mitford accepted this and despised British or Japanese aristocrats who exploited those beneath them.

Mitford did not expect *Tales of Old Japan* to sell well and if necessary was prepared to publish it at his own expense, 'as I know that the fact of having undertaken the job would do me good in the [diplomatic] service'.[22] The books that had been written so far about Japan had been either plodding and worthy, or sensational and fanciful, so there was certainly a gap in the market for something better. The *Tales* should have seemed like a commercial proposition, but Mitford was unsure of it and in his desperation to see it in print, accepted very poor terms from

MacMillan, receiving only £240 for it, which was nearly what it had cost him to put it together, and it came out in 1871. The book turned out to be a bestseller, becoming an essential addition to any serious bookshelf. 'The mistake which I made', he wrote later, 'was in selling the copyright out and out.'[23]

The key to its success was its timing, fitting the need for authentic information about Japan just when it had become the rage in the West. A guest to the British Legation watched Mitford's former colleagues struggling to get their hands on the one copy which had just arrived from London.[24] It even did well long after it was originally published, going through more than a dozen editions and impressions (a new one came out in 2012).[25] It became a given that anybody interested in Japan must have read it; Lafcadio Hearn, in a 1904 book on the country, wrote that 'There is probably none of my readers unacquainted with Mitford's ever-delightful *Tales of Old Japan*'.[26]

Writers and artists were universally enthusiastic. Robert Louis Stevenson named it as one of the books that had most influenced him and Dante Gabriel Rossetti thought it 'the first Western revelation that has ever been made of the soul of the Japanese'.[27] Painters were particularly interested in it because it helped to make sense of the art that was coming to the West and creating such a sensation. As Edmund Gosse put it, before the book, artists like Rossetti and Whistler were 'bewildered by the specimens … of … rich and fascinating art' from Japan, which was like 'a beautiful maze without a plan'.[28]

Mitford was not only praised for his insights into Japan, but also for his writing style, the *Japan Weekly Mail* considering that 'Mr. Mitford's book possesses special charms in the ease and elegance with which it is written, qualities which seem to be an intellectual inheritance in the members of a family to which English literature already owes lasting obligations.'[29] This was a particularly nice compliment for Mitford, who prided himself on his ancestry. Even in Japan there was interest in it; one of the country's most famous writers (he used to be on the 5,000 yen note), Nitobe Inazō, in *Bushido and the Soul of Japan*, quoted Mitford's account of the Taki hara-kiri in full, as he thought it could not be bettered.[30]

These reactions were hugely gratifying to Mitford and they showed how much he had progressed. Before he went to Japan, he had been little more than a promising paper-pusher. Now he was being lionised by some of the most famous people in the country. He had also changed inwardly – in the early days of his time in Japan, he had been uncertain about his future path. He never seems to have doubted that he had talent, but he did not know how he could achieve the kind of success he yearned for. Now he had found it. It is hard to imagine how he could have got this far had he stayed in Britain – the chance he had taken in going to China and Japan was now paying dividends.

The reason that Mitford hit gold with the *Tales* derived from his natural interest in people. While his letters are not exactly gossipy, they focus much more on the characteristics and actions of individuals rather than events. He knew he did not have the talent to be a great writer, but he realised that by showing the Japanese as personalities with emotions and motives that the Western reader could relate to, rather than as types, that he could produce something that readers would respond to on an emotional level. As Gosse put it, he 'made the Japanese man or woman, for the first time, an interesting human being'. Gosse compared the *Tales* with Pierre Loti's hugely popular *Madame Chrysanthème*, which Puccini's opera *Madame Butterfly* was partly based on. He thought Mitford 'less brilliantly equipped as a writer', but he gave a 'truer … deeper impression of reality'. In the *Tales*, Gosse believed, 'there was an exposition, never achieved before by a European, of the inner life of the Empire, of its religion, its morals, its ways of thought, the hidden springs by which its citizens moved'.[31]

The press wrote about the *Tales* at length, clearly considering their appearance to be newsworthy. The *Times* declared that 'we do not venture too high praise when we say that a strange country and people have never been the theme of a more entertaining and informing work than *Tales of Old Japan*'.[32] Other newspapers were less keen, many questioning how representative the stories were of Japanese society. The *Saturday Review* commented that the characters in them resembled 'caricatures in which the most noticeable traits of certain well-known classes are brought into distorted prominence, [more] than reflections of the real life of the people at large'.[33] It was a fair point – Mitford thought that while the stories might not be of an everyday kind, that they nonetheless shed light on Japan's customs and values. That said, he certainly emphasised the traits he admired most, 'the chivalry, the heroism celebrated in many an old-world legend, the poetry of myth and fable which cast a glamour over all those … coming from the humdrum and commonplace of the West'.[34]

One unfortunate impression that the *Tales* gave was that the Japanese were casual about human life and even about performing the *hara-kiri*. Bizarrely, in Britain at the time it was commonly referred to as the 'happy despatch', which many people thought was what the words literally meant (they simply mean 'cut the stomach').[35] The *Saturday Review* commented: 'Living perpetually within arm's-length of death, life ceases to be in their eyes more than a very transitory affair … murders or suicides of sons, husbands, and fathers are matters of indifference, and often of pride'.[36] Mitford had not wanted to say this at all; what he had tried to show was that the Japanese sense of honour and duty overrode the terror that any human would feel when facing a violent death. In fact, Mitford had greatly exaggerated how prevalent the *hara-kiri* was. Admittedly he had been in Japan during a time of unrest when it was more common than usual; however, we know that of five thousand *hatamoto* (retainers of the Shogun) who lived in Tokugawa Japan (1603–1868), only eight died by *hara-kiri* and at least six of these were forced, contradicting Mitford's assertion that a samurai who had been defeated or disgraced would usually choose to die in that way in order to preserve his honour.[37] However, this fits with the overall theme of the *Tales*, that the Japanese of the time were not very different to any other group of humans. In reality, all but the most fanatical samurai viewed the *hara-kiri* as we would: something to be avoided at absolutely any cost.

Although Mitford's picture of Japan was generally accurate and sympathetic, it was unfortunate that he so firmly lodged the idea that the Japanese were a particularly bloodthirsty race in the Western brain. The *Tales* encouraged works like *The Mikado*, which ridiculed Japan by exploiting the comic potential of the bloodshed. In Mitford's stories, so many of the deaths stem from trivial matters – the vendetta in *The Forty-Seven Rōnin* originates in nothing more than insulting behaviour. Such stories seem to invite the kind of parody they get in *The Mikado*, such as the scheme to save Ko-Ko from death for flirting, which almost appears realistic after reading *Tales of Old Japan*:

> And so we straight let out on bail
> A convict from the county jail,
> Whose head was next,
> On some pretext,
> Condemned to be mown off,
> And made *him* Headsman, for we said,
> "Who's next to be decapitated
> Cannot cut off another's head
> Until he's cut his own off."

*

Once Mitford had finished the *Tales* he had plenty of time on his hands. He visited Palestine and Syria where he met up with the explorer, Richard Burton, with whom he had worked in the African Department at the Foreign Office and was now British Consul in Damascus. Burton had tried to persuade Mitford to take a post in Fernando Po (the island now known as Bioko, part of Equatorial Guinea) so that they could explore west Africa together. Mitford had difficulty saying no to anything that sounded like an adventure but his father refused to allow him to go. Maybe Mitford could have talked him round had he really wanted to but this perhaps shows that in the final resort, Mitford accepted his father's authority. This would surely have been tied in with the allowance Mitford depended on until his marriage – it could always be stopped if his father was really upset with him.

Burton would have been a wonderful companion, being utterly exceptional both as a scholar and traveller. His achievements make Mitford's look tame: his was the first translation into

English of *One Thousand and One Nights* and he collaborated on translating the *Kama Sutra* (both unexpurgated). He was also, with John Speke, the first European to visit the Great Lakes of Africa and he spoke something in the order of thirty languages. He was, in Mitford's words, 'ignorant of fear' and 'his powers of endurance were simply marvellous'.[38] But equatorial Africa had a far worse survival rate than China and Japan for Europeans – it was the 'White Man's Grave', and with Burton encouraging him to take risks, Mitford would have been lucky to survive it.

*

In 1873, Mitford returned to Japan for two months. This seems a surprising decision, considering how much the journey would cost, how much time it would take and how little he liked sea journeys. It also had him in Japan in the middle of summer (he arrived on 9 July), which was far from his favourite time to be there. Mitford tells us nothing at all about this stay in Japan in his memoir, simply writing that it was something 'of which I need say nothing here', although he does describe the voyage from San Francisco: the Pacific was 'anything but pacific' with 'a succession of gales, in one of which our starboard paddle was smashed, and we had to steam the second half of our voyage steering against the remaining one'.[39] However, there is enough evidence to piece together the probable reasons for the trip.

Certainly one of the purposes was to negotiate with the Japanese Government about a submarine telegraph cable between Japan and the United States. The telegraph had revolutionised international communication, making it possible to send messages to distant parts of the world in minutes – an effective cable had been working from Europe to the United States since 1866, to India since 1870, and to Australia since 1872. In his memoir Mitford mentions having many meetings with the fantastically wealthy John Mackay in San Francisco, whose company would be responsible for the laying of two trans-Atlantic cables. They must have put together a proposal for a cable to Japan because on 22 July, Mitford submitted one to the Emperor's chief minister, Sanjō Sanetomi, and thereafter, carried on a correspondence about it with officials. It seems extraordinary that the Japanese side would consider a scheme of this magnitude presented by someone who had no official standing, but they clearly did, responding with enthusiasm at the start, although it eventually came to nothing, which must be why Mitford left it out of his memoir. Perhaps it was an all-or-nothing gamble for Mitford – one that would have made him a fortune if it had been successful, but because it failed, left him with nothing.

However, it looks like the trip had another purpose, which may have been its primary one: to see a woman called 'Tomi'. Mitford was very good at covering his tracks and we only know about her because of two stray letters in his archive, one from Tomi herself, written in 1870, telling him that a child called Omitsu ('mitsu' being the 'mit' of Mitford) was beginning to walk and eat cakes. She said she hoped Mitford would come back soon to see how the child was growing.[40]

This simple letter is not at all the kind of importuning, vaguely threatening one that we might expect someone in Tomi's position to send. Its gentle tone is poignant when we consider the jeopardy Tomi had placed herself in by getting involved with Mitford and how hard Omitsu's life would have been. Tomi had been breaking the law having a relationship with a foreigner, and the mixed race Omitsu would have been proof of it. She showed courage in keeping Omitsu – for many women, the prospect of having such a child was so frightening that they killed themselves or risked their lives by going to an abortionist, rather than have one. Sometimes the babies were abandoned – a home was started in Yokohama for such children by a foreign woman horrified by what was happening to them. Mixed race children faced discrimination and their mothers had no right to keep them; Omitsu legally belonged to Mitford, who could have taken him or her (the gender of the child is unclear) away when he left Japan. Foreign fathers taking their children home with them was not uncommon; in Puccini's *Madame Butterfly*, Pinkerton intends to take his and Butterfly's son to the United States, his American wife having agreed to bring him up. Tomi did not have to face that tragedy, and her letter shows that she was not living in a fool's paradise, believing that Mitford was coming back to live with her, as Butterfly does.

It is possible that Mitford intended to somehow remain true to Tomi. In 1868, he had told his father 'I am never likely to marry' which may have been a hint that he could not because he felt bound to her.[41] Perhaps he considered marrying her; Dr Willis married his Japanese mistress, but such an act meant social death in Britain and Mitford had a lot to lose. It was also not accepted in Japan and indeed had not been possible while Mitford was living there: marriage between Japanese and foreigners only became legal in 1873. Satow was in a similar position, having two sons with a Japanese woman named Takeda Kane. Kane was luckier than Tomi in that Satow spent far longer in Japan than Mitford and he seems to have remained true to her for the rest of his life, although he never married her and never took her to England with him.

If he had promised Tomi that he would return to her, Mitford had at least kept that promise. However, there is a family story that he had proposed to the ultra-eligible Lady Clementine Ogilvy, daughter of the Earl of Airlie, and she had turned him down, which is why he took the trip to America and Japan.[42] Perhaps he only went back to see Tomi because he had been rejected by Clementine. During the two months he was in Japan, he must have explained his situation to Tomi, which she would surely have understood, lovers kept apart by circumstances being a very common thing there. He surely made certain that she would be financially secure, a standard thing for men in Mitford's situation – the cheapness of Japan compared to Britain meant this would not have cost him a great deal. Very likely Satow would have taken care of this for him. But after he left, they may very likely never have heard from each other again, although it would be nice to think of him seeing Tomi and Omitsu when he returned to Japan in 1906.

When he got back to Britain, Mitford tried again with Clementine at an afternoon party at Holland House in west London. She was standing with another admirer beside a lily pond and told him that a water-lily would be just the thing to wear with her gown at the ball that evening. Mitford, as always, immaculately dressed, stepped into the middle of the pond and picked it for her. She wore it in her dress that evening, and when he proposed to her, she accepted him.

They had a successful marriage, having five sons and four daughters, although Mitford, who remained attractive and sexually active into old age, had many affairs. A daughter-in-law, Sydney Bowles' first impression of him, written when he was fifty-seven, was that he was 'the best looking old man' she had ever seen, 'with pure white hair and glittering … blue eyes, together with a bony rather hooked nose and a good figure'. Clementine, on the other hand 'had a fine presence and much personality. She was beautiful in her youth but … was too fat.'[43] She gave birth to twins when Mitford was fifty-eight and she forty-one, which suggests that they kept some spark in their marriage for a long time. A portrait of her painted in middle age, emphasises her enormous bust and has her looking commandingly, but coquettishly at the viewer, head cocked slightly to one side.[44] She looks both sensual and like someone who would stand no nonsense. Mitford liked forthright, opinionated women who took an equal part in conversation with men, not caring for the shy, servile types he had met in Japan; he thought that these characteristics were a 'defect', 'bred by the seclusion and abased condition in which women are kept' there.[45] Clementine's great-grandson, who spoke to her youngest daughter (who lived to a hundred), portrayed her as a conventional woman, a 'bit stuffy' but fairminded.[46] It seems that she ruled the roost indoors, but Mitford was allowed to do what he wanted outside.

As for the affairs, it was said that Mitford used to take the Prince of Wales 'wenching'.[47] His most interesting relationship was with Clementine's older sister, Blanche Hozier, the mother of Winston Churchill's wife, another Clementine.[48] The Churchills' daughter, Mary Soames, wrote that her mother was certain that Henry Hozier was not her real father, and the poet Wilfrid Scawen Blunt (who himself had a brief affair with her), recorded gossip that there were ten lovers. Soames puts forward

Captain William Middleton and Mitford as the two likeliest candidates to be the father of Clementine and her older sister Kitty, but says that she cannot make a judgment on which it was.[49] Both Clementine's other main biographers lean towards Mitford.[50] Joan Hardwick thinks that it explains why, when Kitty died, Blanche went to Mitford's country estate, and had her buried there, rather than her family's castle in Scotland. In addition, Edward VII, who Mitford seems to have confided in, knowing that he would not be censorious, told a courtier that Mitford was Clementine's father.[51] Some people have said that their noses were strikingly similar, and that the 'Mitford eyes' – large and blue – can be seen in the Churchill descendants, if not in Clementine herself.[52] Admittedly, Blanche told people that Middleton was the father of Kitty and Clementine, but Hardwick believes this may have been in order to create a credible rumour that would hide a much more scandalous fact: that she was sleeping with her sister's husband.

Clementine Mitford, only twenty when she got married, had an unworldliness about her at the start which may have helped her husband get away with his adventures. When they married, he opened a bank account for her and she was delighted to see that the more money she spent, the higher the balance, printed attractively in red, seemed to be. Mitford, who was not all that clever with money himself, had to explain the concept of an overdraft to her.

The family settled in Lindsey Row in Chelsea, which had been the site of Sir Thomas More's house. Now these houses are some of the most expensive in London – Roman Abramovich, the Russian billionaire, bought one in 2011 for £25 million. Mitford in fact had two of them joined together. How could he have afforded them? The answer must be that Clementine came with a substantial dowry, which would have made her an exceptionally sought-after marriage partner.

Chelsea was a gathering place for artists and writers and had only recently become fashionable – when the historian Thomas Carlyle and his wife moved there in 1834, they had only done so because it was cheap. Most people found Carlyle intimidating, but Mitford had known him since childhood and had a relaxed relationship with him. Carlyle was curious about Japan and Mitford thought it was a 'bright feather' in his cap that he had read *Tales of Old Japan*, although Carlyle did not like the stories – too much blood and murder in them for him.[53]

The artist James McNeill Whistler lived next door to Mitford, and he and Mitford were constantly wandering into each other's houses. Whistler was the pioneer of *japonisme* in Britain and so must have talked endlessly about Japan with Mitford. Whistler painted him in Van Dyck costume and his wife in Chinese blue silk but unfortunately, both paintings were slashed to pieces by Whistler to prevent them from falling into the hands of his creditors.

Whistler was unquestionably a genius in Mitford's eyes, 'always original. He was himself, he imitated nobody.'[54] Mitford contrasted him with Oscar Wilde, who he also knew: Wilde was 'the great plagiarist ... brilliantly clever ... [but he] never hesitated to copy'.[55] Whistler agreed with this; when, after a clever remark of his Wilde said 'I wish I had said that Whistler', Whistler replied 'You will, Oscar, you will.'

Mitford was very interested in art, but while he enthused about traditional Japanese painting, he does not seem to have truly grasped it and never wrote analytically about it. He went to great lengths to get authentic illustrations for *Tales of Old Japan*. He tells us in the preface that he employed an artist named Ōdake to draw the illustrations for the book and that they were cut on wood by a famous engraver, making them 'genuine specimens of Japanese art'.[56] Ōdake has proved impossible to track down; there were three Ōdake brothers, all prominent woodblock artists, but they were born between 1868 and 1880 and so cannot have been Mitford's Ōdake. But as trades ran in families, he was probably related to them, perhaps being their father.

The prints in *Tales of Old Japan* are not in the league of the Ōdake brothers, much less the likes of Hokusai and Hiroshige, whose work would have been all over Edo, but which Mitford never mentioned. But their prints were art for the masses and their subject matter was mostly everyday life (government censorship had restricted depictions of anything associated with the Shogun). At the time, the idea of an art gallery would have seemed ridiculous in Japan because, as the Australian artist Mortimer Menpes, who visited the country in 1887 noticed, art formed 'part and parcel of the very life of the people' and 'every Japanese is an artist at heart'.[57] Art could be appreciated by the poor as much as by the rich in Japan – Hiroshige's prints could be bought for the cost of a bowl of noodles which was probably what made Mitford feel they were not worthy of consideration.

The Japanese woodblock artists had a great influence on another group of painters that now have a high reputation but that Mitford disliked: the French Impressionists. In 1914, as a trustee of the National Gallery in London, he did everything he could to stop a collection of their paintings being displayed there. Describing it as a 'degraded craze', he wrote: 'I should as soon expect to hear of a Mormon service being conducted in St. Paul's Cathedral as to see an exhibition of the modern French art-rebels in the sacred precincts of Trafalgar Square.'[58]

To those who thought that hanging the Impressionists would do no harm, Mitford responded that this would be a desecration because they were lazy, the work of cynics, having been tossed off, rather than laboured over to make them perfect. It is easy to imagine Mitford being censorious for the same reason about Japanese woodblock artists like Hiroshige, who produced more than four thousand prints in his career (compare him with, say, Vermeer, who has just thirty-four paintings attributed to him). Also, Hiroshige was linked to the Impressionists, which would have been another black mark in Mitford's eyes; Camille Pissarro wrote: 'Hiroshige is a wonderful Impressionist. Monet, Rodin and I are enthusiastic.'[59] The Japanese art that Mitford thought was good was that of diligent craftsmen who respected the work of their forebears. He chose three artists whose work he thought worth collecting: 'Myochin', 'Seimin' and 'To-un', but none have stood the test of time and all are now very obscure, apart from Myochin, which is the name of a family who have been making armour from the 1500s to the present day.

However, Whistler, whose paintings Mitford did admire, was greatly influenced by the work of Hiroshige and Hokusai. Perhaps his most famous Japan-inspired work is *Nocturne: Blue and Gold – Old Battersea Bridge* which, with its fireworks in the distance and exaggeratedly high, curving wooden bridge, strongly resembles Japanese woodcuts. The bridge, which could be seen from Lindsey Row was a dangerous and dilapidated wooden structure (it was demolished in 1885), disliked by the people who had to use it, but loved by artists. Whistler's depiction of it fused Japan with Impressionism but we do not see Mitford criticising him for this. This would probably have been because he and Whistler were so close – a friendship would always be more important to Mitford than a style of painting. It is also the case that Whistler was eclectic – much of his art, such as his most famous painting, his portrait of his mother, is more conventional by the standards of the day, and would have been easier for Mitford to like.[60] Most people now would probably consider Mitford to be a philistine for his inability to appreciate the French Impressionists or (we assume because he never mentioned them) the likes of Hiroshige and Hokusai. He would have been mortified to be thought of in this way; looking at his artistic taste from a 21st-century perspective, perhaps it would be fairer to call it 'of its time and of his origins'.

*

The year of Mitford's marriage, 1874, was significant in another way for him, as it saw him gain an important appointment from Benjamin Disraeli, who had just become Prime Minister again. He was made Secretary to the Board of Works, the senior permanent civil servant in the department, whose job was to look after the parks and government buildings. Mitford was just the kind of handsome, confident aristocrat that Disraeli liked and he had long had Mitford in mind for a job; when Mitford was just starting out at the Foreign Office, Mrs Disraeli had told him, 'Dizzy has got his eye upon you'.[61] On the face of it the appointment was a strange one. At thirty-six he was young for the position and he had no experience of civil service work. But Disraeli was not one to worry about details like this and Mitford turned out to be ideal for the post. Unfortunately, Disraeli appointed another attractive aristocrat, Lord Henry Lennox, as the minister in the department, with far less successful results. He had been extremely close to Lennox – in one letter to him Disraeli had written, 'I can only tell you I love you'.[62] But Lennox was lazy, incompetent and resentful, believing that he deserved better from Disraeli and he made Mitford's life impossible, taking very little interest in the job and not listening properly when he was being briefed. Disraeli wanted the department completely reformed and Mitford was ready to carry this out. Lennox, however, opposed it tooth and nail and was backed up by other senior staff. Mitford wrote Disraeli a letter of resignation, but Disraeli refused to accept it and instead set up a Cabinet committee to look into the workings of the department. The committee backed Mitford and in 1876, Lennox went.

From then on, Mitford had good relations with his political chiefs from both parties, which included an up-and-coming Lord Rosebery, who went on to be a Liberal Prime Minister. In spite of his Conservative sympathies, he got along very well with Gladstone, joining the small band of people who managed to be friendly with both him and his rival Disraeli. He and Gladstone had a large amount of correspondence about the placing of a reproduction of the old city cross in Edinburgh to mark his victory in the 'mid-Lothian campaign' of 1880. The victory itself must have been galling for Mitford, as it saw the defeat of his friend Disraeli and started a tradition of mass political rallies, which was loathed by the upper classes.

Many of Britain's historic buildings had fallen into decay and Mitford was responsible for restoring some of the most important, including the Tower of London, Hampton Court Palace and Windsor Castle. His sense of style was very much of his time and he hated Georgian architecture, writing of the 'prevailing dearth of taste' of that time.[63] But otherwise his instincts were sound and those buildings would not be standing the way they do today without his work on them. His interest in horticulture made him passionate about the royal parks and he remodelled the gardens in them. He wanted to redesign Hyde Park Corner, which was becoming very busy, but Disraeli rejected the idea, saying: 'Do away with the congestion of traffic at Hyde Park Corner? Why, my dear fellow, you would be destroying one of the sights of London!'[64] Another, much more ambitious scheme of Mitford's was to build a chain of public offices between Trafalgar Square and Parliament Square, to replace the haphazard set of buildings that were there at the time. He says that his plan was generally approved, but was not adopted 'owing to the costly timidity of Ministers' – it would have saved the country a huge sum of money because of the subsequent huge increase in the value of the land, Mitford later claimed.[65]

When he left the Board of Works, in 1886, Gladstone, who was Prime Minister at the time, went beyond the conventional pleasantries for a departing official:

> I received with very great regret the announcement of your resignation, which at the same time I admit to be no desertion on your part, but to be reasonable and just.
>
> But it will, I fear, be very difficult to fill your place with a person possessed in the same degree with yourself of the varied and high qualifications which it requires.[66]

The reason Gladstone did not consider Mitford to have deserted was that he had just inherited a magnificent house and estate called Batsford from his cousin, Earl Redesdale, near Moreton-in-Marsh in Gloucestershire. As the youngest of three brothers, Mitford was very lucky to get it. Redesdale was childless, and his will directed that it be left to Percy, and then his male heirs – Henry, still in disgrace, would only get an annuity of a measly (in upper class terms) £400 a year. However, because Percy died childless in 1884, Bertie got virtually everything: a cool quarter of a million pounds in cash – approaching £20 million today – along with an estate producing an income of £17,000 a year. He used some of that fortune to knock down the Georgian house standing there and build an immense new one on a site nearby. It is striking how alien Mitford's taste is to that of today. The previous house would now be rated far more highly than the neo-Gothic Victorian one he put up. This house has been altered since Mitford lived there, but its main hall remains the same, with the air of a large German hunting lodge. Mitford's granddaughter, the Duchess of Devonshire, did not like it: 'What a bugger that house is, no redeeming feature of any kind, cruel proportions, frightfully cold because of being so huge and impossible to heat'.[67] From the outside, however, the building is magnificent, built in lovely local stone that melds into the idyllic landscape, its elevated position giving it sweeping views across the Cotswolds.

Mitford probably gave more attention to the unique garden he created there. He was fortunate that the slope behind the house was south-facing and sheltered, thus enabling him to create a micro-climate that would allow plants from much warmer climes to survive there. He had observed natural groupings of plants in China and Japan and sought to copy that style in his own garden. He loved Japanese gardens when they mimicked nature but did not like the celebrated stone gardens because he thought they were contrived and unnatural. Mitford's great passion was bamboo, and by 1890, there were fifty-three species growing on the estate, making it probably the most comprehensive collection anywhere in the world (a few survivors are still thriving there). He had made himself an expert on identifying different species of bamboo, which is such a difficult topic that there is still not agreement on some classifications. At the time, gifted amateurs were able to make significant contributions to science and he wrote a respected book on the topic, *The Bamboo Garden*, in 1896, helping make the plant fashionable in Britain. He built a Japanese-style rest house, with two tablet boards on it with the following messages written in Japanese: 'better to live without meat than without bamboo' and 'how can one live without this gentleman [bamboo]?' He also planted Japanese cherry trees and maples to create the two quintessential markers of the seasons in Japan: the flowering of the cherry blossoms in the spring, and the brilliant reds of the maple leaves in the autumn.

In the early 1890s, Batsford was starting to feel a bit quiet for Mitford, because he briefly returned to public life, being elected as a Conservative MP for Stratford-on-Avon, in 1892, although he stood down in the General Election of 1895. He was still only in his fifties and could have hoped for ministerial office had he remained in Parliament, but he did not. What he really enjoyed about the place was meeting the people and witnessing great events. In the past, he had been ambitious, but now he was more relaxed, having reached a comfortably high position in society.

The death of Queen Victoria in 1901 enabled him to move even higher. She had had many dealings with Mitford over the years, and had respected him – when he resigned from his position at the Board of Works, she had her secretary tell him he had done his duty 'not only to her entire satisfaction, but also in a manner which has proved to be of great benefit to the public'.[68] That said, because he was such an intimate friend of her eldest son, whom she had serious doubts about, she would still have suspected him of being 'fast'. Nevertheless, on Gladstone's recommendation, she made him a Companion of Bath in 1882, ironically, the very reward Mitford had complained to his father he would not get, years earlier, from Japan:

> They are lavish in honours to those who are nearest home, but we get nothing. For two years I have had to run into continual danger and to take upon myself grave responsibilities, but I suppose my position in the service is too low for them to be acknowledged. CBs and the like are only for … [those] who went through less danger and less hardship than any of us. It is not encouraging.[69]

Clearly Mitford's status had changed in the intervening years from a discontented outsider to a very comfortable insider, although it would have been difficult for him to advance any further while the high-minded Victoria was on the throne. It was a different story when Edward VII succeeded her. In his coronation honours list, in which he could choose men to honour without the advice of the Prime Minister, the King made him Baron Redesdale, which gave him a seat in the House of Lords. This started a flow of honours: three years later he received the Grand Cross of the Royal Victorian Order, awarded for distinguished personal service to the Sovereign, and in 1906 he became a Knight Commander of the Order of the Bath.

We should now call him Lord Redesdale, but somehow, having got to know him as plain old Mitford, it seems easier to continue using that name for the last part of his life.

10

THE RETURN

February – March 1906

℘

In 1906, MITFORD – Lord Redesdale – is now nearly seventy, but still has plenty of spring in his step. Edmund Gosse penned an affectionate portrait of him in his later years, describing him as a sort of 'Prince Charming':

> [W]ith his fine features, sparkling eyes, erect and elastic figure and … his burnished silver curls, he was a universal favourite, a gallant figure of a gentleman, solidly English in reality, but polished and sharpened by travel and foreign society'.

He would, Gosse continued, stroll 'down Pall Mall, exquisitely dressed, his hat a little on one side, with a smile and a nod for every one'.[1]

It was now thirty-three years since he had last been in Japan and he had probably given up on visiting it again. There was no chance that he could in any way acknowledge Tomi and Omitsu, his high position in British society depending upon a respectable front that they could not be a part of. And a return as a dimly-remembered bit player in the Meiji Restoration, attempting to trade on connections made so long before, would not have been a good way to go back.

Fortunately, the perfect opportunity arose to revisit in style: sent by the King to assist his nephew in bestowing Britain's oldest order of chivalry, the Order of the Garter, on Emperor Meiji. Mitford would get the chance to relive the greatest adventure of his life and be feted as Britain's highest-ranking expert on the country. With the added elements of royalty and honours, combined with the most luxurious travelling arrangements possible, it was a dream come true for him. In addition, it would give him the chance to publish another book on the country – an account of the trip – this time certain that it would be gobbled up by the public; the triumphant reception of Puccini's *Madame Butterfly* two years earlier was evidence that enthusiasm for Japan in the West was still going strong.

The British had been very reluctant to give the Garter to non-Christians, the Shah of Persia being the only one who had received it so far, so it did seem to be a distinct honour, even for an Emperor. The *Spectator* complacently suggested that 'nothing could prove more clearly the inclusion of our ally among the great Kings of the world'.[2] The prince who was undertaking this mission was a junior member of the royal family, the twenty-three-year-old Arthur of Connaught, son of Edward VII's younger brother, the Duke of Connaught. Up to this point, Prince Arthur had not achieved very much. Like Mitford he had been to Eton (the first British prince to be educated there) and then had gone into the army, fighting in the Boer War – later he went on to be Governor-General of South Africa (1920–1923). He found public duties difficult, being described as a 'tall, stooping figure, known for his shyness and reticence'.[3] But he would have to do his best because he otherwise fitted the bill: a male member of the family who could be spared for the four months or so that it would take and – bearing in mind the assassination attempt on the future Tsar Nicholas II in Ōtsu in 1891 – one whose loss would not be catastrophic. In spite of Arthur's relatively junior rank, this Mission would be a historic event, being the first official royal visit to Japan – on all the previous visits the royalty had been stopping on the way to somewhere else or had come as tourists.

Mitford could be fairly sure of being well-received in Japan, if for no other reason than as a link to the Restoration, now seen as the glorious event which had propelled Japan towards becoming a great nation. He could also hope to be fondly regarded for having presented such a sympathetic picture of the country in *Tales of Old Japan*.

However, he had badly damaged his reputation among senior Japanese in 1900. At that point the country had recently defeated China and was on the way to building up an Empire, having acquired Taiwan, a foothold in China (the Liaodong Peninsula) and was gaining control of Korea. No other nation in history had ever achieved so much from such a low starting point. What might it lead to? Mitford had sounded an alarm bell, predicting in a letter to *The Times* that sooner or later Manchuria would be taken over by Russia or Japan (it would be Japan).

> Let us hope that it [is] … not … Japan. It must be remembered that barely a quarter of a century has elapsed since Japan was murdering foreigners with … wild fanaticism. True, in the interval she has donned a veneer of Western civilization. But how deep does it go? … The national character of Japan is restless, ambitious and aggressive in the highest degree … Once give Japan a foothold on the continent of Asia, place her in command of the countless hordes of Tartars and Chinese … drilled and licked into shape by her marvellous power of organization … and you will have given shape and substance to … [the] yellow terror. You will have conjured into existence a disturbing force that may alter the map of Asia, if not the world.[4]

In Japan, this letter produced, according to *The Times* correspondent in Tokyo, a 'profoundly painful impression in official circles'. The correspondent was told that they felt 'such baseless suspicions must inevitably shock and discourage the nation's friendly impulses'.[5] It is amazing to see Mitford adopting such a hostile tone with respect to Japan because it is so out of keeping with the rest of his published writing, if not all his private letters – his use of the phrase 'yellow terror' is particularly jarring, sounding appalling to twenty-first century ears, although it would have seemed unexceptional to his contemporaries.

As usual, Mitford bounced between extreme positions and shortly afterwards became Japan's most passionate advocate in

Britain. Probably he partly changed his mind because he decided he cared about what the Japanese thought of him. But what really caused him to alter his view was the signing of the Anglo-Japanese alliance in 1902 and the close relationship that developed between the two countries, which was extraordinary given how distant they were, both culturally and geographically; the Tokyo journal *Jiji* commented that the 'feelings existing between the British and Japanese people are in perfect sympathy', adding, 'the existence of such cordiality and sympathy between two Courts and peoples is unprecedented in the annals of the world'.[6]

Up until this point, Britain had always shunned alliances on the grounds that any potential ally would gain far more from one than it could. But Britain was starting to feel the strain of ruling the waves, and the idea of having a friend in the Pacific, that was as safe from invasion as it was, and could help rein in Russia's ambitions, made a lot of sense.

Japan's potential as a powerful partner was realised when it won a stunning victory over Russia in 1905. Britain took no part in the fighting but gave vital assistance without which Japan would almost certainly have lost.[7] It was the first time a Western power had been defeated by an Asian one and the Russians kept coming back for more, refusing to accept that they could lose. Mitford was impressed not just by the victories themselves but by the way Japan had won them. He told *The Times* (having returned to being Japan's champion): 'The world stands amazed at the magnanimity of the Japanese', adding,

> After a war which from beginning to end has been an unbroken series of triumphs, by his noble act of renunciation the Emperor of Japan has achieved the crowning victory of all. He has added the olive branch to his wreath of laurels.[8]

Mitford did not realise that the victories had come at such a cost to Japan that it was not magnanimity but exhaustion that stopped them pushing home their advantage.

*

In spite of the warm feelings between Britain and Japan, Emperor Meiji was not at all keen on meeting the Mission. 'I can't stand receiving British envoys', he told the Imperial Household Minister, Tanaka Mitsuaki, 'Tell them not to come.' The shocked Tanaka replied:

> Prince Connaught will have already have left his country. Such an act would violate the trust that must prevail among allies in matters affecting them both. It is absolutely impossible. All Your Majesty can do now is to await the prince and receive him.[9]

Meiji's contemporary, Queen Victoria, would have completely understood his feelings, having a similar hatred of meeting foreign royalty. She wrote in 1867, that she was 'UTTERLY incapable (overwhelmed with work, and the responsibility of her arduous position ...) of entertaining any Royal personage as she would wish to do'.[10] Both Meiji and Victoria would relent, with very bad grace, and would be in a foul mood in the days leading up to the audience, lashing out at their staff for arranging it. However when they actually met the guests, they would behave with perfect politeness and friendliness.

The Prime Minister asked the Emperor to go to Yokohama to meet the Prince on his arrival there on 19 February, but Meiji refused, meeting him instead at Shimbashi station, the Tokyo terminal. Mitford, unaware of this exchange, marvelled at his doing that:

> [H]ere at Shimbashi ... there took place a ceremony which must have stirred to their profoundest depths the hearts of all the Japanese who witnessed it. Never before, since the first creation of Japan, was such a compliment paid as that which awaited Prince Arthur ... the Emperor had come in person to greet his guest. This august Sovereign ... as heir of a god-descended line of kings, had come, for the first time in all the history of the country, publicly to acclaim a foreign prince. It was an act of kingly hospitality most graciously conceived, most graciously carried out ... When the Emperor so warmly shook hands with the Prince it was a message to his people which said in unmistakable terms, "This is MY friend."[11]

Huge numbers gathered to cheer the Prince in the streets, Mitford saying that it felt like every person who lived in the city was there. For the Duke of Edinburgh, the people had silently kneeled in the streets, but this crowd was standing, 'both hands raised high above the head, with palms turned outward, feet parted, mouth wide open, eyes sparkling' shouting *banzai!* – hooray.[12] The difference in the response gives a good idea of how much Japan had changed in the intervening years – the people now had a feeling of being Japanese, rather than belonging to a domain, and they were able to express themselves, rather than remain in reverential silence when in the presence of their superiors. The country appeared to be as Mitford had described it in a talk given in 1904: the 'gayest, the sunniest, the brightest nation in the whole world'.[13]

The enthusiasm was real, a sign of how special ordinary people thought the visit was. There was a feeling of gratitude that a prince from such a great nation as Britain should have come all the way to their humble, insignificant country, in order to honour their Emperor. The *Yomiuri* newspaper wrote that it was 'incumbent upon us – the whole Japanese nation – to welcome our exalted guest with due deference and sincere enthusiasm worthy of the occasion'.[14]

Mitford was excited to be presented to the Emperor again. The Meiji he met in 1906, was very different from the sixteen-year-old that had greeted the Duke of Edinburgh in 1869. He now had a towering reputation; 'until a few short years ago' he had been 'as great a mystery even to his own people as ... [his] ancestors'. But now, Mitford thought, he was 'a Ruler whom all may see, and whom all revere ... [H]e has raised his country from the obscurity of Hermit Nation to the proud position which she now occupies among the great Powers of the world.'[15] Mitford reflected that 'the Emperor ... must be a strong man to have scattered to the winds all the trammels of tradition by which his ancestors had for so many generations been fettered'.[16] There was truth in this, but once Japan had decided it wanted to be considered the equal of the great European powers, it accepted that it had to largely follow their conventions.

Nevertheless, Meiji was determined that he would not cave in completely. When told that it was a violation of etiquette to wear any other decorations while receiving the Garter, he reluctantly removed the Order of the Chrysanthemum, Japan's highest order of chivalry, but kept another, the Paulownia Leaf, pinned to his chest. These orders could not begin to rival the Garter (founded in 1348) for antiquity, having been established in 1876 and 1888 respectively, but the Emperor nonetheless sent the message that they could sit beside the Garter and that it did not exceed them.

At the ceremony itself, the nervous Prince Arthur had to buckle the garter on the Emperor's leg, but unfortunately he pricked himself and got blood on the decoration.[17] He may have jumped when the band suddenly struck up with 'God Save the King' while he was in the middle of the operation. Mitford, keen to praise anything the Japanese did, described the effect of this as 'electric', lending 'a charm to the whole ceremony'.[18] The Emperor's Chamberlain, Hinonishi Sukehiro, recorded that fortunately, the Emperor took the spilling of blood in his stride, and later expressed admiration for the fact that the Prince had remained composed in spite of it. He adopted a good humoured air throughout the proceedings and on retiring to his private quarters, he took off the large black plumed hat with a white feather which Garter knights wore, with a laugh, as much as to say, 'What am I supposed to do with this thing?'[19]

The Emperor followed European etiquette by paying a return visit to the Prince and, Mitford tells us, expressed 'great admiration of the ceremonial and of the smoothness with which it had been conducted', which was generous in the circumstances.[20] He then produced a lacquer box which contained the ribbon and star of the Order of the Chrysanthemum and pinned it to the Prince's breast. This was the highest Japanese honour and only three men who were not members of the Japanese Imperial Family had received it, all Japan's most distinguished statesmen. This was the first time the Emperor had pinned the order on someone personally; before he had always simply handed over the box, another fact that Mitford got excited about: 'Never before, not even in the case of the Crown Prince, has His Majesty deigned to invest a recipient... [n]o man save Prince Arthur alone can boast that the Emperor put on the ribbon or fixed the star for him.'[21]

Then Mitford himself was taken into an inner room and presented with a lacquer box containing the Order of the Rising Sun – the second highest decoration in Japan. It was also given to two other members of the Mission which may have peeved Mitford slightly – with his efforts to spread knowledge about Japan, he had done far more to merit it. He also would have hoped to have received it directly from the Emperor. But it was still a magnificent addition to his collection of British honours and he was excited: 'It is something to have the privilege of wearing the same ribbon and star as a Tōgō [victor of the key naval battle in the Russo-Japanese War]'.[22]

At a state dinner that evening, Mitford noted a further departure towards European conventions, when the Emperor proposed a toast for the first time. He saw the day as one that had 'broken all records and established many precedents'.[23]

Mitford basked in his unique position: 'I was the only European present who could remember the old days of mystery and seclusion in which the Emperors of Japan had lived for upward of eight centuries.'[24] In fact, there were not many Japanese around who had been involved in the Meiji Restoration, early deaths, including several assassinations, having wiped out most of them. The most significant survivor other than the Emperor was the former Shogun, Yoshinobu. The Emperor had been generous to him, raising him to the rank of prince in 1902, and he had been pretty well rehabilitated. He still had his good looks and charm. To Mitford, he stated the obvious: 'Things have changed a good deal since you and I met in Osaka'. The fact that Mitford did not record anything else that passed between them probably means that they had found themselves without anything to say to each other. There may have been some embarrassment – Mitford would have been a reminder to Yoshinobu of his last desperate days as Shogun. Mitford ended up thinking that he was 'happier perhaps in his calm old age than ever he was in the stormy days of a glory which he himself felt to be an anachronism, false and untenable'.[25]

These events were followed by a series of receptions, performances, concerts and excursions. One of the most interesting was a *jujutsu* demonstration which involved a woman tossing a full-grown man over her head. Mitford was struck by the fact that girls were taught martial skills, with both sexes learning to march in perfect time. He defended the militarism he saw, ignoring the worries about where it would lead that he had expressed before:

> The spirit of Bushidō [the way of the warrior] is fostered and worked up to the highest pitch. First of all things duty. Duty to the Fatherland. Duty before life itself ... Some there may be who will sneer at this and call it jingoism, militarism. Let them sneer. This it is that builds up the strength of a nation and makes it rise above its fellows. In each man it breeds the determination to be himself at his best, – that such faculties as he possesses shall be so developed, so improved that, should his country want him, he can offer up, in sacrifice if so it must be, the highest capabilities of which he is the heir.[26]

Prince Arthur was spared the *nō* that had been inflicted on his uncle in 1869, but had a variety of other performances to sit through, including a display of *bugaku*. This form of dance was over a thousand years old, and had been performed exclusively at the Court, meaning that very few people had seen it. Like the *nō*, it was very slow and just as painful to watch for the uninitiated – Mitford tactfully described it as 'very solemn and semi-religious'.[27] It seems that even the Emperor had trouble with it, suddenly giving an order for it to stop after the first half.

On their last two days in the area around Tokyo, Prince Arthur went to Nikkō, famous for its lavishly decorated shrines and temples. Mitford wanted to go, having missed out on seeing it on his previous stay (Parkes had gone while he was stuck in Osaka) but had things to do in Tokyo and Yokohama. In his account of the Mission, Mitford sounds like he filled these days with plenty of activity, but if he did see Tomi and Omitsu this would have been when he could have done it.

Meiji saw the party off on the following morning and they would now spend another three weeks touring Japan. They were supposed to be moving around in a semi-private capacity, but were nevertheless rapturously greeted wherever they went. At every station they passed, troops were assembled and school children from all around came to see the Prince and presentations of flowers and gifts were made. When they visited Kagoshima in southern Kyushu, Mitford thought that a million people, many transported on special trains from around the island, lined the streets to greet them. Amazingly, the Governor and Mayor described the British bombardment of Kagoshima in 1863 as having been largely instrumental in bringing reform to Japan, which was a very positive spin on an event that had destroyed around five hundred houses in the city.

They also went to Kyoto, Mitford finding that it was 'full of memories, mostly sad, – but it is the sad memories that are the most abiding … It is a living link with the buried past, a past that was many centuries old when it vanished thirty-eight short years ago [when the capital moved to Edo].'[28] There is something affected about Mitford's nostalgia here. He had not spent much time in Kyoto and had not been particularly taken with it when he was there. Apart from the attack on the British delegation and the first meeting with the Emperor, it was not a city of many memories for him.

They were shown entertainments that were more fun for a young Prince than those they had to sit through in Tokyo – indeed, they were rather on the margins of what was considered seemly for someone of his rank. In Kyoto they watched geisha performing the celebrated Cherry Dance, specially done a month early, which, Mitford thought, was 'an exceptional compliment' to the Prince. Mitford reflected that in the West, dancing was an art which appeals to the senses, while in Japan, it appealed to the imagination. 'We can praise the beauty, the decorous grace, the poise of the neck … the dainty flutter of the fan; but behind all there is a magic, something hidden, something which we can see means so much to the enlightened, but as to which we remain perforce in the dark.'[29] The venues went to incredible lengths to please the Prince. At a theatre in Nagoya, a green carpet had been laid so that his eyes 'might be rested from looking at the brightness of the stage'.[30]

These performances were all part of a wonderful, but gruel-ling programme of public events and private entertainments that involved late nights and early morning starts. Mitford writes of having to go duck hunting in freezing rain: 'I got up, hoping against hope that a merciful telegram might arrive to say the hunt was put off.'[31] There had been a boar hunt scheduled on a day of similarly awful weather that involved a 5am start, but Prince Arthur decided he could not face it, missing it 'owing to slight indisposition' according to a newspaper report.[32]

When they finally left, after a month in the country, they were satisfied by how well the tour had gone, but were shattered. One newspaper commented that the Prince 'had but just escaped with his life from the hail of festivities, dinners and addresses with which he had been pelted by the hospitable subjects of the Mikado'.[33] That said, they had obviously enjoyed it, helped by the fact that they got along well among themselves. Mitford could have gone on and on about his experiences in 1860s Japan, but he seems to have been careful not to become a bore. A chatty letter from Arthur to Mitford after they returned ('Hoping to see you again soon') suggests that they had a relaxed relationship, although Mitford never forgot who he was addressing.[34]

Mitford's account of the Mission – a collection of the letters he wrote home while on it – was published very soon after his return. It was an unashamed celebration of the event which his great-grandson, Jonathan Guinness, described as 'unctuous to the point of caricature', although strangely, Mitford himself wrote was 'the piece of work that I like better than anything else that I have done'.[35] He certainly raved at length and in detail about the wel-come they received in it, but so did Miles Lampson, another mem-ber of the Mission ('Nothing could have surpassed the kindness, forethought, and care of our Japanese' hosts), which suggests that Mitford's account was essentially truthful.[36] Mitford was, however, critical of some of the changes he saw. When he revisited his old neighbourhood around Sengakuji, he was very disappointed, not-ing that it had been 'one of the prettiest spots in all the suburbs of the great city' and his house had been 'as dainty as Japanese art could make it. Now it has all gone to rack and ruin.' He added:

the whole suburb of Takanawa is altered, and not for the better. Abbots and monks have parted with much of their land for building purposes, so the temples which stood in groves sacred to the gods have been shorn of much of their glory. Nor do I see that the money so acquired has been devoted to the maintenance of the holy buildings; on the contrary, they seem to me to be shabbier and less well-cared-for than they were in the olden time. Perhaps there was less wealth and more piety in those days.[37]

However, the tone of the book is overwhelmingly upbeat, reflecting the extraordinarily enthusiastic response that greeted the Mission. Guinness's use of the word 'unctuous' implies that it was not sincere, but it probably was; it was the climactic moment of Mitford's life, when so many threads came together – his intimate knowledge of Japan, his instinctive understanding of courtly etiquette both there and in Britain, and his personal knowledge of many of the leading players on both sides. Above all, it must have been so satisfying to see the successful results of the revolution which he had been involved in, and have the part Britain played in it so lauded.

Unfortunately, it was the last great moment in his life, as deafness, money troubles and a terrible family tragedy closed in on him to darken his last years.

11

THE LEGACY

1906 –

ℰℴ

THE INHERITANCE MITFORD had received from Earl Redesdale was immense. As Satow put it, 'there was plenty of money there at the outset. But he never denied himself anything that took his fancy.'[1] If he was generous with himself, he was also generous to others. He built the imposing Redesdale Hall in the centre of Moreton-in-Marsh as a memorial to Earl Redesdale, a building that is still much in use there – if you want to play badminton, have a wedding reception, do TaeKwonDo or go ballroom dancing in the town, Redesdale Hall is the place to do it. He was also a generous landlord; one example of this was in 1891, his telling the poorer families on his estate that he would refund them any money they paid out for their children's education.

His money diminished to such an extent that in 1910 he had to leave Batsford and rent it out. Mitford's daughter-in-law Sydney maintained that this state of affairs was down to the simple fact that the cost of the house and garden improvements were more than he could afford, but Satow reports Mitford telling him he had been 'greatly robbed' and his great-grandson writes of a family story that he had been embezzled by a trusted employee, but that this was hushed up.[2]

He moved to a large house on the corner of Kensington Court and Kensington High Street in London. The loss of Batsford was devastating to him, but to ordinary eyes, the new place does not look too bad: a grand building overlooking Kensington Gardens, a stone's throw from Kensington Palace, which is now part of a luxury hotel.

The deafness cruelly crept up on him at the same time, curtailing his social life. He filled his days with writing, publishing his immense two-volume memoir, *Memories* in 1915. This was his most successful work since *Tales of Old Japan*; Edmund Gosse, always his most generous critic, told him, 'I firmly believe you have added a permanent work to English literature.'[3] However, the *Saturday Review*, which forty-five years earlier had accused him of faking his Japanese sermons, was still as hostile, writing sardonically that all his life he had been 'outrageously and unfairly happy' so it was

> only natural that in his old age he should allow his joyous memories to overflow in two bulky volumes without much sense of perspective, and evidently without any regard for his own or his readers' time.[4]

It seems like he followed Mark Twain's advice that with autobiography, you should forget about the dates and simply set things down as they come into your head. Reading the book feels very much like sitting with him in his living room, listening to him reminisce about his life, tolerating digressions because you know that soon there will be a well-told anecdote, an atmospheric description, or a pithy character sketch. But this casualness was surely intentional. Aristocrats like Mitford wanted it to look like they had not tried too hard at anything. He deliberately made the book read more like the life of someone who had drifted along enjoying serendipitous pieces of good fortune, than of the man who had carefully calculated his route to success that he really was.

It became one of the best-selling autobiographies of its day, probably because people were interested to read the stories it contained about famous people Mitford had known. It has some twenty-one pages of reminiscences about Benjamin Disraeli, for example, who was still an object of public fascination. But probably what interested people most was his extensive treatment of Edward VII. The late King's reputation was of public interest because in 1912, Sidney Lee had written a piece about him for the *Dictionary of National Biography* that portrayed him as a fun-loving man of limited intellect, who had contributed little to domestic or foreign affairs while king.[5] Mitford devoted twenty-six pages to refuting this picture, portraying him as hard working and conscientious, and making the bold claim that he had earned an 'influence such as no British monarch had ever before achieved'.[6] While ostensibly Mitford was defending the King, he also made sure that in the process, his readers realised just how highly-placed he was. To take one example of many, he quotes the letter telling him he had been elected Chairman of the Committee of the Marlborough Club: 'you were proposed for the office by His Majesty the King, seconded by His Royal Highness the Prince of Wales'.[7]

As a result of Mitford's efforts, he was seriously considered by the Royal Household to be Edward VII's official biographer. There were no worries that he would not be sympathetic and he was seen as a good enough writer. The thing that told against him was that he had only known the King socially, and did not know enough about his official work. In the end, Lee, who was a specialist biographer, was given the job, in spite of the unheroic picture he had painted of the King in the *Dictionary of National Biography*.

Memories also contains Mitford's considered account of his time in Japan. It seems amazing, especially given the success of *Tales of Old Japan*, that he waited forty-five years before publishing the full story of his time there. He explained that he felt that 'there was much that could hardly be written without indiscretion until a considerable time should have elapsed'.[8] It is hard to see what he said in 1915 that would have been unsayable in the 1870s, as he was supportive of the overthrow of the Shogun and the transfer of power to the Emperor and his ministers, a stance which would have been welcomed by official Japan at any time from 1868 onwards. But waiting to see how the situation panned out certainly made writing his account easier and it is significant that Satow waited even longer (until 1921) before publishing his version of those years.[9] By the time these accounts were written, the men who had led the Meiji Restoration were revered as the founding fathers of the new Japan, and both Satow and Mitford praised them and exaggerated the support Britain had given them.

As we have seen, Mitford smoothed out the story of his own relationship with Japan in the account, portraying himself as falling in love with the country pretty much from the start, while, in truth, he had blown hot and cold about it for the first two years. Nevertheless, his memoir stands the test of time and is still widely quoted in histories of the Meiji Restoration because it is frank and relatively unbiased, written by someone who saw the events at first hand.

More difficult for Mitford was writing about Germany in the memoir while the First World War was raging. He adored the country and its culture and he wrote lovingly about his experiences in Germany, and in particular, his feeling for Wagner: 'the one master who could stir the feelings ... the one man who could make his own art an article of faith in others'.[10] As for the war itself, Mitford viewed it in black and white terms, having no doubt that it had to be fought whatever the cost. Anything connected with matters of honour could not be compromised over. Britain's guarantee to Belgium had to be upheld and the fight had to been seen through to the end. As it dragged on, Mitford's attitude hardened; he wrote of the 'coarse-fibred soul of the German ... which seem[s] to urge him on to new cruelties and new crimes'.[11] He railed against the 'half measures' being employed: 'We must protect our women and children ... If Germany uses poison gas and liquid fire, so must we. If she drops bombs from airships upon innocent civilians, women, and children, we must follow suit.'[12]

All five of his sons joined up immediately, in spite of the fact that his second son, David, had lost a lung in the Boer War, and his fourth, Jack, had been married to the heiress to one of the biggest fortunes in Germany, Marie Anne von Friedlander-Fuld. The wedding, in Berlin in January 1914, had been a big social event, with talk of the Kaiser attending, but the marriage collapsed after only five months.

During the war, there were accusations that the aristocracy pulled strings to keep their sons out of danger, but this cannot be said of Mitford. His eldest, Clement, received the Distinguished Service Order (the second highest award for bravery, one below the Victoria Cross) from the King – to the 'rapturous exaltation' of his father.[13] This was during the first Battle of Ypres in October 1914, where he was badly wounded. He nevertheless returned to fight and on 15 May 1915, his family received the dreaded telegram: 'He died gallantly.'[14] Clement was buried in the Vlamertinghe Military Cemetery in Belgium and on his gravestone there is a quotation from *The Pilgrim's Progress* by John Bunyan: 'And so he passed over, and all the trumpets sounded on the other side.'[15] Mitford presented the set of wrought iron gates that still stand at the entrance to the cemetery. He dealt with his grief by holding it in, Gosse writing that he seemed 'to clench his teeth in defiance of the blow', determined not to be crushed by it.[16]

After Clement's death, he wanted to return to Batsford, and fortunately his tenant was happy to vacate it. It was an 'unspeakable joy' to be back in his own house again', but his days were empty.[17] He still received invitations; Cambridge University asked him to lecture on Russian history, impressed by his Russian chapters in *Memories*, but these were one-offs and his deafness prevented most social activities. Gosse suggested he fill his days by writing a series of essays on general subjects, but bound together by the themes of his wild garden of bamboos and the Buddha in his secret grove, as if he were talking to a friend. This conversational style suited Mitford and he took up the idea. His thoughts strayed back to Japan. Many visitors, he wrote, had called his garden a Japanese one, but Mitford explained that a Japanese garden outside Japan was impossible: 'We must not imitate them, for if we do, we shall merely parody them. Bamboos and stones and lanterns will not make a Japanese garden.'[18]

Mitford had a mish-mash of plants and objects in his garden: a large bronze statue of Buddha, which still stands there, facing east; palms from China; bamboos from the Himalayas and life-size bronze representations of Japanese deer, one of the strangest elements, something that would be alien to a Japanese garden, yet also odd in an English one. He quotes the Japanese proverb, 'Meeting is the beginning of parting' to justify his collection, explaining that those objects could soften the sorrow of missing people from his past. 'Is not that the chief sanity of the collector's madness?'[19]

Mitford was still fit and active for a man of almost eighty – Gosse described him as being more like nineteen: 'In a suit picturesquely marine, with his beautiful silver hair escaping from a jaunty yachting cap, he was the last expression of vivacity and gaiety.'[20] But in June 1916, it seems, simply from lying on some wet grass while fishing, he caught a feverish chill. He nonetheless insisted on going to London to attend various meetings ('nothing vexed … [him] more than not to keep a pledge', Gosse lamented) and while there he became seriously ill. He returned to Batsford and seemed not to be in any danger – he was, after all unusually healthy for his age. But he developed hepatitis and, gradually sinking, died peacefully on 17 August 1916.

The *Times* wrote the following day that Mitford had been 'one of the most picturesque and courtly figures' in the social life of the previous half-century.[21] His time in Japan had only been a little over three years of his life but more than half of the obituary was about his experience of and writings about that country. Nothing else Mitford did could compete with it.

*

Although Mitford's books are still read by those interested in Japan, he has pretty much been forgotten by the Japanese, while Ernest Satow is widely known there. This is fair. Satow spent a lot longer there and went on to become the British Minister in Tokyo. He also authored the most respected book by a Westerner on the Meiji Restoration, *A Diplomat in Japan*. Although there are some good descriptions in it, the book is rather hard work for anyone who does not want to know every detail. Mitford was more conscious of his reader and consequently a better writer than Satow, although he knew he was outside the top league. Edmund Gosse put it kindly: 'He retained, in spite of all the labour which he expended, a certain stiffness, an air of the amateur'.[22] His granddaughters, the 'Mitford sisters', achieved more enduring fame than he did, with four out of the six of them far outstripping him as authors. Indeed, outside the field of Japan studies, if he is remembered at all today, it is for having been their grandfather. They were the daughters of David who, because Clement had died without having any sons, succeeded to the title of Lord Redesdale on his father's death. David, the second son, was very much second-best in his father's mind. He was not considered bright enough to enter Eton and when he tried for a military career, failed to get into Sandhurst. But he lives on in the work of his daughters, his eccentricities providing wonderful material for them. He was Uncle Matthew in Nancy Mitford's novel *The Pursuit of Love* and his strange ways have been described in many other books by and about the Mitfords.

Two of the sisters, Diana and Unity, became prominent British Fascists in the 1930s. Their biographers, looking for the origins of their extreme views have worked their way back to A.B. Mitford, who we must now call Bertie again to avoid confusing him with his relations. In a 2013 biography of Unity, he is described as 'a rank fascist', with the added comment that it was a quality that 'most of the Mitfords would inherit in various degrees'.[23]

Diana Mitford could have been a poster girl for Aryan beauty – Winston Churchill described her as 'Dina-mite', and Evelyn Waugh wrote that her beauty 'ran through the room like a peal of bells'.[24] In 1936, she married the leader of the British Fascist party, Oswald Mosley, in Germany. The only guests at their wedding, held in Goebbels' dining room, were Hitler and Goebbels, with Unity as a witness. The glory days ended when war broke out, and she and Mosley were interned in 1940. Churchill saw to it that they could stay together, making Mosley the only male inmate in Holloway Prison – they lived in a house in the grounds. (They did not suffer much: Diana wrote that the best strawberries she ever tasted were those she grew in the prison garden.) When Mosley fell ill in 1943, they were transferred to house arrest, in spite of being entirely unrepentant. Diana, who lived to 2003, never recanted on her affection for Hitler.

Unity went one stage further and fell in love with the *Führer*. Less beautiful than Diana, but more fanatical and even blonder, Unity effectively stalked Hitler. In spite of his being Chancellor, he would go to cafes in a predictable way and she spent ten months sitting in them until he finally invited her to his table. They soon became intimate, Unity being to him 'a perfect specimen of Aryan womanhood'.[25]

Hitler's attraction to Unity was based on more than her looks. Bertie had unwittingly created a link between them, even though he had died when she was only two. He had asked that she be given the middle name Valkyrie, a strange choice at any time, but especially four days after Britain had declared war on Germany in 1914. Bertie pointed out that the Valkyrie were Scandinavian, not German, war maidens, but the choice was a reflection of his love of the music of the quintessential German composer, Richard Wagner. The name Valkyrie became important because when Hitler found out about it, it immediately drew him to her – he thought that it made Unity into a talisman of good fortune for him. Eva Braun, Hitler's jealous mistress, thought it highly appropriate, writing that her 'replacement' had a Valkyrie's looks and legs.[26] It took a suicide attempt by Eva to wrest back the attention of the *Führer* from her English rival.

Hitler knew of and admired Bertie because in 1909, Bertie had written a long introduction to a book that had greatly inspired him, *The Foundations of the Nineteenth Century*. When he was showing Diana and Unity the grave of Wagner, Hitler told them it was an honour to be visiting it with the great Lord Redesdale's granddaughters.[27] The book was by Houston Stewart Chamberlain, a British writer who lived in Germany and wrote in German. It is obvious what attracted Hitler to it: 'Physically and mentally', the Aryans (actually all the European races, but predominantly the Germanic ones) were 'pre-eminent among all peoples', and 'for that reason they are by right ... the lords of the world.'[28] As for the Jews, they were

> everlastingly alien ... indissolubly bound to an alien law that is hostile to all other peoples – this alien people has become precisely in

the course of the nineteenth century a disproportionately important and in many spheres actually dominant constituent of our life
... The Indo-European ... opened the gates in friendship: the Jew
rushed in like an enemy, stormed all positions and planted the flag
of his, to us, alien nature.[29]

To be fair to Chamberlain, he adds that to revile the Jews would
be 'as ignoble as it is unworthy and senseless'.[30] In his introduction, Bertie agrees with Chamberlain's criticisms of the Jewish
religion, writing of the 'dreary forebodings of the Old Testament,
where all is vanity, life is a shadow, we wither like grass', but
he is admiring of the Jewish people: 'In all countries and ages
the Jew has been a masterful man', adding that he had 'wonderful self-confidence ... [and] toughness of character, which could
overcome every difficulty, and triumph over the hatred of other
races'.[31] He does skate over Chamberlain's anti-Semitism here,
but in an article five years later, he admitted it, and completely
detached himself from it by reinforcing his admiration of the
Jewish race in Britain at least, writing of their 'many charities,
the single-hearted generosity of their nature, their true nobility of character'.[32] If Hitler saw Bertie as some kind of fellow-
traveller, he was mistaken; had Bertie lived long enough to hear
Unity's thoughts – once when shooting at targets she said, 'I'm
practising to kill Jews' – he would have been horrified.[33]

Because of his link to Hitler, most attention has been paid to
Chamberlain's attacks on Jews, but his attitude towards other
non-Christians was worse. They had

> no history; their story is but a chronicle on the one hand of ruling
> houses, butcheries and the like, and on the other, represents the dull,
> humble, almost bestially happy life of millions that sink in the night
> of time without leaving a trace.[34]

In his introduction Bertie, unbelievably, picks out this particular
passage to quote approvingly. He seems to be agreeing that the
history and culture of the Japanese (along with the other non-
Christian races he had been interested in) was devoid of meaning. We are left to wonder why, if he had thought that, had he

devoted so much energy to sympathetically introducing Japan to the West? As we know, Bertie bounced between extremes and his admiration for Chamberlain at this point was unqualified:

> To few men has been given in so bountiful a measure the power of seeing, of sifting the true from the false, the essential from the insignificant … the wide horizon of Chamberlain's outlook furnishes him with standards of comparison which are denied to those of shorter sight: his peculiar and cosmopolitan education, his long researches in natural history, his sympathy and intimate relations with all that has been noblest in the world of art … point to him as the one man above all others worthy to tell the further tale of a culture of which he has so well portrayed the nonage [period of immaturity] and which is still struggling heavenward.[35]

However, Bertie repented of his enthusiasm for Chamberlain after he read an article of his written in 1915 which proclaimed that England was 'rotten unto its very marrow' and that the English could 'be saved only be a wise, strong, and victorious Germany'.[36] 'I am heartily ashamed of having been connected with him', Mitford wrote. 'How could one suspect such treachery from a man belonging to a family of brave and distinguished soldiers and sailors?'[37]

*

How, then, to link Mitford's life together and – more important for the purposes of this book – link it back to Japan? It is not easy. Gosse thought that few had done so much 'in so many directions as he', generously adding, 'or, aiming widely, failed in so few'.[38]

Certain traits never changed. He remained curious and optimistic throughout his life. He was always 'best foot forward' but his sense of humour and lack of religious conviction stopped him becoming a classic Victorian self-sacrificing, heroic achiever in the David Livingstone or General Gordon mould – he could not take himself that seriously. At the same time, he had some absolute beliefs; the rough upper-class education he received at Eton had instilled in him the importance of honour which, powerfully reinforced by his experiences in Japan, became the foundation of his world view. It enabled him to fearlessly face down groups of samurai warriors on his own, but also meant that he had to encourage his sons to go to the trenches. In this respect he was of his time – as he was in his reluctance to show any emotion. He managed to write nearly eight hundred pages of memoir without betraying any of his inner feelings – he simply ignored unpleasant things like his parents' divorce or Clement's death. He is more frank about Japan in his letters to his father, but gave no hint even in them that he had fathered a child there. In biography we have to base our accounts on the words that are left to us. The deepest feelings of some subjects are just unknowable.

But for the purposes of this book, this does not matter much, because we are interested in him in relation to Japan. In his reading of this country, he was way ahead of his time, judging its people by their own set of values rather than his own. At the same time, he had a paternalism which was very Victorian – he felt a responsibility to those beneath him, which he translated into a responsibility towards Japan to depict it in a fair and generous way. He was acutely conscious of his class, which again was typical of his age, but he was genuinely friendly to anybody he met, curious about their lives and wanting to record what he saw.

What makes him such an endearing recorder of events is that it was the people involved in them that interested him, enabling him to bring to life the Japan of the 1860s, a time that is little known about outside Japan. For him a story about, say, a poor farmer or a low-caste woman could illuminate aspects of a culture far better than a more detached description, however penetrating. In his writing he sought not just to appeal to his reader's intellects, but to also touch their hearts. He tried to turn the Japanese he described into people who could almost be his readers' next-door neighbours. The Japan that he wrote about was real and alive. Better than anyone else, he was able to put into human terms the events that saw Japan transformed from a feudal pre-industrial nation into one that could take on the world. It is one of the world's most remarkable stories and in Mitford it found its storyteller.

NOTES

སྐ

Preface

[1] *Saturday Review* (London), 14 August 1869.
[2] *Saturday Review*, 11 March 1871.
[3] Lord Redesdale, *Memories*, Vol. I (London: Hutchinson, 1915), 389.

Chapter 1: Yokohama

[1] A.B. Mitford to H.R. Mitford, 27 June 1867.
[2] Redesdale, *Memories*, vol. I, 374. To be precise the company was the P&O.S.N.C. – the Peninsular and Oriental Steam Navigation Company.
[3] A.B. Mitford to H.R. Mitford, 8 September 1866.
[4] Ibid., 30 March 1867.
[5] A.B. Freeman-Mitford, *The Attaché at Peking* (London: Macmillan, 1900), 95.
[6] Redesdale, *Memories*, vol. I, 353.
[7] A.B. Mitford to H.R. Mitford, 17 August 1866. The date Mitford wrote on this letter is incorrect – it was written very soon after his arrival in Japan, so sometime after 3 October 1866.
[8] Ibid., 24 August 1866.
[9] It looks from *Memories* as if the position in Russia was a more senior second secretary post: 'I agreed to make an exchange for six months with Mr. Locock, the second secretary of Embassy at St. Petersburg' (Redesdale, *Memories*, vol. I, 204), but when speaking to a House of Commons committee, Mitford said that he was third secretary there. (Select Committee on Diplomatic and Consular Services, *Parliamentary Papers* 1870, 382, VII, 299.) Incidentally, the diplomatic service and the Foreign Office were distinct. So, Mitford transferred from the Foreign Office to the diplomatic service when he went to Russia, returning to the Foreign Office when he went back to London. He then re-entered the diplomatic service when he went to China.
[10] Redesdale, *Memories*, vol. I, 374.
[11] Hugh Cortazzi, 'The First British Legation in Japan', *Collected Writings of Sir Hugh Cortazzi* (Richmond, Surrey: Japan Library, 2000), 218.
[12] F.G. Notehelfer (ed.), *Japan Through American Eyes: The Journal of Francis Hall, Kanagawa and Yokohama, 1859–1866* (Princeton: Princeton University Press, 1992), 514.
[13] Ibid., 515.

14   Ernest Satow, *A Diplomat in Japan* (Tokyo: Oxford University Press, 1968), 24.
15   Redesdale, *Memories*, vol. I, 374.
16   Ibid.
17   A.B. Mitford to H.R. Mitford, 14 December 1866; Ibid., 17 August 1866.
18   Ibid., 30 March 1867.
19   Redesdale, *Memories*, vol. I, 375.
20   The figure of £40 million was given by the First Lord of the Admiralty, Henry Lowry-Corry, in Parliament, *Hansard*, 11 May 1868, CXCII, col. 43. To be exact, China accounted for 4.8% of British exports and 3.2% of British imports in 1870. Janet Hunter and S. Sugiyama, *The History of Anglo-Japanese Relations, 1600–2000* (Basingstoke: Palgrave Macmillan, 2002), vol. IV, 15.
21   Yokohama-shi (ed.), *Yokohama-shi Shi*, vol. II (Yokohama: Yurindo, 1959), 570.
22   A.B. Mitford to H.R. Mitford, 28 January 1868.
23   Redesdale, *Memories*, vol. I, 376.
24   Ibid.
25   Satow, *A Diplomat in Japan*, 141.
26   Hugh Cortazzi, *Dr. Willis in Japan, 1862–1877*, (London: Athlone, 1985), 123.
27   Sanjō Sanetomi to Lord Clarendon, undated but probably sent in February 1871. FO46/142.
28   Harold Williams, *Shades of the Past: Indiscreet tales of Japan* (Rutland, Vermont: Tuttle, 1959), 220.
29   Stanley Lane-Poole, *The Life of Sir Harry Parkes*, vol. I (London: Macmillan, 1894), 467–468.
30   A.B. Mitford to H.R. Mitford, 15 November 1866.
31   Ibid., 31 October 1866.
32   Redesdale, *Further Memories* (London: Hutchinson, 1917), xvii.
33   Satow, *A Diplomat in Japan*, 141–142.
34   *Saturday Review*, 11 March 1871.
35   Select Committee on Diplomatic and Consular Services, *Parliamentary Papers* 1870, 382, VII, 307.
36   Redesdale, *Memories*, vol. I, 373.
37   A.B. Mitford to H.R. Mitford, 15 November 1866.
38   Ibid., 24 December 1866.
39   Ibid., 23 April 1867.
40   Isabella L. Bird, *Unbeaten Tracks in Japan: An Account of Travels in the Interior Including Visits to the Aborigines of Yezo and the Shrines of Nikkô and Isé* (London: Murray, 1880), 19.
41   Admittedly, this is open to debate. See Susan Hanley, *Everyday Things in Premodern Japan: The Hidden Legacy of Material Culture* (Berkeley: University of California Press, 1997) for an extensive discussion of the traditional Japanese diet and how healthy it was.
42   Gail Honda, 'Differential Structure, Differential Health: Industrialization in Japan, 1868–1940' in *Health and Welfare during Industrialization*, eds.

Richard H. Steckel and Roderick Floud (Chicago: University of Chicago Press, 1997), 258. The Japanese themselves decided that they should consume dairy products and meat so as to become bigger; the Emperor led the way by starting to eat meat in 1872.

43   Redesdale, *Memories*, vol. I, 383.
44   A.B. Mitford, 'A Ride Through Yedo', *Fortnightly Review* XLI (1 May 1870), 514.
45   Satow, *A Diplomat in Japan*, 210.
46   Draft note to Parkes, No.83, 9 July 1869. FO46/105/13.
47   A.B. Mitford to H.R. Mitford, 15 November 1866.
48   Ibid., 20 April 1868.
49   Hunter and Sugiyama, *The History of Anglo-Japanese Relations, 1600–2000* (Basingstoke: Palgrave Macmillan, 2002), vol. IV, 11.
50   F.G. Notehelfer (ed.), *Japan Through American Eyes*, 81.
51   A.B. Mitford, *Tales of Old Japan* (Ware: Wordsworth, 2000), 55.
52   A.B. Mitford to H.R. Mitford, 31 October 1866.
53   Edward Barrington de Fonblanque, *Niphon and Pe-che-li; or, Two Years in Japan and Northern China* (London: Saunders, Otley, 1863), 135.
54   Harold Williams, *Shades of the Past: Indiscreet tales of Japan* (Rutland, Vermont: Tuttle, 1959), 216.
55   Shibusawa Keizō, *Japanese Life and Culture in the Meiji Era*, trans. Charles S. Terry (Tokyo: Ōbunsha, 1958), 159.
56   A.B. Mitford, *Tales of Old Japan*, 54.
57   Edward Barrington de Fonblanque, *Niphon and Pe-che-li*, 44.
58   Laura Nenzi, *Excursions in Identity: Travel and the Intersection of Place, Gender, and Status in Edo Japan* (Honolulu: University of Hawaii Press, 2008), 1. A later writer, Kuki Shūzō, argued that the Edo ideal of style (*iki*) had a threefold structure: coquetry (*bitai*), pride (*ikiji*) and resignation (*akirame*).
59   Harold Williams, *Shades of the Past*, 217.
60   A.B. Mitford, *Tales of Old Japan*, 43.
61   Charlotte Mosley (ed), *The Mitfords: Letters between Six Sisters* (London: Fourth Estate, 2007), 682. I asked Mrs Mosley if I could see it, but was told that it had been leant to another researcher and had never been returned.
62   A.B. Mitford, *Tales of Old Japan*, 53.
63   Henry Norman, *The Real Japan: Studies of Contemporary Japanese Manners, Morals, Administration, and Politics* (London: T. Fisher Unwin, 1908), 293–294.
64   A.B. Mitford, *Tales of Old Japan*, 54.
65   Ibid., 58.
66   Norman, *The Real Japan*, 280.
67   A.B. Mitford, *Tales of Old Japan*, 58.
68   Ibid.
69   A.B. Mitford to H.R. Mitford, 31 October 1866.
70   Ibid.
71   Ibid., 24 December 1864.

[72] Lord Redesdale, *A Tragedy in Stone and other papers* (London: John Lane, 1913), 155–156.

[73] A.B. Mitford to H.R. Mitford, 28 January 1868.

[74] Cortazzi, *Dr. Willis in Japan, 1862–1877*, 33–4.

[75] A.B. Mitford to H.R. Mitford, 1 December 1866.

[76] Ibid. Mitford ended up claiming £715 in losses – far more than any of his colleagues (Satow claimed £440).

[77] Ibid.

[78] Ibid.

[79] Ibid., 26 January 1868.

[80] Ibid., 30 November 1867.

[81] Ibid., 24 December 1866.

[82] Ibid.

[83] Ibid.

[84] Ibid., 30 March 1867.

[85] Ibid., 14 December 1866.

[86] The dollars were Mexican dollars, the trading currency that had been used in east and southeast Asia since the 1500s.

[87] A.B. Mitford to H.R. Mitford, 26 August 1867.

[88] Ibid., 24 December 1866.

[89] Ibid., 26 January 1868.

[90] Ibid., 14 December 1866.

[91] Ibid., 15 November 1866.

[92] Ibid., 24 December 1866.

[93] Ibid.

[94] Ibid.

[95] It was a bank, called the Yokohama Shōkin Ginkō (横浜正金銀行), and is now the Kanagawa Prefectural Museum of Cultural History.

[96] A.B. Mitford to H.R. Mitford, 24 December 1866.

[97] Ibid., 24 December 1866.

[98] Redesdale, *A Tragedy in Stone*, 266.

Chapter 2: Edo

[1] It is known as the Great Ansei Earthquake.

[2] It is impossible to establish how many people in Edo were killed in the epidemics – estimates vary between 30,000 and 280,000 (in a population of around one million). For a considered assessment, see Ann Bowman Jannetta, *Epidemics and Mortality in Early Modern Japan* (Princeton: Princeton University Press, 1987), 170.

[3] A.B. Mitford to H.R. Mitford, 31 October 1866.

[4] A.B. Freeman-Mitford, *The Attaché at Peking*, 59.

[5] Edward Seidensticker, *Low City, High City* (New York: Knopf, 1983), 34.

[6] A.B. Mitford, 'A Ride Through Yedo'; *Fortnightly Review*, 7/41 (May 1870): 514.

[7] A.B. Mitford to H.R. Mitford, 31 October 1866.

8   A.B. Mitford, *Tales of Old Japan*, 42.
9   'Long houses' is a literal translation of the Japanese word for them, '*nagaya*'.
10   A.B. Mitford to H.R. Mitford, 3 April 1868.
11   Hugh Cortazzi (ed.), *Mitford's Japan: The Memoirs and Recollections, 1866–1906, of Algernon Bertram Mitford, the first Lord Redesdale* (London: Athlone, 1985), 15.
12   A.B. Mitford, 'A Ride Through Yedo'; *Fortnightly Review*, 7/41 (May 1870): 517–518.
13   Satow, *A Diplomat in Japan*, 53.
14   Parkes to Hammond, 4 December 1869, FO391/15.
15   A.B. Mitford, *Tales of Old Japan*, 23.
16   A.B. Mitford, *Tales of Old Japan*, 104.
17   Ibid., 101.
18   Ibid., 102.
19   A.B. Mitford to H.R. Mitford, 30 November 1867.
20   Ibid., 22 April 1867.
21   Redesdale, *A Tragedy in Stone and other papers*, 165.
22   Fukuzawa Yukichi, *The Autobiography of Fukuzawa Yukichi*, trans. Eiichi Kiyooka (Lanham: Madison, 1992), 145. Fukuzawa is writing about the crisis triggered by the murder of Charles Richardson in 1862.
23   A.B. Mitford to H.R. Mitford, 1 October 1867.
24   Ibid., 16 March 1868.
25   Ibid., undated.
26   A.B. Mitford to H.R. Mitford, 31 January 1867.
27   Cortazzi, 'The First British Legation in Japan', *Collected Writings of Sir Hugh Cortazzi*, 214.
28   A.B. Mitford to H.R. Mitford, 24 December 1866.
29   A.B. Mitford, *Tales of Old Japan*, 22.
30   Henry D. Smith II, 'The Capacity of Chūshingura', *Monumenta Nipponica* 58/1 (Spring 2003): 1.
31   Kira Kōzukenosuke is the standard reading of the name – Kōtsuke no Suke is being used because this is what Mitford called him.
32   A.B. Mitford, *Tales of Old Japan*, 36.
33   Ibid., 29.
34   Quoted in Henry D. Smith II, 'Rethinking the Story of the 47 Ronin: Chūshingura in the 1980s'. http://www.columbia.edu/~hds2/47ronin.htm.
35   A.B. Mitford, *Tales of Old Japan*, 38.
36   Ibid., 40.
37   Redesdale, *Memories*, vol. I, 384.
38   Ibid.
39   A.B. Mitford to H.R. Mitford, 24 December 1866.
40   Parkes to Hammond, 1 December 1866, FO391/14.
41   Redesdale, *Memories*, vol. I, 384.
42   Ibid.
43   A.B. Mitford to H.R. Mitford, 24 December 1866.
44   Ibid.

[45]   Redesdale, *Memories*, vol. I, 383.
[46]   Ibid., 384–385. Mitford called it Monriu-in and Satow, Monriō-In.
[47]   A.B. Mitford to H.R. Mitford, 30 March 1867.
[48]   Bernard M. Allen, *The Rt. Hon. Sir Ernest Satow G.C.M.G.* (London: Kegan Paul, 1933), 49.
[49]   Ibid.
[50]   Satow, *A Diplomat in Japan*, 196.
[51]   Parkes to Hammond, 19 July 1866, FO391/14.
[52]   Mark Ravina, *The Last Samurai: The Life and Battles of Saigo Takamori* (Hoboken: Wiley, 2004), 230.
[53]   Redesdale, *Memories*, vol. I, 385.
[54]   Satow, *A Diplomat in Japan*, 196.
[55]   Select Committee on Diplomatic and Consular Services, *Parliamentary Papers* 1870, 382, VII, 303.
[56]   A.B. Mitford to H.R. Mitford, 29 May 1867.
[57]   A.B. Mitford to H.R. Mitford, 12 June 1867.

Chapter 3: The Shogun

[1]   Emperor Kōmei to Shogun Iemochi, 28 February 1864, W.G. Beasley, trans. & ed., *Select Documents on Japanese Foreign Policy, 1853–1868* (London: Oxford University Press, 1955), 264. The foreign powers represented in Japan at this time were Britain, France, the USA, the Netherlands and Prussia. In addition, Russia had a consulate in Hakodate.
[2]   A.B. Mitford to H.R. Mitford, 11 December 1868.
[3]   Redesdale, *A Tragedy in Stone*, 166.
[4]   A.B. Mitford to H.R. Mitford, 31 October 1866.
[5]   This was said to Léon Roches at a meeting in April 1867, John McMaster, *Sabotaging the Shogun: Western Diplomats Open Japan, 1859–69* (New York: Vantage, 1992), 153.
[6]   Tokugawa Yoshinobu to the Imperial Court, 9 April 1867, W.G. Beasley, trans. and ed., *Select Documents on Japanese Foreign Policy*, 309.
[7]   Parkes to Hammond, 1 February 1867, FO391/14.
[8]   Satow, *A Diplomat in Japan*, 186. In *Emperor of Japan*, Donald Keene examines the evidence for and against the idea that Kōmei was poisoned but in the end, he does not offer an opinion as to what happened (Donald Keene, *Emperor of Japan: Meiji and His World, 1852–1912*; New York: Columbia University Press, 2002, 96–97).
[9]   A.B. Mitford to H.R. Mitford, 30 March 1867.
[10]   Parkes to Captain Courtenay, 6 February 1867, FO46/78.
[11]   Memorandum of Instructions for Mr. Mitford, Signed, Harry S. Parkes, Yedo, 6 February 1867, FO46/78.
[12]   Parkes to Captain Courtenay, 6 February 1867, FO46/78.
[13]   To be precise they landed at Hyōgo – Kobe was the name of the tiny village near it that was chosen as the site for the foreign settlement. As the whole place became known as Kobe, for the convenience of readers it is called by that name

throughout, although Mitford and his colleagues more often referred to it as Hyōgo (spelling it Hiogo).

14 Mitford to Parkes, 26 February 1867, FO46/78.
15 Satow, *A Diplomat in Japan*, 186.
16 Mitford to Parkes, 26 February 1867, FO46/78.
17 A.B. Mitford to H.R. Mitford, 22 April 1867.
18 Mitford to Parkes, 26 February 1867, FO46/78.
19 Ibid.
20 A.B. Mitford to H.R. Mitford, 24 December 1866.
21 Redesdale, *The Garter Mission to Japan*, (London: Macmillan, 1906), 219.
22 Mitford to Parkes, 26 February 1867, FO46/78.
23 Ibid.
24 Ibid.
25 Satow, *A Diplomat in Japan*, 200.
26 Mitford to Parkes, 10 February 1867, FO46/78.
27 A.B. Mitford to H.R. Mitford, 3 April 1868.
28 Parkes to Lord Stanley, 14 February 1867, FO46/78.
29 Mitford to Parkes, 26 February 1867, FO46/78.
30 Redesdale, *Memories* vol. I, 377.
31 Ibid., 377–378.
32 Ibid., 378.
33 John McMaster, *Sabotaging the Shogun*, 153.
34 This building no longer exists, having been destroyed in the mayhem of the 1871 Commune – it used to close off the Louvre Courtyard, where the glass pyramid now stands.
35 Redesdale, *Memories* vol. I, 32.
36 Ibid., 34.
37 Mitford to Parkes, 12 July 1868, Cambridge University Library, MS Parkes 1/F25.
38 Redesdale, *Memories* vol. I, 377.
39 Roches tells the story in full in his memoirs, *Trente-Deux Ans à travers l'Islam (1832–1864)*, 2 vols (Paris: Firmin-Didot, 1884–1887). A summary in English may be found in John-Pierre Lehmann, 'Léon Roches – Diplomat Extraordinary in the Bakumatsu Era: An Assessment of His Personality and Policy', *Modern Asian Studies*, 14/ 2 (1980), 275–276.
40 John-Pierre Lehmann, 'Léon Roches', *Modern Asian Studies*, 14/ 2 (1980), 276.
41 Redesdale, *Memories* vol. I, 378.
42 A.B. Mitford to H.R. Mitford, 1 March 1867.
43 Ibid.
44 Parkes to Stanley, 28 February 1867, FO46/78.
45 Redesdale, *Memories*, vol. I, 389.
46 A.B. Mitford to H.R. Mitford, 6 May 1867.
47 Redesdale, *Memories*, vol. I, 390.
48 A.B. Mitford to H.R. Mitford, 6 May 1867.
49 Redesdale, *Memories*, vol. I, 392.

50   Ibid., 393.
51   Memorandum sent to Mitford by Matsuno Magohachiro and Takenouchi? no
      Kami, 16 February 1867, FO46/78.
52   A.B. Mitford to H.R. Mitford, 6 May 1867.
53   Redesdale, *Memories*, vol. I, 394.
54   A.B. Mitford to H.R. Mitford, 6 May 1867.
55   Ibid., 29 December 1868.
56   Ibid., 21 August 1868.
57   Ibid., 14 September 1867.
58   Ibid., 26 August 1867.
59   Ibid., 15 January 1869.
60   Ibid., 22 July 1867.
61   Ibid.,? August 1866. In fact, Emperor Chenghua reigned from 1464 to 1487.
62   Redesdale, *Memories*, vol. I, 395.
63   Parkes to Hammond, 6 May 1867, F.O. 391/14.
64   Redesdale, *Memories*, vol. I, 394.
65   A.B. Mitford to H.R. Mitford, 6 May 1867.
66   Ibid.
67   Ibid.
68   Redesdale, *Memories*, vol. I, 396.
69   Satow, *A Diplomat in Japan*, 200–201.
70   Ibid., 201.
71   Ibid., 202.
72   A.B. Mitford to H.R. Mitford, 6 May 1867.
73   Ibid., 22 April 1867.
74   Parkes to Hammond, 27 June 1867, FO 391/14; Parkes to Hammond,
      14 June 1867, FO 391/14.
75   A.B. Mitford to H.R. Mitford, 30 March 1867.
76   Ibid., 13 July 1867.
77   Ibid.
78   Ibid., 30 November 1867.
79   Redesdale, *Memories*, vol. I, 396.

Chapter 4: An Adventurous Journey

1   Cortazzi, *Dr. Willis in Japan*, 1862–1877, 68.
2   A.B. Mitford to H.R. Mitford, 13 July 1867; A.B. Mitford to H.R. Mitford,
     27 June 1867.
3   Redesdale, *Memories*, vol. II, 397.
4   These comments were made during a visit two years earlier. Entry for 2
     October 1865. Robert Morton & Ian Ruxton eds., *The Diaries of Sir Ernest
     Mason Satow, 1861–1869* (Kyoto: Eureka, 2013), 134.
5   Redesdale, *Memories*, vol. I, 208.
6   Ibid.
7   Ibid., 210.
8   Satow, *A Diplomat in Japan*, 233.

9 Redesdale, *Memories*, vol. I, 1.
10 Ibid., 26.
11 Alan Hager (ed.), *Encyclopedia of British Writers* (New York: Book Builders, 2003), 170.
12 Redesdale, *Memories*, vol. I, 30.
13 Ibid., 33.
14 Ibid., 30.
15 The *Times* (London), 22 February 1842.
16 Redesdale, *Memories*, vol. I, 25
17 A.B. Mitford to H.R. Mitford, 14 October 1867.
18 It is now possible to drive about half-way up the mountain and most people start from there.
19 Lane-Poole, *The Life of Sir Harry Parkes*, vol. I, 198.
20 Cortazzi, *Dr. Willis in Japan*, 80.
21 Frederick Victor Dickins and Stanley Lane-Poole, *The Life of Sir Harry Parkes*, vol. II (London: Macmillan, 1894), 287.
22 Andrew Roberts, *Salisbury, Victorian Titan* (London: Phoenix, 1999), 10.
23 Christopher Hollis, *Eton: A History* (London: Hollis & Carter, 1960), 233.
24 Redesdale, *Memories*, vol. I, 52.
25 Ibid., 104.
26 F.E. Durnford to H.R. Mitford, 20 July 1852, Gloucestershire County Archives, D2002/4/.
27 Redesdale, *Memories*, vol. I, 94.
28 Ibid.
29 Satow, *A Diplomat in Japan*, 236.
30 Redesdale, *Memories*, vol. II, 398.
31 Ibid., 411.
32 Ibid., 398.
33 Ibid., 399.
34 Ibid., 398–399.
35 Entry for 6 August 1867. Morton &Ruxton eds., *The Diaries of Sir Ernest Mason Satow*, 223.
36 Redesdale, *Memories*, vol. II, 399.
37 Entry for 3 June 1867. Morton &Ruxton eds., *The Diaries of Sir Ernest Mason Satow*, 217.
38 Redesdale, *Memories*, vol. II, 402.
39 Ibid., 400. The quotation is from Shakespeare's *Othello*.
40 Bird, *Unbeaten Tracks in Japan*, 85.
41 A.B. Mitford, 'Wanderings in Japan – II', *Cornhill Magazine* 25/47 (March 1872), 319.
42 Satow, *A Diplomat in Japan*, 241.
43 Redesdale, *Memories*, vol. II, 402.
44 Ibid., 405.
45 A.B. Mitford to H.R. Mitford, 26 August 1867.
46 Ibid.
47 Ibid., 1 October 1867. 'Unter den Linden' literally means 'under the linden trees' and is the name of the best-known street in Berlin.

Chapter 5: The Birth of the New Japan

1   Letter from W.S. Gilbert to the *Morning Leader*, reported in the *Gloucester Citizen*, 2 May 1907.
2   Henry Coke, *Tracks of a Rolling Stone* (London: Smith, Elder & Co., 1905), 292.
3   A.B. Mitford to H.R. Mitford, 14 September 1867.
4   Ibid., 29 October 1867.
5   Parkes to Hammond, 28 November 1867, FO 391/14.
6   A.B. Mitford to H.R. Mitford, 29 October 1867.
7   Ibid., 6 December 1867.
8   W.G. Beasley, *The Meiji Restoration* (Stanford: Stanford University Press, 1972), 293.
9   Redesdale, *Memories*, vol. II, 414.
10   A.B. Mitford to H.R. Mitford, 29 December 1867.
11   Redesdale, *Memories*, vol. II, 414.
12   A.B. Mitford to H.R. Mitford, 23 April 1867.
13   Mitford to Parkes, 6 December 1867, ed. Kenneth Bourne & D. Cameron Watt, part 1, series E, ed. Ian Nish, *British Documents on Foreign Affairs*, vol. I ([Frederick, MD?]: University Publications of America, 1989), 105.
14   A.B. Mitford to H.R. Mitford, 6 December 1867.
15   Ibid., 24 December 1866.
16   Ibid., 6 December 1867.
17   Parkes to Hammond, 16 December 1867, FO 391/14.
18   Satow, *A Diplomat in Japan*, 285.
19   Redesdale, *Memories*, vol. II, 416.
20   A.B. Mitford to H.R. Mitford, 29 December 1867.
21   Satow, *A Diplomat in Japan*, 290.
22   Ibid., 286.
23   A.B. Mitford to H.R. Mitford, 4 July 1868.
24   Ibid., 4 January 1868.
25   Redesdale, *Memories*, vol. II, 418.
26   A.B. Mitford to H.R. Mitford, 4 January 1868.
27   Ibid.,? May 1868.
28   Ibid., 18 March 1868.
29   Ibid., 13 May 1869.
30   Ibid., 27 May 1869.
31   Ibid., 20 March 1869.
32   Ibid., 29 May 1867.
33   Redesdale, *Memories*, vol. II, 418.
34   Ibid., 419.
35   Ibid.
36   Ibid., 420.
37   Ibid.
38   Ibid.
39   A.B. Mitford to H.R. Mitford, 28 January 1868.

40 A.B. Mitford, *Tales of Old Japan*, 73.
41 Redesdale, *Memories*, vol. II, 416.
42 Quoted in M. William Steele, *Alternative Narratives in Modern Japanese History* (London: Routledge Curzon, 2003), 19.
43 A.B. Mitford to H.R. Mitford, 14 February 1868.
44 Ibid., 25 February 1868.
45 Ibid., 24 February 1869.
46 Redesdale, *Memories*, vol. II, 427.
47 Ibid.
48 Ibid.
49 Parkes to Stanley, 13 February 1868, ed. Kenneth Bourne & D. Cameron Watt, part 1, series E, ed. Ian Nish, *British Documents on Foreign Affairs*, vol. I, 130.
50 A.B. Mitford, *Tales of Old Japan*, 139.
51 Ibid., 140.
52 Ibid., 155 and 182.
53 Redesdale, *Memories*, vol. II, 433.
54 Ibid., 428.
55 A.B. Mitford to H.R. Mitford, 25 February 1868.
56 Ibid., 6 October 1868.
57 Ibid., 29 January 1868.
58 Ibid.
59 Satow, *A Diplomat in Japan*, 347. The last public execution in Britain was on 26 May 1868, a little less than three months after this *hara-kiri*.
60 'The Execution by Hara-Kiri', *Cornhill Magazine*, vol. XX (November 1869), 549–554. Satow wrote a similar account in his diary entry for 2 March 1868. Morton &Ruxton eds., *The Diaries of Sir Ernest Mason Satow*, 327–329.
61 A.B. Mitford, *Tales of Old Japan*, 292–294.
62 A.B. Mitford to H.R. Mitford, 3 March 1868.
63 Ibid.
64 Satow, *A Diplomat in Japan*, 346.
65 A.B. Mitford, *Tales of Old Japan*, 297.
66 A.B. Mitford, *Tales of Old Japan*, 298.
67 Ibid.
68 M. William Steele, *Alternative Narratives in Modern Japanese History*, 66.
69 A.B. Mitford to H.R. Mitford, 24 December 1866.
70 A.B. Mitford to H.R. Mitford, 3 March 1868.

Chapter 6: Kyoto

1 I am grateful to Dr Charles De Wolf for suggesting this poem and translating it for me.
2 A.B. Mitford to H.R. Mitford, 29 May 1867.
3 Ibid.
4 Ibid., 25 February 1868.
5 Ibid.

[6]   Ibid.

[7]   Ibid., 14 September 1867.

[8]   Satow, *A Diplomat in Japan*, 31.

[9]   A.B. Mitford to H.R. Mitford, 16 March 1868.

[10]   Ibid.

[11]   Ibid.

[12]   Ibid.

[13]   Redesdale, *Memories*, vol. II, 439.

[14]   Ibid., 442.

[15]   Parkes to Roches, 13 March 1868, FO46/92. This letter was written in English, rather than French as diplomatic etiquette required because Mitford was not at hand to translate it for Parkes.

[16]   Mitford to Parkes, 14 March 1868, FO 46/92.

[17]   Satow, *A Diplomat in Japan*, 347.

[18]   A.B. Mitford to H.R. Mitford, 16 March 1868.

[19]   Ibid.

[20]   Ibid.

[21]   Entry for 18 February 1868. Morton &Ruxton eds., *The Diaries of Sir Ernest Mason Satow*, 317.

[22]   Redesdale, *Memories*, vol. II, 444.

[23]   A.B. Mitford to H.R. Mitford, 16 March 1868.

[24]   Keene, *Emperor of Japan*, 133–4.

[25]   For more about Nakai, see Eleanor Robinson, 'Nakai Hiromu (1838–94): A Forgotten Hero of Anglo-Japanese Relations' in Hugh Cortazzi (ed.), *Britain and Japan: Biographical Portraits*, vol. VII (Folkestone: Global Oriental, 2010), 33–43.

[26]   It was the corner of Shinmonzen and Nawate.

[27]   Redesdale, *Memories*, vol. II, 451. The phrase 'sensation diplomacy' was something of an in – joke. It is taken from an article entitled 'Sensation Diplomacy in Japan' in *Blackwood's Magazine* that was critical of British policy. *Blackwood's Edinburgh Magazine* 93/570 (April 1863), 397–413.

[28]   A.B. Mitford to H.R. Mitford, 25 March 1868.

[29]   Redesdale, *Memories*, vol. II, 450.

[30]   Satow's accounts can be found in the entry for 23 March 1868 in Morton & Ruxton eds., *The Diaries of Sir Ernest Mason Satow*, 337–339, and in Satow, *A Diplomat in Japan* (Tokyo: Oxford University Press, 1968), 359–360. Parkes' account can be found in Parkes to Stanley, 25 March 1868, *British Documents on Foreign Affairs*, ed. Bourne & Watt, part 1, series E, ed. Nish, vol. I, 173. The Legation guard witnesses were Alexander Aberdein, Thomas Cole, Patrick Duffey, Robert Green, Henry Harding, Edmund Hatton, Charles Kingston, Peter Peacock, Henry Reeve and William Wood. Only two of them even mentioned Mitford in their statements: Aberdein wrote that he 'saw Mr. Mitford with his sword drawn coming up' and Green reported, 'when I reached the 9th I met Mr. Mitford coming up'. MS Parkes 30/2.

[31]   Redesdale, *Memories*, vol. II, 455.

[32]   Redesdale, *Memories*, vol. II, 409.

33   Redesdale, *The Garter Mission to Japan*, 247.
34   A.B. Mitford to H.R. Mitford, 25 March 1868.
35   Ibid.
36   Ibid.
37   Parkes to Stanley, 25 March 1868, *British Documents on Foreign Affairs*, ed. Bourne & Watt, part 1, series E, ed. Nish, vol. I, 174.
38   A.B. Mitford, 'Wanderings in Japan II', *The Cornhill Magazine* 25/147 (March 1872), 307.
39   A.B. Mitford to H.R. Mitford, 3 April 1868.
40   Ibid.
41   Ibid.
42   Ibid.
43   Ibid.
44   Ibid.
45   Quoted in Keene, *Emperor of Japan*, 145.
46   Quoted in Hugh Cortazzi, *Victorians in Japan* (London: Athlone, 1987), 334.
47   A.B. Mitford to H.R. Mitford, 3 April 1868.

Chapter 7: Osaka

1   Mitford to Parkes, 4 April 1868, MS Parkes 1/F21.
2   Redesdale, *Memories*, vol. II, 474.
3   John Black, *Young Japan*, vol. II (New York: Baker, Pratt & Co., 1883), 196.
4   Mitford to Parkes, 14 April 1868, *British Documents on Foreign Affairs*, ed. Bourne & Watt, part 1, series E, ed. Nish, vol. I, 191.
5   Black, *Young Japan*, vol. II, 197.
6   A.B. Mitford to H.R. Mitford, 20 April 1868.
7   Ibid.
8   Parkes to Henry Keppel, 29 April 1868, FO46/98/Inclosure 1 in No. 93.
9   Entry for 17 May 1868. Morton & Ruxton eds., *The Diaries of Sir Ernest Mason Satow*, 340.
10   Satow, *A Diplomat in Japan*, 371.
11   Redesdale, *Memories*, vol. II, 462.
12   Ibid., 464.
13   A.B. Mitford, *Tales of Old Japan*, 61.
14   A.B. Mitford to H.R. Mitford, 14 April 1868.
15   Mitford to Parkes, 14 April 1868, MS Parkes 1/F24.
16   Ibid., 1/F23.
17   Redesdale, *The Garter Mission to Japan*, 246.
18   A.B. Mitford, *Tales of Old Japan*, 117.
19   A.B. Mitford to H.R. Mitford, 24 May 1868.
20   Ibid., 11 December 1868.
21   Ibid.
22   Mitford to Parkes, 14 April 1868, MS Parkes 1/F23.
23   A.B. Mitford to H.R. Mitford, 14 April 1868.
24   Ibid., 11 December 1868.

25 Ibid., 29 October 1867.
26 Ibid., 18 September 1868.
27 Parkes to Hammond, 26 June 1869, FO 391/14.
28 Ibid., 17 March 1867.
29 Hugh Cortazzi, *Dr. Willis in Japan*, 80.
30 Mitford to Parkes, 4 April 1868, Parkes Papers, 1/F21.
31 Mitford to Parkes, 6 April 1868, ibid., 1/F22.
32 Redesdale, *Memories*, vol. II, 467.
33 For more on Itō's time in the U.K., see Andrew Cobbing, 'Itō Hirobumi in Britain' in J.E. Hoare (ed.), *Britain and Japan: Biographical Portraits*, vol. III (Richmond: Japan Library, 1999), 13–24.
34 Quoted in Chushichi Tsuzuki, *The Pursuit of Power in Modern Japan, 1825–1995* (Oxford: Oxford University Press, 2000), 101.
35 Kuroda Kiyotaka, prime minister 1888–1889, was rumoured to have beaten his wife to death so Itō may not be the only murderer.
36 Redesdale, *Memories*, vol. II, 383.
37 A.B. Mitford to H.R. Mitford, 24 December 1866.
38 Mitford to Parkes, 12 April 1868, MS Parkes 1/F23.
39 A.B. Mitford, 'Wanderings in Japan II', *The Cornhill Magazine* 25/147 (March 1872), 314.
40 Redesdale, *Memories*, vol. II, 465.
41 Parkes to Stanley, 18 April 1868, FO 46/93.
42 Mitford to Parkes, 14 July 1868, MS Parkes 1/F27.
43 Redesdale, *The Garter Mission to Japan*, 173.
44 Mitford to Parkes, 12 July 1868, MS Parkes 1/F25.
45 Keene, *Emperor of Japan: Meiji and His World, 1852–1912*, 111.
46 Mitford to Parkes, 28 May 1868, *British Documents on Foreign Affairs*, ed. Bourne & Watt, part 1, series E, ed. Nish, vol. I, 208.
47 Mitford to Parkes, 5 May 1868, FO46/94.
48 Redesdale, *Memories*, vol. II, 466.
49 Mitford to Parkes, 19 June 1868, *British Documents on Foreign Affairs*, ed. Bourne & Watt, part 1, series E, ed. Nish, vol. I, 234.
50 Satow, *The Family Chronicle of the English Satows*, Vol. I of *Collected Works of Ernest Mason Satow* (Bristol: Ganesha / Tokyo: Edition Synapse, 1998), 35.
51 Satow to Mrs Dickins, 8 November 1889, I. Ruxton (ed.), *Sir Ernest Satow's Private Letters to W.G. Aston and F.V. Dickins* (Tokyo: Lulu, 2008), 168.
52 List of donors to the English Episcopal Church establishment in Yokohama, 1868, FO46/106.
53 Jonathan and Catherine Guinness, *The House of Mitford* (London: Hutchinson 1984), 85.
54 Lord Redesdale, Introduction to Houston Stewart Chamberlain, *The Foundations of the Nineteenth Century*, trans. John Lees (London: John Lane, 1911), xxxi.
55 A.B. Mitford to H.R. Mitford, 27 May 1869.
56 Mitford to Parkes, 19 June 1868, *British Documents on Foreign Affairs*, ed. Bourne & Watt, part 1, series E, ed. Nish, vol. I, 234.
57 Redesdale, *Memories*, vol. II, 470.

58   F.O. Adams to Lord Granville, 12 December 1871, FO46/143. For more on
     Iwakura and Great Britain, see Andrew Cobbin, 'Iwakura Tomomi (1825–83)'
     in Hugh Cortazzi (ed.), *Britain and Japan: Biographical Portraits*, vol. VIII
     (Leiden: Brill, 2013), 1–12.
59   Parkes to Stanley, 21 August 1868, *Correspondence Respecting the Change of
     Constitution in Japan, 1867–1868*, Part 2 (London: Foreign Office, 1869),
     332.
60   A.B. Mitford to H.R. Mitford, 12 January 1869.
61   Redesdale, *Memories*, vol. II, 471.

Chapter 8: Tokyo

1   M. William Steele, *Alternative Narratives in Modern Japanese History*, 80.
2   A.B. Mitford to H.R. Mitford, 6 October 1868.
3   Sidney DeVere Brown and Akiko Hirota (eds.), *The Diary of Kido Takayoshi*,
     vol. I: 1868–1871 (Tokyo: University of Tokyo Press, 1983), 78.
4   A.B. Mitford, 'Wanderings in Japan I', *The Cornhill Magazine* 25/146
     (February 1872), 196.
5   A.B. Mitford, *Tales of Old Japan*, 181.
6   A.B. Mitford to H.R. Mitford, 6 October 1868.
7   Meiji did not start living in Tokyo until 1869 and it was never officially
     announced that the city was his capital – this however became clear from the
     fact that he did not return to Kyoto for any extended period until 1877.
8   A.B. Mitford to H.R. Mitford, 18 September 1868.
9   Satow, *A Diplomat in Japan*, 366.
10   A.B. Mitford to H.R. Mitford, 18 September 1868.
11   Ibid., 6 October 1868.
12   Redesdale, *Memories*, vol. II, 472.
13   A.B. Mitford to H.R. Mitford, 21 August 1868 and 8 August 1868.
14   Ibid., 21 August 1868.
15   Adams would become a key figure in British-Japan relations, serving as Chargé
     d'affaires while Parkes was on leave in 1871–1872. He also wrote a two volume
     history of Japan: F.O. Adams, *The history of Japan* (London: Henry S. King,
     1874–1875). For more on his career in Japan, see Hugh Cortazzi, 'Sir Francis
     Ottiwell Adams, KCMG, CB, British Diplomat (1826–89)' in Hugh Cortazzi
     (ed.), *Britain and Japan: Biographical Portraits*, vol. VII (Folkestone: Global
     Oriental, 2010), 96–111.
16   Ibid., 8 August 1868.
17   A.B. Mitford, 'Wanderings in Japan I', *The Cornhill Magazine* 25/146
     (February 1872), 196.
18   A.B. Mitford to H.R. Mitford, 31 October 1866; Satow, *A Diplomat in Japan*,
     289.
19   A.B. Mitford, 'Wanderings in Japan II', *The Cornhill Magazine* 25/147 (March
     1872), 315.
20   A.B. Mitford to H.R. Mitford, 29 April 1869.
21   Redesdale, *A Tragedy in Stone*, 88.

22   A.B. Mitford to H.R. Mitford, 11 December 1868.
23   Ibid.
24   A.B. Mitford, 'A Ride Through Yedo'; *Fortnightly Review*, 7/41 (May 1870): 506.
25   A.B. Mitford to H.R. Mitford, 11 December 1868.
26   Ibid., 10 February 1869.
27   Ibid., 29 December 1868.
28   Ibid., 26 June 1869.
29   Date Chiunagon (Principal Minister for Foreign Affairs) & Terashima Shi-i (Assistant Minister for Foreign Affairs) to Parkes, 15 July 1869, John Black, *Young Japan*, vol. II, 266.
30   Keene, *Emperor of Japan: Meiji and His World*, 184.
31   A.B. Mitford to H.R. Mitford, 27 May 1869.
32   A.B. Mitford to H.R. Mitford, 4 September 1869.
33   Ibid., 12 June 1869.
34   Parkes to Hammond, 28 July 1869, FO391/15.
35   Redesdale, *Memories*, vol. II, 496.
36   A.B. Mitford to H.R. Mitford, 9 August 1869.
37   Ibid.
38   Ibid., 23 August 1869.
39   Ibid.
40   Ibid.
41   Dickins and Lane-Poole, *The Life of Sir Harry Parkes*, vol. II, 143.
42   Redesdale, *Memories*, vol. II, 497.
43   Keene, *Emperor of Japan*, 185.
44   Redesdale, *Memories*, vol. II, 500.
45   Ibid., 499.
46   Parkes to Clarendon, 23 August 1869. Keene, *Emperor of Japan*, 186.
47   Memorandum by A.B. Mitford. John R. Black, *Young Japan*, vol. II, 271.
48   Keene, *Emperor of Japan*, 186.
49   Parkes to Hammond, 23 October 1869, FO391/15.
50   Beverley Curran, 'Nogami Toyoichirō's Noh Translation Theories and the Primacy of Performance,' Silvia Bigliazzi, Paola Ambrosi, Peter Kofler (eds.), *Theatre Translation in Performance* (New York: Routledge, 2013), 212. For more about Shaw's time in Japan, including an article he wrote on Japan in 1934, see Bernard F. Dukore, 'George Bernard Shaw (1856–1950) on Japan', in Hugh Cortazzi (ed.), *Britain and Japan: Biographical Portraits*, vol. VII (Folkestone: Global Oriental, 2010), 250–254.
51   A.B. Mitford, *Tales of Old Japan*, 112.
52   Henry Keppel, *A Sailor's Life under Four Sovereigns*, vol. III (London: Macmillan, 1899), 291.
53   The future Edward VIII told his father on a visit in 1922, 'My chief disappointment is not being able to get *tattooed* in Japan; but it seems that it's been made illegal, though I can't think why.' (Noboru Koyama, 'Japanese Tattooists and the British Royal Family during the Meiji Period', in Hugh Cortazzi ed., *Britain & Japan: Biographical Portraits*, vol. VI, Folkestone: Global Oriental, 2007, 80.)
54   Machida (*Gaimu Saijo*); Mumawatari (*Gaimu Shojo*); Miyamoto (*Gaimu Gon Shojo*) to Mitford, 9 October 1869, FO46/113.

55   Clarendon to Parkes, 16 December 1869. *Japan No. 3 (1870), Correspondence respecting affairs in Japan: 1868–70* (London: Harrison & Sons, 1870).
56   A.B. Mitford, 'A Ride Through Yedo', *Fortnightly Review* XLI (1 May 1870), 505.
57   A.B. Mitford, 'Wanderings in Japan I', *The Cornhill Magazine* 25/146 (February 1872), 197.
58   A.B. Mitford, 'Wanderings in Japan II', *The Cornhill Magazine* 25/146 (March 1872), 305.
59   Ibid., 313–314.
60   Ibid., 314.
61   Sidney DeVere Brown and Akiko Hirota (eds.), *The Diary of Kido Takayoshi*, vol. I, 275.
62   Redesdale, *The Garter Mission to Japan*, 122–123.
63   A.B. Mitford to H.R. Mitford, 18 December 1869.
64   A.B. Mitford to H.R. Mitford, 23 August 1869.
65   A.B. Mitford to H.R. Mitford, 23 April 1867.
66   Select Committee on Diplomatic and Consular Services, *Parliamentary Papers* 1870, 382, VII, 301.
67   A.B. Mitford to H.R. Mitford, 23 April 1867.
68   Advertisement for the Central Pacific Railroad of California. *The Hiogo News*, 7 January 1870.
69   A.B. Mitford to H.R. Mitford, 23 August 1869. At the time, Hawaii was not part of the USA.
70   Gordon Daniels, *Sir Harry Parkes: British Representative in Japan 1865–83* (Richmond, Surrey: 1996), 181.
71   Letter of commendation, probably sent to Mitford by Hammond, 6 April 1870, Gloucestershire County Archives, D2002/7/1/1.
72   Redesdale, *Memories*, vol. II, 514.
73   A.B. Mitford to H.R. Mitford, 13 July 1867.
74   *The Hiogo News*, 5 January 1870.
75   Hunter and Sugiyama, *The History of Anglo-Japanese Relations, 1600–2000*, vol. IV, 34.
76   Redesdale, *Memories*, vol. II, 503.
77   Ibid., 515.
78   Ibid., 522.

Chapter 9: After Japan

1   Redesdale, *Memories*, vol. II, 552.
2   Ibid., 552–553.
3   Redesdale, *A Tragedy in Stone*, 180.
4   Redesdale, *Memories*, vol. I, 109.
5   Select Committee on Diplomatic and Consular Services, *Parliamentary Papers* 1870, 382, VII, 299.
6   Ibid., 301.
7   'Adams Report. Cost of Living', 27 January 1870, MS Parkes 26/5.

8   Select Committee on Diplomatic and Consular Services, *Parliamentary Papers* 1870, 382, VII, 12.
9   Redesdale, *Memories*, vol. I, 111.
10   Cortazzi, *Mitford's Japan*, xx.
11   A.B. Mitford to H.R. Mitford, 8 June 1868 and 12 June 1869.
12   Redesdale, *Memories*, vol. II, 555.
13   A.B. Mitford to H.R. Mitford, 24 March 1869.
14   *Saturday Review*, 14 August 1869.
15   A.B. Mitford, *Tales of Old Japan*, 240.
16   Ibid., 255.
17   Ibid., 263.
18   A.B. Mitford to H.R. Mitford, 8 June 1868.
19   Redesdale to Edmund Gosse, 24 October 1912 (Gosse Collection, University of Leeds).
20   *Saturday Review*, 14 August 1869.
21   Redesdale, *A Tragedy in Stone*, 233–234.
22   A.B. Mitford to H.R. Mitford, 18 November 1868.
23   Redesdale, *Memories*, vol. II, 554.
24   Baron de Hübner, *Promenade autour du monde – 1871*, vol. I (Paris: Librairie Hachette et Cie, 1873), 439.
25   Published by DanielDi Marzio.com, whose website says it is 'exploring the world through martial arts'.
26   Lafcadio Hearn, *Japan: An Attempt at Interpretation* (New York: Macmillan, 1905), 323.
27   William Lyon Phelps (ed.), *Essays of Robert Louis Stevenson*, (Rockville, MD: Arc Manor, 2008), 121; Edmund Gosse, 'The Writings of Lord Redesdale' *Edinburgh Review* 217: 444 (1913): 320.
28   Gosse, 'The Writings of Lord Redesdale' *Edinburgh Review* 217: 444, (1913): 320.
29   The *Japan Weekly Mail*, 6 May 1871.
30   Inazo Nitobe, *Bushido: The Soul of Japan* (Tokyo: Teiei, 1908), 106–111.
31   Gosse, 'The Writings of Lord Redesdale' *Edinburgh Review* 217/444 (April 1913), 321.
32   The *Times*, 26 May 1871.
33   *Saturday Review*, 11 March 1871.
34   Redesdale, *A Tragedy in Stone*, 153.
35   As does the more formal term for it, *seppuku*.
36   *Saturday Review*, 11 March 1871.
37   This information is based on a study by Kozo Yamamura in *A Study of Samurai Income and Entrepreneurship: Quantitative Analyses of Economic and Social Aspects of the Samurai in Tokugawa and Meiji Japan* (Cambridge, Mass.: Harvard University Press, 1974), 79.
38   Redesdale, *Memories*, vol. II, 563.
39   Ibid., 636–637.
40   Cortazzi, *Mitford's Japan*, xxi.
41   A.B. Mitford to H.R. Mitford, 8 August 1868.
42   Jonathan and Catherine Guinness, *The House of Mitford*, 73–4.

NOTES217

43 Ibid., 106.
44 The painting is reproduced in ibid. Unfortunately there is no indication given as to when it was painted or by whom.
45 A.B. Mitford, 'Wanderings in Japan – II', *Cornhill Magazine* 25/47 (March 1872), 312.
46 Jonathan and Catherine Guinness, *The House of Mitford*, xxiii. Jonathan Guinness (Lord Moyne) is the son of Diana Mosley (née Mitford).
47 Ibid., xxv. It was the hostess, Lady Cunard, who used to say this – she found it out from her husband, Sir Bache Cunard.
48 Blanche, known as Aunt Natty, was by far the favourite relation of the Mitford sisters. She would tell them endless stories about her past, but what they liked most, according to Diana Mosley was that she was 'the first unprincipled grown-up who came our way'. Ibid., 244.
49 Mary Soames, *Clementine Churchill: The Biography of a Marriage* (New York: Mariner, 2003), 5–9.
50 Sonia Purnell, *First Lady: The Life and Wars of Clementine Churchill* (London: Aurum, 2015) and Joan Hardwick, *Clementine Churchill: The Private Life of a Public Figure* (London: John Murray, 1997).
51 The courtier was Lord Esher. Jane Ridley, *Bertie: A Life of Edward VII* (London: Vintage, 2013), 447.
52 Soames, *Clementine Churchill*, 8.
53 Redesdale, *Memories*, vol. II, 650.
54 Ibid., 648.
55 Ibid.
56 A.B. Mitford, *Tales of Old Japan*, 19.
57 Mortimer Menpes, 'A Personal View of Japanese Art. A Lesson from Khiosi', *Magazine of Art*, vol. 11, April 1888, 199.
58 James Fenton, *Leonardo's Nephew: Essays on Art and Artists* (Chicago: University of Chicago Press, 1998), 118.
59 Melanie Trede and Lorenz Bichler, *Hiroshige, Meisho Edo Hyakkei* (Cologne: Taschen, 2007), 36.
60 Although the painting is colloquially known as *Whistler's Mother*, its official name is *Arrangement in Grey and Black No.1*.
61 Redesdale, *Memories*, vol. II, 661.
62 Disraeli to Lord Henry Lennox, 1 September 1852, Monypenny & Buckle, *The Life of Benjamin Disraeli*, vol. I (New York: MacMillan, 1929), 1203. In his classic biography of Disraeli, Robert Blake tells us that the 'language must be discounted as the hyperbole of the time'. (Robert Blake, *Disraeli*, London: Prion, 1998, 327.)
63 Redesdale, *A Tragedy in Stone*, 19.
64 Redesdale, *Memories*, vol. II, 695.
65 Redesdale, *Further Memories*, 158.
66 Jonathan and Catherine Guinness, *The House of Mitford*, 80.
67 Charlotte Mosley (ed.), *The Mitfords: Letters between Six Sisters*, 700.
68 Jonathan and Catherine Guinness, *The House of Mitford*, 80.
69 A.B. Mitford to H.R. Mitford, 20 October 1868.

Chapter 10: The Return

1   'Mitford, Algernon Bertram Freeman-, first Baron Redesdale in the second creation (1837–1916),' Edmund Gosse in *Dictionary of National Biography* [Third] Supplement 1912–1921, ed. Leslie Stephen et. al. (London: OUP, 1927); online ed., http://odnb2.ifactory.com/view/olddnb/35048 (accessed May 1, 2015).

2   The *Spectator* (London), 18 August 1906.

3   'Arthur, Prince (1883–1938),' Hugo Vickers in *Oxford Dictionary of National Biography*, ed. H.C.G. Matthew and Brian Harrison (Oxford: OUP, 2004); online ed., ed. Lawrence Goldman, October 2007, http://oxforddnb.com. ezproxy.library.uq.edu.au/view/article/30461 (accessed April 3, 2015).

4   The *Times*, 12 July 1900.

5   Ibid., 23 July 1900.

6   Quoted in the *Japan Weekly Chronicle* (Kobe), 8 March 1906.

7   The Japanese needed British guns for their battleships and armoured cruisers and Britain supplied 20,000 tons of coal a month for their ships. More information can be found in Iguchi Kazuki, *Nichiro Sensō no Jidai* (Tokyo: Yoshikawa Kōbunkan, 1977), 127–128.

8   The *Times*, 1 September 1905.

9   Keene, *Emperor of Japan*, 633.

10 Queen Victoria to Lord Derby, 5 June 1867, *The Letters of Queen Victoria*, Series 2, vol. I, p. 430.

11 Redesdale, *The Garter Mission to Japan*, 7–8.

12 Ibid. *Banzai* literally means '10,000 years'.

13 An address delivered by Lord Redesdale, K.C.V.O., C.B., on the opening of the new buildings of the Campden School of Arts and Crafts. October 20, MDCCCCIV (Campden, Glous.: Essex House Press, 1904), 5.

14 Quoted in the *Japan Weekly Chronicle* (Kobe), 8 March 1906.

15 Redesdale, *The Garter Mission to Japan*, 21.

16 Ibid., 8–9.

17 Accounts vary on this point; some say the decoration was stained with blood, some that a little blood went on to the Emperor's breeches. Compare the accounts in Keene, *Emperor of Japan*, 634 and in Momoko Williams & Peter Pagnamenta, *Falling Blossom*, (London: Century, 2006), 62.

18 Redesdale, *The Garter Mission to Japan*, 20.

19 The Japanese was '*Nanda, konna mono wo.*' Quoted in Keene, *Emperor of Japan*, 634.

20 Redesdale, *The Garter Mission to Japan*, 22.

21 Ibid., 23.

22 Ibid.

23 Ibid., 29.

24 Ibid., 8.

25 Ibid., 33 and 34.

26 Ibid., 64–65.

27 Ibid., 26.

28 Ibid., 214–215.

29 Ibid., 188 and 190.
30 Ibid., 226.
31 Ibid., 53.
32 The *Japan Weekly Chronicle* (Kobe), 15 March 1906.
33 *Eastern World*, 17 March 1906.
34 Prince Arthur of Connaught to Mitford, 'Tuesday' (almost certainly in June 1906), Gloucestershire County Archives, D2002/7/1/1.
35 Jonathan Guinness with Catherine Guinness, *The House of Mitford*, 106 and Redesdale to Gosse (Gosse Collection), 17 October 1912.
36 'Mr. Lampson's Private Diary of the Garter Mission to Japan, January 10 to May 2, 1906', Ian Nish (ed.), *British Documents on Foreign Affairs*, Part 1, Series E, vol. X, 86.
37 Redesdale, *The Garter Mission to Japan*, 93 and 94.

Chapter 11: The Legacy

1   Ernest Satow to Mrs. Dickins, 20 May 1917, Ian Ruxton ed., *Sir Ernest Satow's Private Letters to W.G. Aston and F.V. Dickins*, 312.
2   Jonathan Guinness with Catherine Guinness, *The House of Mitford*, 84; Ernest Satow's Diary, 12 January 1912, PRO 30/33/16/12.
3   Gosse to Redesdale, 3 April 1915, Gloucestershire County Archives, D2002/7/1/1.
4   *Saturday Review*, 20 November 1915.
5   Sidney Lee (ed.), *Dictionary of National Biography*, second supplement, vol I, (London: Smith, Elder & Co., 1912), 607.
6   Redesdale, *Memories*, vol. I, 181.
7   Ibid., vol. II, 520. The club had been founded by the Prince of Wales, because White's had not allowed him to smoke where he wanted.
8   Ibid., vol. I, 373.
9   Satow, *A Diplomat in Japan*, first published in 1921.
10 Redesdale, *Memories*, vol. II, 775.
11 Redesdale, *Further Memories*, 79.
12 Ibid., 92.
13 These are Edmund Gosse's words. Redesdale, *Further Memories*, xi.
14 Redesdale to Edmund Gosse, 16 May 1915 (Gosse Collection).
15 The quotation is slightly abbreviated on the gravestone; in full it reads, 'And so he passed over, and all the trumpets sounded for him on the other side.'
16 Redesdale, *Further Memories*, xi.
17 Redesdale to Edmund Gosse, 27 May 1915 (Gosse Collection).
18 Redesdale, *Further Memories*, 5.
19 Ibid., 45.
20 Ibid., xiv.
21 The *Times* (London), 18 August 1916.
22 Redesdale, *Further Memories*, ix.
23 David Litchfield, *Hitler's Valkyrie: The Uncensored Biography* (Stroud: History Press, 2013), 15.

24 Soames, *Clementine Churchill: The Biography of a Marriage*, 283; Alison Maloney, *Bright Young Things: Life in the Roaring Twenties* (London: Virgin, 2012), 171.

25 Megan Gressor and Kerry Cook, *All For Love* (Miller's Point, NSW: Murdoch, 2005) 182.

26 Diary of Eva Braun, 10 May 1935, http://www.humanitas-international.org/holocaust/evadiary.htm.

27 Story told by Diana Mosley to Selina Hastings, who passed it on to the author.

28 Houston Stewart Chamberlain, *The Foundations of the Nineteenth Century*, 542.

29 Ibid., 330.

30 Ibid., 331.

31 Redesdale, Introduction to ibid., xxxviii-xxxix.

32 Redesdale, 'Houston Stewart Chamberlain' *Edinburgh Review* 219/447 (January 1914), 81.

33 David Pryce-Jones, *Unity Mitford: A Quest* (London: Weidenfeld & Nicolson, 1976), 127.

34 Houston Stewart Chamberlain, *The Foundations of the Nineteenth Century*, 5.

35 Redesdale, Introduction to Chamberlain, *The Foundations of the Nineteenth Century*, lv.

36 Houston Stewart Chamberlain, 'England', *North American Review*, 202/716, July 1915, 52.

37 Redesdale to Edmund Gosse, 27 May 1915 (Gosse Collection).

38 Ibid., x.

BIBLIOGRAPHY

∞

Primary Sources

Letters from A.B. Mitford to H.R. Mitford. (Copies held among the Sir Hugh
Cortazzi papers at the Japan Society, London and at the Sainsbury Institute for
the Study of Japanese Arts and
Cultures, Norwich).
Papers of Algernon Bertram Freeman-Mitford, 1st Baron Redesdale of the 2nd
creation
(Gloucestershire County Archives, Gloucester).
Eton College Archives
Foreign Office Files (National Archives, Kew, London).
Great Britain, Foreign Office General Correspondence, *Japan*
Great Britain, Embassy and Consular Archives, *Japan Correspondence*
The Hammond Papers
The Gosse Collection (University of Leeds, Leeds)
Government Publications
Hansard 1803–2005 (http://hansard.millbanksystems.com/)
Correspondence Respecting the Change of Constitution in Japan, 1867–1868, Part 2
  Parliamentary Papers, 1870
Japan No. 3 (1870), Correspondence respecting affairs in Japan: 1868–70, presented
  to both Houses of Parliament by Command of Her Majesty (London: Harrison
  & Sons, 1870)
The Jardine Matheson Archive (Cambridge University Library, Cambridge).
The Parkes Papers (Cambridge University Library, Cambridge)
The Royal Archives (Windsor Castle, Windsor).
The Satow Papers (National Archives, Kew, London).

Secondary Sources

Allen, Bernard M. *The Rt. Hon. Sir Ernest Satow G.C.M.G.* London: Kegan Paul,
  1933.
Auslin, Michael. *Negotiating with Imperialism: The Unequal Treaties and the
  Culture of Japanese Diplomacy.* Cambridge, Mass.: Harvard University Press,
  2004.
Beasley, W.G. *The Meiji Restoration.* Stanford: Stanford University Press, 1972.
———, trans. and ed. *Select Documents on Japanese Foreign Policy, 1853–1868.*
  London: Oxford University Press, 1955.

Bennett, Terry, ed. *Japan and the Illustrated London News: Complete Record of Reported Events, 1853–1899*. Folkestone: Global Oriental, 2006.

Bird, Isabella L. *Unbeaten Tracks in Japan: An Account of Travels in the Interior Including Visits to the Aborigines of Yezo and the Shrines of Nikkô and Isé*. London: Murray, 1880.

Black, John Reddie, *Young Japan, Yokohama and Yedo: A Narrative of the settlement and the city from the signing of the treaties in 1858 to the close of the year 1879, with a glance at the progress of Japan during a period of twenty one years*. 2 vols. New York: Baker, Pratt, 1883.

Blake, Robert. *Disraeli*. London: Prion, 1998.

Bourne, Kenneth and D. Cameron Watt, eds. *British Documents on Foreign Affairs*. Vol. I part 1, series E, ed. Ian Nish. [Frederick, MD?]: University Publications of America, 1989.

Braun, Eva. *Diary*. http://www.humanitas-international.org/holocaust/evadiary.htm.

British Parliamentary Papers Catalogue: Area Studies: China and Japan: Japan: General Affairs 1864–1870. Vol. II: Reports and Correspondence Relating to Japan, 1864–70. Edgware, Middlesex: Irish University Press.

Brown, Sidney DeVere and Akiko Hirota, eds. *The Diary of Kido Takayoshi*. Vol. 1: 1868–1871. Tokyo: University of Tokyo Press, 1983.

Buckle, George Earle, ed. *The Letters of Queen Victoria, Second Series: A Selection from Her Majesty's Correspondence between the years 1862 and 1878*. Vol 1. London: John Murray, 1926.

Chamberlain, Basil Hall. *Japanese Things: Being Notes of Various Subjects Connected with Japan*. Rutland, Vermont & Tokyo: Tuttle, 1979.

Chamberlain, Houston Stewart. *The Foundations of the Nineteenth Century*. Translated by John Lees. London: John Lane, 1911.

Coke, Henry. *Tracks of a Rolling Stone*. London: Smith, Elder & Co., 1905.

Cortazzi, Hugh. *Dr. Willis in Japan, 1862–1877*. London: Athlone, 1985.

———. 'The First British Legation in Japan.' In *Collected Writings of Sir Hugh Cortazzi*. Richmond, Surrey: Japan Library, 2000.

———, ed. *Mitford's Japan: The Memoirs and Recollections, 1866–1906, of Algernon Bertram Mitford, the first Lord Redesdale*. London: Athlone, 1985.

———. *Victorians in Japan*. London: Athlone, 1987.

———, ed. *Britain and Japan: Biographical Portraits*. Vol IV. London: Japan Library, 2002.

———, ed. *Britain and Japan: Biographical Portraits*. Vol V. Folkestone: Global Oriental, 2005.

———, ed. *Britain and Japan: Biographical Portraits*. Vol VI. Folkestone: Global Oriental, 2007.

———, ed. *Britain and Japan: Biographical Portraits*. Vol VII. Folkestone: Global Oriental, 2010.

———, ed. *Britain and Japan: Biographical Portraits*. Vol VIII. Leiden: Brill, 2013.

———, ed. *Britain and Japan: Biographical Portraits*. Vol IX. Folkestone: Renaissance Books, 2015.

Curran, Beverley. 'Nogami Toyoichirō's Noh Translation Theories and the Primacy of Performance.' In Silvia Bigliazzi, Paola Ambrosi, Peter Kofler, eds. *Theatre Translation in Performance*. New York: Routledge, 2013.

Daniels, Gordon and Chushichi Tsuzuki, eds. *The History of Anglo-Japanese Relations 1600–2000*. Vol V. Basingstoke: Palgrave Macmillan, 2002.

Daniels, Gordon. *Sir Harry Parkes: British Representative in Japan 1865–83*. Richmond, Surrey: Japan Library, 1996.

de Fonblanque, Edward Barrington. *Niphon and Pe-che-li; or, Two Years in Japan and Northern China*. London: Saunders, Otley, 1863.

de Hübner, Baron. *Promenade autour du monde – 1871*. Vol. I. Paris: Librairie Hachette et Cie, 1873.

Dickins, Frederick Victor and Stanley Lane-Poole. *The Life of Sir Harry Parkes*. Vol. 2. London: Macmillan, 1894.

Fenton, James. *Leonardo's Nephew: Essays on Art and Artists*. Chicago: University of Chicago Press, 1998.

Fox, Grace. *Britain and Japan, 1858–1883*. Oxford: Clarendon Press, 1969.

Freeman-Mitford, A.B. *The Attaché at Peking*. London: Macmillan, 1900.

Fukuzawa Yukichi. *The Autobiography of Fukuzawa Yukichi*. Translated by Eiichi Kiyooka. Lanham: Madison, 1992.

Gow, Ian, Yoichi Hirama and John Chapman, eds. *The History of Anglo-Japanese Relations, 1600–2000*. Vol. III. Basingstoke: Macmillan, 2003.

Gressor, Megan and Kerry Cook. *All For Love*. Miller's Point, NSW: Murdoch, 2005.

Guinness, Jonathan and Catherine. *The House of Mitford*. London: Hutchinson 1984.

Hager, Alan, ed. *Encyclopedia of British Writers*. New York: Book Builders, 2003.

Hanley, Susan. *Everyday Things in Premodern Japan: The Hidden Legacy of Material Culture*. Berkeley: University of California Press, 1997.

Hardwick, Joan. *Clementine Churchill: The Private Life of a Public Figure*. London: John Murray, 1997.

Hearn, Lafcadio. *Japan: An Attempt at Interpretation*. New York: Macmillan, 1905.

Hoare, J.E. *Japan's Treaty Ports and Foreign Settlements: The Uninvited Guests, 1858–1899*. Folkestone: Japan Library, 1994.

———. *Embassies in the East: The Story of the British Embassies in Japan, China and Korea from 1859 to the Present*. Richmond: Curzon, 1999.

———, ed. *Britain and Japan: Biographical Portraits*, Richmond: Japan Library, 1999.

Hollis, Christopher. *Eton: A History*. London: Hollis & Carter, 1960.

Honda, Gail. 'Differential Structure, Differential Health: Industrialization in Japan, 1868–1940.' In *Health and Welfare during Industrialization*. Edited by Richard H. Steckel and Roderick Floud. Chicago: University of Chicago Press, 1997.

Hunter, Janet and S. Sugiyama, eds. *The History of Anglo-Japanese Relations, 1600–2000*, vol. IV. Basingstoke: Palgrave Publishers, 2002.

Iguchi Kazuki. *Nichiro Sensō no Jidai*. Tokyo: Yoshikawa Kōbunkan, 1977.

Jannetta, Ann Bowman. *Epidemics and Mortality in Early Modern Japan*. Princeton: Princeton University Press, 1987.

Keene, Donald. *Emperor of Japan: Meiji and His World, 1852–1912*. New York: Columbia University Press, 2002.

Keppel, Henry. *A Sailor's Life under Four Sovereigns*, vol. 3. London: Macmillan, 1899.

Lane-Poole, Stanley. *The Life of Sir Harry Parkes*. Vol. 1. London: Macmillan, 1894.

Lehmann, John-Pierre. 'Léon Roches – Diplomat Extraordinary in the Bakumatsu Era: An Assessment of His Personality and Policy.' *Modern Asian Studies*. 14/2 (1980): 273–307 . http://www.jstor.org/stable/312415.

Litchfield, David. *Hitler's Valkyrie: The Uncensored Biography*. Stroud: History Press, 2013.

Maloney, Alison. *Bright Young Things: Life in the Roaring Twenties*. London: Virgin, 2012.

Matthew, H.C.G. ed. *The Gladstone Diaries*. Vol. VII, January 1869–June 1871. Oxford: Clarendon, 1982.

McMaster, John. *Sabotaging the Shogun: Western Diplomats Open Japan, 1859–69*. New York: Vantage, 1992.

Medzini, Meron. *French Policy in Japan during the Closing Years of the Tokugawa Regime*. Cambridge, Mass.: East Asian Research Center, Harvard University, 1971.

Menpes, Mortimer. 'A Personal View of Japanese Art. A Lesson from Khiosi.' *Magazine of Art*. Vol. 11 (April 1888):255–261.

Mitford, A.B. *Tales of Old Japan*. Ware: Wordsworth, 2000.

Monypenny, William Flavelle and George Earle Buckle. *The Life of Benjamin Disraeli Earl of Beaconsfield*. Vol. I. New York: MacMillan, 1929.

Mosley, Charlotte, ed. *The Mitfords: Letters between Six Sisters*. London: Fourth Estate, 2007.

Morton, Robert and Ian Ruxton, eds. *The Diaries of Sir Ernest Mason Satow, 1861–1869*. Kyoto: Eureka, 2013.

Nenzi, Laura. *Excursions in Identity: Travel and the Intersection of Place, Gender, and Status in Edo Japan*. Honolulu: University of Hawai'i Press, 2008.

Nish, Ian, ed. *British Documents on Foreign Affairs*, Part 1, Series E.Vol. X. [Frederick, MD?]: University Publications of America, 1989–1995.

———, ed. *Britain and Japan: Biographical Portraits*, Folkestone: Japan Library, 1994.

———, ed. *Britain and Japan: Biographical Portraits*. Vol. II. Richmond: Japan Library, 1997.

Nish, Ian and Yoichi Kibata, eds. *The History of Anglo-Japanese Relations*. Vol. I: The Political-Diplomatic Dimension, 1600–1930. Basingstoke: Macmillan, 2000.

Nitobe Inazo. *Bushido: The Soul of Japan*. Tokyo: Teiei, 1908.

Norman, Henry. *The Real Japan: Studies of Contemporary Japanese Manners, Morals, Administration, and Politics*. London: T. Fisher Unwin, 1908.

Notehelfer, F.G., ed. *Japan Through American Eyes: The Journal of Francis Hall, Kanagawa and Yokohama, 1859–1866*. Princeton: Princeton University Press, 1992.

Phelps, William Lyon, ed. *Essays of Robert Louis Stevenson*. Rockville, MD: Arc Manor, 2008.

Platt, D. C. M. *Finance, Trade, and Politics in British Foreign Policy, 1815–1914*. Oxford: Clarendon Press, 1968.

————. *The Cinderella Service: British Consuls since 1825.* Hamden, Conn: Archon, 1971.

Pryce-Jones, David. *Unity Mitford: A Quest.* London: Weidenfeld & Nicolson, 1976.

Purnell, Sonia. *First Lady: The Life and Wars of Clementine Churchill.* London: Aurum, 2015.

Ravina, Mark. *The Last Samurai: The Life and Battles of Saigo Takamori.* Hoboken: Wiley, 2004.

Redesdale, Lord. *The Garter Mission to Japan.* London: Macmillan, 1906.

————. *Memories.* 2 vols. London: Hutchinson, 1915.

————. *A Tragedy in Stone and other papers.* London: John Lane, 1913.

Ridley, Jane. *Bertie: A Life of Edward VII.* London: Vintage, 2013.

Roberts, Andrew. *Salisbury, Victorian Titan.* London: Phoenix, 1999.

Roches, Léon. *Trente-Deux Ans à travers l'Islam (1832–1864).* 2 vols. Paris: Firmin-Didot, 1884–1887.

Ruxton, Ian, ed. *Sir Ernest Satow's Private Letters to W.G. Aston and F.V. Dickins.* Tokyo: Lulu, 2008.

Sansom, G.B. *The Western World and Japan: A Study in the Interaction of European and Asiatic Cultures.* New York: Knopf, 1950.

Satow, Ernest. *A Diplomat in Japan.* Tokyo: Oxford University Press, 1968.

Seidensticker, Edward. *Low City, High City.* New York: Knopf, 1983.

Shibusawa Keizō. *Japanese Life and Culture in the Meiji Era,* trans. Charles S. Terry. Tokyo: Ōbunsha, 1958.

Soames, Mary. *Clementine Churchill: The Biography of a Marriage.* New York: Mariner, 2003.

Steele, M. William. *Alternative Narratives in Modern Japanese History.* London: Routledge Curzon, 2003.

Trede, Melanie and Lorenz Bichler. *Hiroshige: Meisho Edo Hyakkei.* Cologne: Taschen, 2007.

Tsuzuki Chushichi, *The Pursuit of Power in Modern Japan, 1825–1995.* Oxford: Oxford University Press, 2000.

Turnbull, Stephen. *The Kakure Kirishitan of Japan: A Study of the Development, Beliefs and Rituals to the Present Day.* Richmond: Japan Library, 1998.

Williams, Harold. *Shades of the Past: Indiscreet Tales of Japan.* Rutland, Vermont: Tuttle, 1959.

Williams, Momoko and Peter Pagnamenta. *Falling Blossom.* London: Century, 2006.

Yamamura Kozo. *A Study of Samurai Income and Entrepreneurship: Quantitative Analyses of Economic and Social Aspects of the Samurai in Tokugawa and Meiji Japan.* Cambridge, Mass.: Harvard University Press, 1974.

Yokohama-shi (ed). *Yokohama-shi Shi,* vol. II. Yokohama: Yurindo, 1959.

ACKNOWLEDGEMENTS

ℰↃ

THE MOST IMPORTANT source for this biography is the set of precious letters that Mitford sent to his father in England from Japan. Their survival is near-miraculous given that no other significant cache of his correspondence still seems to be in existence. It is thanks to the former British Ambassador to Japan, Sir Hugh Cortazzi, who uncovered them in the 1980s and placed copies of them in his archive in the Sainsbury Institute for the Study of Japanese Arts and Cultures in Norwich and at the Japan Society in London, that they are available to scholars. Without them, and Sir Hugh's generous assistance (which included reading the entire text and giving thoughtful and incisive comments on it), this book could not have been written.

I originally intended to write a biography of Mitford's whole life, something that seemed very feasible because his papers are preserved in the Gloucestershire County Archives and there are Mitford materials all over the place. I spent nearly a week going through his Gloucester archive before realising that a biography could not be written from that material. It was that most painful combination for a researcher of being voluminous but unrevealing, just the odd gem here and there to keep you hopeful. There are plenty of letters from famous people – Churchill, Edward VII, Asquith, Disraeli, Gladstone, Sullivan. Unfortunately almost none are worth quoting: Sullivan recommends a cook; Churchill accepts an invitation. I remained certain that there had to be a set of letters he had written to family members somewhere, and searched and searched for it, but never found it. Now I feel that this was a blessing in disguise because it made me focus on the most exciting time in his life – the Japan experience – compared to which, if we are honest, everything else was fairly tame.

One of the wonders of writing a biography is the places it takes you and the people you meet through it. Lord Dulverton, the present owner of Mitford's house at Batsford, near Moreton-in-Marsh, generously showed me around it and shared his thoughts about him as we sat on the terrace looking over the timeless Cotswold landscape, scarcely changed since Mitford's day. Mitford's descendants, particularly Charlotte Mosley and the present Lord Redesdale, were helpful, as was Nancy Mitford's biographer, Selina Hastings, who generously shared with me her knowledge of the family, and particularly the recollections of Diana Mosley, the granddaughter of 'my Mitford', as I generally call him in such company. One sadness of the project was that the last Mitford sister, the Dowager Duchess of Devonshire, expressed interest in it, but was not well enough to talk to me (she died on 24 September 2014, at the age of 94). Lord Dulverton introduced me to Edward Burman, who had independently become interested in A.B. Mitford (although not – thankfully – to the extent of writing a competing biography of him). I met him on a research trip in Beijing, and he guided me to places Mitford had known. I feel bad that, in the end, I did not write much about China in this book. But with a biography, about 90% of what you discover does not go into it; the trouble is that you do not know until you have been to the places and read the sources what the magic 10% will be.

You realise working on a project like this how precious archives and libraries are. Of the different places I worked in, I want to express special thanks to the Sainsbury Institute for the Study of Japanese Arts and Cultures in Norwich, and its librarian, Akira Hirano, who helped me so much with obtaining Mitford's letters from Japan. Eton College was generous not only with information, but also giving me the feeling of what it was like to be a boy there in the 1840s. I would strongly advise anybody who is writing about an old boy of that school to consult their remarkable records. Another exceptionally hospitable place to conduct research is at the Royal Archives, stored in the Round Tower of Windsor Castle. Its hard-pressed staff manage to carefully protect their priceless documents while bending over backwards to help writers. I am grateful to Jardine Matheson and the Syndics of Cambridge University Library for permission to view and quote from the Parkes papers. In Japan, the Yokohama Archives of History was invaluable, the scope of its collection spreading way beyond the city of Yokohama. I would like to express my special gratitude to the library of the International House of Japan, where much of this book was written, and especially its head librarian, Rie Hayashi. It provides researchers interested in Japan with a calm, comfortable, beautiful space and all the resources they could wish for. May it never change.

At the University of Queensland, Dr Stuart Glover, Professor Gillian Whitlock and Dr Tomoko Aoyama used their talismanic skills to help me turn the book from a pedestrian narrative into a proper biography. While I was working on it, I also co-edited an annotated edition of the 1861–1869 diaries of Mitford's closest colleague in Japan, Ernest Satow, with Ian Ruxton. Having to explain tricky Japanese names and events to readers in footnotes forced me to ensure that I really understand them myself – that work was indescribably useful for writing this book. I am grateful to Ian for including me in that project, which he initiated. Professors Emeriti Ciaran Murray and Charles De Wolf were both generous with practical help and morale-boosting encouragement. I also thank Dr J.E. Hoare who read the text and guided me towards valuable sources, while saving me from embarrassing errors. I am deeply thankful to Chuo University for giving me a sabbatical which allowed me the time to research and write the book. And most important of all, Kazuo Tominari, who traipsed around Mitford's haunts in Japan with me; without him, life could not go on, much less this book have been written.

INDEX

ℰℴ